Gendering the International Asylum and Refugee Debate

Gendering the International Asylum and Refugee Debate

Jane Freedman

Marie Curie Professor of Politics, Universite Panthéon – Sorbonne (Paris 1), France

First published 2007 by
PALGRAVE MACMILLAN
Houndmills, Basingstoke, Hampshire RG21 6XS and
175 Fifth Avenue, New York, N.Y. 10010
Companies and representatives throughout the world

PALGRAVE MACMILLAN is the global academic imprint of the Palgrave Macmillan division of St. Martin's Press, LLC and of Palgrave Macmillan Ltd. Macmillan® is a registered trademark in the United States, United Kingdom and other countries. Palgrave is a registered trademark in the European Union and other countries.

ISBN-13: 978–0–230–00653–9 hardback
ISBN-10: 0–230–00653–1 hardback

This book is printed on paper suitable for recycling and made from fully managed and sustained forest sources. Logging, pulping and manufacturing processes are expected to conform to the environmental regulations of the country of origin.

A catalogue record for this book is available from the British Library.

A catalog record for this book is available from the Library of Congress.

10 9 8 7 6 5 4 3 2 1
16 15 14 13 12 11 10 09 08 07

Printed and bound in Great Britain by
Antony Rowe Ltd, Chippenham and Eastbourne

Contents

Preface

In September 2005, I moved with my family from the United Kingdom to France, a move which brought with it some degree of upheaval. But the minor inconveniences and difficulties which my family and I experienced moving from one European city to another quickly pale into insignificance when compared with the stories and experiences of those women asylum seekers and refugees whom I interviewed for this research. These women told stories which were very varied, but all had shown enormous courage and persistence to leave their own countries and families and travel to Europe. Sadly, the reception that was waiting for them when they arrived was far from welcoming. This book is inspired by those women and by their stories of determination and courage in the face of great difficulty. I would like to thank them all for taking the time to talk to me and to share their stories which form the basis of the analysis contained within the book. Thanks also to all of those working in NGOs, government offices, international organisations or legal firms, who agreed to spare me some time to talk about their perceptions and experiences of asylum and refugee policies and processes. Without their help, this book would not have been possible.

I was able to devote time to this research thanks to the generous funding from several sources. So I would also like to thank the Mairie de Paris for their research grant allowing me to spend a year at the Sorbonne, and to the European Commission's Marie Curie programme for funding my continued presence in Paris. Thanks also to the Agence National de Recherche who funded the "Frontières" programme of which I have been a part, and which has allowed me both to fund research trips, and to exchange and discuss my findings with colleagues. The Fondation du Roi Baudoin and the Observatoire de l'Egalite Hommes-Femmes de la Ville de Paris both provided funds to support an international conference organised at the Sorbonne in September 2006 on the theme of Gender Related Persecutions and the Right to Asylum, so I would like to thank them for providing the opportunity for researchers and activists from around the world to talk about these issues.

I have been lucky to be able to discuss my ideas with colleagues who have provided me with both useful criticisms and inspiration. In particular, thanks go to Jérôme Valluy and the members of the TERRA research network. I would also like to thank the Centre de Recherches Politiques de la Sorbonne for hosting me whilst I carried out my research, and in particular thanks to Catherine Bailleux for all her help and support.

Finally, I would not have been able to write this book without the patience and support of my family. Thanks in particular to Stanley Freedman and Donna Hirsh for the interesting discussions about my work, and also for all the time they have spent looking after their grandchildren whilst I was working. And last but not least, thanks to Stuart, Olivia, Juliette and Sophia, and sorry that I've spent so long in front of my computer instead of with you.

1
A Gendered Approach to Refugee and Asylum Studies

In recent years asylum seekers have made the headlines of many newspaper and television reports in European countries and other richer nations around the world like Canada, the United States or Australia. These asylum seekers and refugees are often seen as a problem and a threat to these societies. Reports express fears of huge masses of asylum seekers flooding into countries of the West with the governments powerless to stop them. These asylum seekers, they say, are not "real" refugees fleeing violence and persecution, but "bogus asylum seekers" or "false refugees" coming to benefit from the economic and material benefits available in Western states. And particularly since the attacks of 11 September 2001 in the United States, and subsequent terrorist attacks in Madrid and London, fears have been raised about the connections that might exist between asylum seekers and terrorists. All these fears can be argued to be without foundation in facts, but they have become part of the everyday understandings of what an asylum seeker is. And at the same time our televisions and newspapers are showing us images of refugees massed in camps in Africa, the Middle East or Asia, living in tents or makeshift shelters, lacking sufficient food supplies, drinking water or basic washing facilities. The people in these camps have fled conflicts, massacres or natural disasters and find themselves still vulnerable and dependent on foreign aid.[1] These lives of extreme insecurity are often revealed to provoke pity[2] in the spectator, to engage support for humanitarian actions or perhaps at the same time to gain public approval for a foreign military intervention.[3] What is the link between these two sets of images and two sets of sentiments? How can we reconcile our "pity" for the refugee in a camp in Africa and our "fear" of the same refugee arriving in our country to seek asylum? And what about all those who have died on the journey from one continent to another?

In December 2006, the Red Cross reported that at least eighty Africans had drowned when their boat sank off the coast of Senegal on its way to the Canary Islands. A month earlier ten children died in a shipwreck off the Spanish coast. These are not isolated incidents but part of an ongoing series of deaths incurred whilst people try to cross the oceans of the world in small and often unseaworthy boats, desperate to reach the coasts of Europe or of Australia. Others have been suffocated whilst hiding in the backs of lorries to try to cross borders to reach the West or have been shot or injured while trying to scale the walls of Ceuta or Melilla, the Spanish compounds in Morocco. It is probably impossible to know how many of them die whilst trying to reach Europe, America, Canada or Australia. Many of these people are refugees fleeing from civil war, conflict and repression of their political and civil rights, economic or environmental crises. But for those who do succeed in reaching a Western country, the reception is more often than not hostile. Suspected of being "false refugees" or "economic migrants" they are subject to a series of interviews and judicial procedures whilst their claims are being examined, usually with no right to work and access to only minimal benefits; they live in poverty and are excluded from the rights of other citizens. More and more often these asylum seekers are housed in reception or detention centres where the living conditions may be poor. In Australia all asylum seekers are kept in mandatory detention until their case is decided, thus extending a prison regime and "criminal" punishment to those who have in fact not committed any criminal offence other than that of entering a country without the correct visas.

So why does the issue of refugees and asylum seekers cause so much debate? And why are people willing to take so many risks to reach another country to claim asylum? The question of refugees is not a new one, indeed the notion of "asylum" or protection to be given to foreigners by another state is one that has been discussed by governments for centuries. However, the scale of forced migrations in recent years has increased massively. At the start of the 1950s about one and half million refugees were registered and under the protection of the United Nations. Most of these people had been displaced by the Second World War or were moving from Eastern to Western Europe as the Cold War began, some had been displaced by the creation of the State of Israel in 1948, and the subsequent war in the Middle East. Just over fifty years later, the United Nations High Commissioner for Refugees (UNHCR) estimates that there are around twenty-one million people worldwide who are "of concern" to them.[4] These include those who have been accorded official refugee status by the UNHCR under the terms of the 1951 Geneva Convention,[5] those who are seeking asylum in a Western state (in other words they have made a claim to be recognised as a refugee under the terms of the Geneva Convention and the national laws of the state in which they have made the claim) and those who have been forced to migrate within their own country of origin and are living in a camp or temporary accommodation within a different region of that country. These figures do not include, however, those who remain undocumented or "clandestine" exiles, those who have fled their country but have not claimed asylum or refugee status from a foreign government or from the UNHCR. Many millions of people forced to flee from their homes are now living in or around cities of Africa, Asia or Latin America, often in desperate conditions, but unregistered by any government, refugee agency or NGO. These refugees then do not figure in the UNHCR statistics (Marfleet, 2006), and as Agier points out, it is often difficult to locate those displaced by forced migration as these people may try to blend discretely into the background, living in conditions of economic or legal clandestinity and thus preferring to remain "silent" (2002: 55). Adding these people would make the figure much greater, but it is impossible to estimate accurately how many people are concerned. What is evident though is that contrary to what some reports might lead us to believe, the great majority of the world's displaced people remain within the countries of the Third World, with very few having the desire or the necessary resources to make the perilous journey to the West. In 2005 Africa, Asia and the Middle East between them hosted over 60 per cent of the total world refugee population (UNHCR, 2006a). Pakistan, for example, was estimated to host about 1.1 million Afghan refugees in UNHCR camps at the end of 2005.[6] Thus those who bear the greatest "costs" in terms of hosting refugees and displaced people are not the rich states of the West (although these states do make contributions to the budget of the UNHCR), but largely the poorer states of the Third World (Chimni, 1998).

Although on paper we can establish simple definitions of a refugee and an asylum seeker, in practice this is not so simple. The definition of a refugee under international law is someone who has been recognised either by a national government or by the UNHCR as deserving international protection under the terms of the 1951 Refugee Convention/Geneva Convention (for a more detailed discussion of this convention and particularly of the understanding of gender-related persecution under the convention see Chapter 4). And an asylum seeker is someone who has asked a particular state to grant him or her refugee status under the terms of this convention. However, these straightforward definitions are challenged by the realities of the current global migratory trends. Can asylum be separated from other migratory phenomena? Are refugees different from other migrants? For some there is a clear difference between an asylum seeker and an economic migrant, one fleeing persecution and the other leaving their country of origin "voluntarily" for economic motives. This distinction is often made in a form that is not neutral, classifying the two groups of migrants within a particular political schema with the real asylum seeker or genuine refugee as a "good" migrant, a poor victim of persecution or oppression worthy of support and protection, and the economic migrant a "bad" migrant, often a fraud trying to make the authorities believe he or she is a refugee but really wanting to enter the countries of the West to benefit from the better economic opportunities and the generous welfare states in these countries. In reality, the division is much more difficult, and perhaps even impossible to make. The reasons that people flee their countries of origin are multiple and diverse, often there are several different reasons combined which finally push people to leave. They may flee because of a particular incident of violence or oppression, an arrest, torture or death threats, but it may also be that the general circumstances in which they are living make it impossible for them to remain. Economic and political causes of migration are not opposites but form part of a continuum and often political conflict is the expression or the result of a failure to bring about economic or social development, or to safeguard human rights (Castles and Loughna, 2005). Further, political conflict may be the cause of economic crises and may thus push many people into untenable conditions of poverty. It is thus nearly impossible to classify migrations as the result of either political or economic circumstances, either as "forced" or "voluntary". Would a man or woman leaving their country of origin because they were unable to find enough food or money to feed themselves or their children be classed as a "voluntary" or "economic" migrant? This type of categorisation seems far too simplistic an understanding. Moreover it is questionable whether truly "voluntary" migration exists other than in a very small minority of cases, with a continuum of different situations between "forced" and "voluntary" migrations existing in practice (Binder and Tosic, 2005). A combination of incidents and circumstances combine to make a refugee, and as Papademetriou comments:

> Increasingly both pure refugees and purely economic migrants are ideal constructs rarely found in real life; many among those who

routinely meet the refugee definition are clearly fleeing both political oppression and economic dislocation.

(1993: 212)

The UNHCR has explicitly recognised that refugees include those who flee "wretched conditions" associated with poverty, marginalisation and discrimination (1995a). But paradoxically as the economic and political situation in many regions has worsened, so the asylum receiving states in the West have tightened up their definitions of who or who is not entitled to asylum in their countries. This means in practice that those who may have been admitted twenty or thirty years ago as refugees are now rejected as "bogus asylum seekers" or economic migrants, subject to detention and expulsion back to their countries of origin. Many of these people do not even make it past the immigration controls at airports – they are held in retention zones and then put on the first aeroplane back to where they came from with only the most cursory examination of their claims for asylum. Others are stopped at sea and turned back. In 2001 a series of boats trying to reach Australia were intercepted and turned back. Those on the boats were not allowed to land on Australian territory but were transferred to other countries in the Pacific – Nauru, Papua New Guinea and Indonesia, for what the Australian authorities called "extraterrestrial processing". This new policy marked a shift in concern from the protection of refugees to the securing of borders (Humphrey, 2003), a shift which is a common feature of Western asylum and refugee regimes. For those who do manage to make a claim for asylum, the likelihood is that it will be rejected. Some countries in the EU now reject over 90 per cent of asylum claims, and in 2003 Greece reached a total of 99.9 per cent of rejections. Valluy (2005) argues that many more European States would now be rivalling Greece in these almost total rejection rates if it were not for the large bureaucracies which have grown up to deal with asylum claimants, and which would become redundant if all asylum claims were summarily rejected. These trends of increasing rejection and repression lead some to conclude that we will shortly witness "the death of the refugee" (Tuitt, 1996: 20) or the refugee as "an endangered species" (Humphrey, 2003: 40).

How have these negative perceptions of asylum seekers and refugees developed? How has the image of a "heroic" refugee fleeing from repression and persecution disappeared to be replaced by that of the "fraudulent" asylum seeker threatening the economic and political stability of Western states? Is it the general public who have suddenly decided that they do not like asylum seekers or have these representations been developed and refined by political elites? Are they a result of the influence of the extreme-Right in Western politics? Or do they stem from more generalised and widespread xenophobia? The answer is not simple and is probably a combination of various factors. Politicians in the West have tended to justify restrictive policies towards asylum seekers in terms of a response to public opinion which is largely "anti-immigration" and which demands tough measures to restrict the numbers of immigrants and asylum seekers admitted to their country. Some researchers share this view. Hansen and King, for example, attribute restrictive tendencies in asylum policy to "illiberal pressures emanating from the basic liberal democratic processes – impulses towards xenophobia, racism and anti-Semitism" (2000: 396). However, this view of the current restrictive policies as a direct result of hostile public opinion is somewhat simplistic. In many European countries the feasibility of maintaining liberal policies with respect to asylum seekers and refugees began to be seriously questioned in the 1970s after the closure of borders to labour migration (Boswell, 2000). Correspondingly the figures for rejected asylum applications began to increase in many countries from the 1970s, that is to say, well before the current politicisation and mediatisation of the asylum issue, and well before asylum became a major topic of public debate (Valluy, 2005). Crépeau points to the emergence of a rhetoric of denial of the right to asylum as early as the late 1970s and early 1980s when the notion of "manifestly unfounded" asylum claims appeared in technocratic language to designate procedural means of expediting the rejection of asylum claims (1995). The start of this rejection of asylum can thus be traced back to a period well before the current debates, a moment when many European States began to close their borders to labour migration and when bureaucratic and political norms began to emerge which treated all forms of incoming migration as a concern for the nation state. These norms were to some degree concealed by particular refugee "crises" such as that of the Vietnamese "boat people" or that of Chilean refugees who were granted asylum in Europe on the basis of specific quotas, but a general tendency to reject asylum claims from nationals of other countries was already emerging.

Linked to explanations of the "rejection" of asylum which attribute restrictionist policies to negative public attitudes to asylum seekers are explanations which posit the emergence of the extreme-Right as a political force as the major causal factor. However, these explanations are also sometimes too reductionist. Although extreme-Right parties have enjoyed electoral successes in some European countries, with manifestos that include anti-immigration policies as a central element, it can be noted as above that anti-asylum rhetoric and practices emerged in the public sphere before the ascendancy of these parties. Further, anti-asylum rhetoric and restrictionist policies have also been evident in countries like the UK where the extreme-Right has had little electoral success or influence. Thus although the extreme-Right and a hostile public opinion may be seen as contributory factors in magnifying the perceptions that asylum seekers are a "threat" that must be dealt with, political and bureaucratic elites must also bear an important part of the responsibility for the xenophobic policies that have emerged with regard to those seeking asylum.

The negative representations and perceptions of asylum seekers as fraudulent or false are reinforced in official discourse by the proportion of asylum claims which are rejected by immigration authorities in different countries. Valluy (2005) describes a cycle of rejection whereby the increasing numbers of asylum seekers rejected in European states are in turn used by politicians as justification for their beliefs that these are false asylum seekers and in turn for their repressive policies towards these people. The then French foreign minister, Dominique de Villepin, announced to the National Assembly in 2002 that:

> Certainly the flood of asylum seekers is a sign of the increase in violations of human rights and of persecution on a global scale. Every day, men and women have no other solution but to flee their country to escape from degrading treatment, torture and death. But those who are really persecuted are far from representing the majority of asylum seekers: not long ago the Ofpra[7] granted refugee status to nearly one asylum seeker in five, today this status is only granted to less than 13 per cent of asylum seekers. The evidence is even clearer in terms of territorial asylum for which the number of favourable decisions was less than 0.3 per cent in 2002. The fact is that many foreigners are claiming asylum in our system, not to obtain the protection of our country, but to stay here for as long as possible, their motivation being purely economic in nature.[8]

This rejection is thus not just a product of the rhetoric of populist right-wing parties or of illiberal public opinion, but has emanated from political institutions and actors themselves. Restrictive and stigmatising discourse on asylum seekers comes politically "from the top down" rather than as a response to public pressure (Statham, 2003). Asylum has increasingly been framed both within a xenophobic and nationalist discourse and within a discourse of security where asylum seekers are seen as threats to the safety of the nation, both through their supposed association with international terrorism and through the amalgam made between asylum seekers, people smugglers and international crime networks, a framing which views the asylum seeker not as a blameless victim of these smugglers but as at least in part complicit in their crime (Morrison, 2001). As Schuster argues, the term "asylum-seeker" is now used to conjure up "cheat, liar, criminal, sponger, someone deserving of hostility by virtue not of any misdemeanour, but simply because he or she is an 'asylum-seeker'" (2003: 244).

In the attempt to continually decrease the number of asylum seekers who reach their countries, and the number of asylum seekers to whom refugee status is eventually granted, governments have put in place procedures for processing and deciding asylum claims, which makes it increasingly difficult for a claimant to formulate a credible claim and for this claim to be "believed" by the relevant officials and judges. In this hostile climate, it is becoming harder and harder for an asylum seeker to prove that he has a genuine claim for protection, and in turn the processes of decision-making have in some cases come to be seen as more and more arbitrary, depending on the personal or discretionary power of individual bureaucrats or judges.[9] As Matas argues, "refugee determination systems around the world share two common features: complexity and unfairness", and these are largely the result of political interventions which are aimed at other ends than those of protecting refugees (2001: 48). Governments continue, however, to label asylum seekers as "bogus" in order to justify their restrictive policies, thus as Boswell explains:

> The characterisation of the asylum crisis as exclusively a problem of abuse by "bogus" asylum seekers is misleading. Many of the restrictive measures introduced by Western governments have been geared towards restricting the definition of who qualifies for refugee status, and so are clearly not intended to target exclusively "bogus" asylum seekers.
>
> (2000: 553)

We could go even further and argue that there are no such things as "bogus" asylum seekers, but only "rejected" asylum seekers, who are a creation of current restrictive asylum policies. These policies transform the question of asylum into one of security (Huysmans, 2006) and at the same time criminalise those who seek refuge in the West.

Migration and globalisation – linked phenomena?

The distinctions between forced and voluntary migration have become, as argued above, increasingly blurred. So when analysing forced migration and exile, and asking why there are now seemingly so many more refugees than in the past, we also have to ask about global patterns of migration. Since the 1960s a number of major developments in global migration patterns have placed the phenomenon at the heart of global politics. The scale of movements has increased exponentially. In the 1960s only a handful of countries, mainly the traditional immigration nations of North America and Oceania, were significantly affected by international migration, but by 2000 the International Organisation for Migration reported that over 2.5 per cent of the world's population was living outside of their country of birth (IOM, 2000)[10] and virtually every nation was influenced in some way by immigration or emigration of various kinds. In addition, the types and causes of migration have changed, and attempts to classify or categorise different varieties of migratory flows have become increasingly difficult and irrelevant as argued above. Many have argued that this migration can be analysed in the context of an increasing globalisation, which Held has argued represents "a widening, deepening and speeding up of worldwide interconnectedness in all aspects of contemporary social life" (Held et al., 1999: 2). Some have argued that the impacts of the end of the Cold War, and of increasing globalisation and free movement of capital would make refugee crises and displacement less of a problem in the twenty-first century (Suhrke, 1997; Adelman, 1999). In fact the reverse appears to be true with conflicts that generate refugees and displacement seemingly on the increase, and with no end in sight. The UNHCR reported in 1995 that successful peace settlements now seem to be the exception rather than the rule, and that they have been overshadowed by a crop of new and very large humanitarian emergencies (UNHCR, 1995a). Ten years later, the world seems to be faced with even more of these large humanitarian emergencies, with the accompanying displacement and forced migration engendered by these emergencies. So what exactly is the connection between globalisation and forced migration? There is a widespread and ongoing debate about the realities and extent of globalisation. For some it is a force of progress which will spread economic prosperity, for others it is a cause of doom. Rather than either of these opposed definitions, however, it seems more realistic to argue that globalisation is not a unified process but instead a set of multiple and varied processes which are sometimes contradictory, and which have uneven and unequal effects in different domains and different geographical areas. As Giles and Hyndman note: "globalisation is not a unitary or unified project that produces positive or negative outcomes but a composite of processes that generate patterns of exclusion, pockets of wealth, and sites of violence" (2004: 302).

It is important to note, however, in the context of migration, that the economic benefits and prosperity that have been promised by some of globalisation's proponents have not been distributed evenly across the world and that there are large areas which have been excluded from these benefits (Castells, 1996; Duffield, 2001) and which indeed have suffered negative consequences as a result of the processes included within the understanding of globalisation. As Marfleet argues: "World markets are not constructed upon even flows of capital which have the capacity to equalise processes of development; rather they are based upon powerful relationships of inequality. Over the past thirty years capital movements have emphasised such relationships, with the result that global differences have been intensified" (2006: 36). The processes of inclusion and exclusion which mark the processes of globalisation (Castells, 1996; Duffield, 2001) have also profoundly affected the way the countries of the West interact with those of the Third World, with a growing fear in the West of uncontrolled migration from the countries of the Third World and a corresponding raising of boundaries and strengthening of borders. Processes of exclusion and inclusion thus also mark the way in which globalisation has restructured the limits of migration, with those from the West becoming freer to move around the world as they wish, whilst those from the Third World find themselves faced with new barriers to their migration (Castles, 2003). As Bauman argues, "mobility has become the most powerful and most coveted stratifying factor" (1998: 2).

These growing inequalities between rich and poor states in the post-Cold War period have fuelled the crises in the Third World that caused increases in forced migration. Inequalities have also been deepened by changes in patterns of aid, with a decrease in long-term development assistance and an increase in funding for humanitarian emergencies as governments in the West seek to "contain" the problem of forced migration (Castles, 2003; Giles and Hyndman, 2004). The desire for "containment" and for political stability has meant that the focus has shifted away from aid for social development and stronger livelihoods. In a parallel modification, the political rationale for aid that accompanied the Cold War has disappeared, making way for a neoliberal regime of fiscal austerity and reform. All these changes have had implications for the ways in which "new" conflicts have been generated (Marfleet, 2006). Whilst each conflict has its own specific character-istics, in terms of the ethnic, racial or class dimensions that it entails, common features are found, particularly in the way in which state struc-tures have been undermined by neo-liberal policies and processes of globalisation. Marfleet describes this process of the weakening of state structures leading to conflict and forced migration:

> As resources are directed away from the state, disrupting food supplies and local economic networks and producing job losses, governments begin to lose legitimacy among the mass of people. Protests are met by repression, further undermining central authority and encouraging factionalism on the basis of regional, religious, sectarian or other differences. The apparatus of state – the police, the army and civil administration – itself becomes an arena for conflict as rival leaders compete for influence. Factional conflict becomes general and the armed forces may collapse or retreat to portions of the territory form-ally under their control. Large numbers of people may flee ahead of armed groups and militias, or may be purposefully displaced by them... For many people choices have run out: they are forced to become migrants.
>
> (2006: 48)

These processes of undermining states and creating situations in which conflicts between different groups within a country can escalate, involving civilians and forcing migration and displacement, are linked to the international structures and policies put in place by countries of the West. However, faced with the consequences in the form of asylum seekers and refugees arriving at their doors, these states prefer to tackle the effects rather than the causes of the problem, penalising those who flee, rather than attempting to deal with the root causes of migration. In the post-Cold War era, refugees are no longer a political symbol which can be used to score points from the "other side", but are rather seen as a menace to be contained. The migrant from Somalia, Iraq or the Demo-cratic Republic of Congo who arrives in Europe or North America is not prized as a sign of the superiority of capitalism as were the dissidents who arrived from the Soviet Union in the 1960s and 1970s. Instead they are treated as the cause of an asylum "crisis" (Castles, 2003). These develop-ments affect both men and women, but this book will focus particularly on the experiences and situations of women who are forced to migrate, and will examine the ways in which gender relations structure both the causes of their flight, and their experiences of displacement either in a refugee camp in the Third World or as an asylum seeker in the West. In situations where nation states fail, leading to conflict and violence, the protection for citizens is marginal and this can be especially the case for women who have been relegated to subordinate social, economic and political positions through gendered relations of power (Yuval-Davis, 1997; Pettman, 2002; Giles and Hyndman, 2004). These women may also have fewer resources to support their migration, and if they do manage to arrive in a country of the West to claim asylum, the construction of their asylum claim within gendered frames will have specific outcomes on their possible reception and integration. In the following section we will examine the ways in which gender has become a variable in research on migration and will ask what exactly a gendered analysis can add to the study of asylum and refugees.

Researching women, gender and migration

What do all these changes mean for women and for gender relations both in countries where the population experiences forced migration and displacement and in the countries which receive asylum seekers and refugees? A study of gender in forced migration is part of a larger move to become aware of the relevance of a gendered analysis of all migratory movements, an analysis which was lacking for many years during which the figure of the migrant was assumed to be male and when women migrants were absent from all research in the area.

One of the first changes in this invisibility of women and gender in studies of migration was the realisation that in fact women have always migrated and that in contemporary times more and more women are migrating. In their analysis of contemporary migration patterns, Castles and Miller point to the "feminisation" of migration as one of the five major tendencies in modern migratory trends (Castles and Miller, 1998). Certainly, recent years have seen an increase in the numbers of women migrating. Most migratory flows contain about 50 per cent of women, and in some migrant populations women far outnumber their male compatriots. In fact, women have outnumbered men in migration to North America (US and Canada) since 1970, and in Europe by 1990 nearly 52 per cent of all migrants were women (Zlotnik, 2003). Whilst historically a large proportion of female migrants moved as dependents of male partners, there have always been women who have migrated independently to work or study in another country. Contemporary female migration is increasingly made up of women migrating independently to escape from impossible conditions in their country of origin and/or to find work in other countries, although again there are still many women who move as part of a "family" migration. So how can we analyse this process of "feminisation" of migration? Is it merely a question of noting how many women are on the move and where they are moving to and from? Or do we need to go further and explore the motives for women's migration and the patterns formed? One of the difficulties in this task of studying feminised migration patterns is that there is a huge diversity in the situation of women who migrate globally, and it is thus almost impossible to generalise about their experiences. Women's migratory experiences are influenced not only by their position as women, but also by their class, race or ethnicity, their age and their sexual orientation. All these factors and others will impact on the causes and means of migration for women, and on their experiences when they reach a new country. In addition, their experiences will be structured by the particular legislative and policy regimes of the countries they have left, those they transit through and those that they finally arrive in. Stratification occurs at all stages of the migration process, caused both by processes of globalisation and by local and national contexts. Faced with all this diversity it is very hard to talk about "migrant women" without making unjustified generalisations. Kofman (2005) argues, for example, that much of the literature on women and migration, and especially that which adopts an integrative approach ignores the experiences of skilled migrants. Even when comparing the experiences of two asylum-seeking women, these will be very different depending on their country of origin and the country in which they claim asylum. Further complexity will be added by factors such as their class and ethnicity, which will have an impact both on the conditions within which they migrate and their reception in the host society.

As will be argued throughout this book, although there are connections to be made between the experiences of different women, we must also be aware of the need to contextualise these experiences and not to create essentialist assumptions on the basis of a common female identity. If we do want to make connections between the varied experiences of women migrants then we need to do this on the basis of an analysis and understanding of the relations of gender which underlie and structure these experiences, and of an examination of the way that these relations of gender interact with other elements of stratification such as class and ethnicity.

Despite the increases in women's migration, which as Zlotnik (2003) notes, are not that recent but date from the 1960s, mainstream migration research has been slow to respond to these changes and to incorporate women into analysis. One of the primary reasons for this invisibility of women in migration research is that the primary models for analysing migration were in terms of labour migration where the migrant worker was assumed to be a man and women were presumed to be economically inactive (Kofman et al., 2000). Castles and Miller's (1998) book on migration was one of the first major studies to consider seriously the "feminisation" of migration even though women academics had already started to research the issue at least a decade earlier (Phizacklea, 1983; Morokvasic, 1984), and the proliferation of such research from the end of the 1980s led one article to describe a "tidal wave" of "research on issues related to gender and human mobility" (Donato et al., 2006: 7). Within this "tidal wave" there is relatively little research which focuses on the gendered politics of migration (Donato et al., 2006; Piper, 2006) and even less which attempts a gendered analysis of the politics of asylum (Freedman, 2007b).

Much of the research and analysis on gender within the asylum process comes from the field of law and focuses on the ways in which gender has been interpreted within national and international laws and jurisprudence (Macklin, 1995; Crawley, 2001; Oswin, 2001; Valji, 2001; Ankenbrand, 2002; Kneebone, 2005). This research is valuable in providing a detailed analysis of the way in which the interpretations of the Geneva Convention prevalent in national legislation and jurisprudence can act to create exclusions within asylum systems or, as Kneebone (2005) describes this process with regard to Australia, trends to "exclusionary inclusion". This legal analysis, however, sometimes fails to take into account other variables in the way that gender is incorporated into the asylum process, such as the gendered impacts of welfare policies for asylum seekers or the unequal integration of female and male refugees into labour markets. These and many other issues all contain a gendered dimension which needs to be analysed in order to obtain a full picture of the way in which women and men will experience asylum and refugee policies in different ways. Moreover, the studies which focus merely on legislation and official policy may overlook the important place of discretionary power in the asylum determination process in Western States. This discretionary power is exercised through gendered lenses which ignore the complexity of the experiences of women seeking asylum and reduce them to a series of stereotyped roles. Further, the great number of actors involved in making and implementing asylum policy and in taking decisions on individual asylum cases means that it is impossible to point to just one source of gendered inequalities in the asylum process. The academic studies of the ways in which asylum legislation relates to women and persecutions specific to women tend to focus on legislation and jurisprudence and thus overlook the complexity of the asylum process and the multiple numbers of actors and agencies involved in determining the outcome of each asylum request. This book will attempt to bring a wider perspective to the study of gender in asylum politics by moving beyond a narrowly legalistic focus to look at the ensemble of actors and processes involved in asylum and to analyse the gendered relations of power which underlie these processes.

In parallel with research on gender in the asylum process we can point to a development of academic research focusing on gender, forced migration and displacement which has come largely from within the academic disciplines of anthropology, sociology and geography and has evolved out of the growing concern with gender and development. Indra (1989) describes the way in which in early academic research on refugees, gender was either not mentioned at all or else was considered as "just another variable like age or occupation...Women's issues were still not well-publicized 'refugee problems', and so little academic research on women was produced". This situation has changed in the last twenty years or so with the emergence of a much greater body of research that considers gender as a primary factor of analysis. This research has led to studies of the operations of gender in conflicts that create refugees and in refugee camps (Indra, 1999; Hyndman, 2000, 2004; Giles et al., 2003; Giles and Hyndman, 2004), and these studies combine with feminist investigations in international relations (Enloe, 1989, 1993, 2000; Whitworth, 1997; Baines, 2004) to provide us with insights into the experiences of gender amongst refugees and the internally displaced, and into the ways in which international organisations such as the UNHCR have sought to respond to the needs of "refugee women". This book will try to build on these studies and to link an analysis of gendered "sites of violence" (Giles and Hyndman, 2004) with an examination of the ways in which this violence is transposed into the experiences of asylum seekers in the West.

Why talk about gender (and not just about women)?

In their introduction to a special issue of the *International Migration Review* focusing on gender in migration studies, Donato et al. (2006) trace a history of scholarship on women, gender and migration showing how this research has moved from efforts to fill in the gaps left by academic studies on migration which focused primarily on male migrants and immigrants, to studies which aim to go beyond this and to reformulate migration theory in the light of gendered analysis. Moving beyond research which merely accounts for the presence of women in migration means analysing not just women's migration, but also the relationships between men and women which underlie this migration and which structure both women's and men's experiences of migration.

Gender is a concept which has been employed by feminist research since the 1970s in order to make a distinction between the fixed characteristics of sex and the socially constructed notions of masculinity and femininity. Gender is sometimes used interchangeably with sex, but in fact the two terms have different meanings. Whilst sex refers to the biological differences between men and women, between male and female, gender refers to the social and cultural constructions and representations which are used to distinguish and classify what is "masculine" and "feminine". Some have argued that sex is in fact just as much a socially constructed division as gender and that to argue that there is a difference between sex and gender is part of a series of "foundationalist fictions" (Butler, 1990; Spijkerboer, 2000). This study, however, will maintain the definitions of sex and gender outlined above, which are considered as useful tools in analysing the ways in which social constructions and representations impact on men and women in different ways, and the ways in which relations between men and women are structured as relations of power. Gender is a relational concept, it is defined in terms of relationships between men and women, between maleness and femaleness, or masculinities and femininities. It is also a dynamic and evolving concept, gender relations should not be understood as fixed across time or place, but rather in constant evolution, and varying according to different local contexts. As Donato et al. (2006) explain:

> Most gender analyses assume that maleness and femaleness are defined in relationship to each other, as other axes of power and difference (class, race, and ethnicity) are. Rather than viewing gender as fixed or biological, more scholars now emphasize its dynamic nature: gendered ideologies and practices change as human beings (gendered as male or female, and sexualized as homosexual, bisexual or heterosexual) cooperate or struggle with each other, with their pasts and with the structures of changing economic, political and social worlds linked through their migrations.

Explaining gender as a relational concept involves several different levels of analysis. Gender is a social relation in that it refers to the conditions and understandings about relationships between women and men and "about the appropriate roles of women and men in society and in the workforce, even about what it is to be a woman or a man" (Whitworth, 1997: 65). But as well as explaining these relationships, gender is also constructed in and through them and thus refers both to the content of the relations and the manner of their construction. Gendered meanings and roles are constructed and maintained, but also contested, through constant struggle and redefinition by actors and institutions. Thus as Whitworth affirms:

> What gender looks like is a result of a wide variety of activities, from the daily rituals of the traditional nuclear family, activities in schools and the workplace through the personal struggles of the single parent, to women and men engaged in anti-sexist demonstrations, demanding the adoption of more egalitarian policies by the state. These experiences, moreover, will be different for the different people involved, and depending where, and under what circumstances they are practised.
>
> (1997: 65)

"What gender looks like" is also not just about women, although women may be the primary subjects of much research on gender because it is they who suffer the primary consequences of gendered inequalities of power. But gendered relations and structures affect men as well as women with constructions of hegemonic masculinities constraining the way that men behave and their social roles. In terms of asylum and refugee policies, gendered inequalities may impact on men in particular ways. If gendered constructions represent women as more "vulnerable" asylum seekers and refugees, then men (and particularly young men) may be constructed as more "threatening" and thus singled out for special attention. Schuster cites the UK Immigration Minister Lord Rooker who disparaged asylum seekers as "single men who have deserted their families for economic gain" (cited in Schuster, 2003: 246). And as Carpenter (2006) points out, the construction of women as "vulnerable" may mean that protection programmes are targeted specifically at them and that the vulnerability of insecurity of men is thus rendered invisible.

One of the difficulties in carrying out a gendered analysis is that these relations of gender and the practices which construct and maintain them are frequently rendered invisible through a process of naturalisation or normalisation. That is to say that relationships between men and women as well as roles and behaviours appropriate for these men and women in all areas of life are seen to be part of a natural order of things. It may thus be considered normal for men to have the role of primary breadwinner in families whilst women take greater responsibility for childcare or during conflict it is men who are the principal combatants and women the civilians. Gender is often normalised in two senses, in that is it normal to talk about differences between men and women, and that in talking about and representing these differences they are reinforced and reconstructed, as Cockburn explains: "difference between men and women is habitually represented. And simultaneously it is reinforced as a norm" (2004: 27). To escape from this normalisation we have to ask questions: questions about why women and men behave in certain ways or experience the same situations differently. Why, for example in situations of conflict is it normally the men who fight and the women who are more often displaced as refugees? Why does rape and sexual violence against women increase in times of conflict? And why is sexual violence used by some men as a strategy of war?

A gendered analysis of the asylum and refugee debate

For a long time the primary images of asylum seekers and refugees were male. Still today in many situations the image we have of an asylum seeker is that of a young man. The high-profile media coverage of the Franco-British dispute over the Sangatte camp in 2002, for example, led to a proliferation of images of young men trying to climb wire fences and jump onto trains to cross to the UK. As we have argued above, asylum policies and legislation have been the focus of academic analysis, but often this analysis lacks any reference to gender or to the effects of policy developments on women. This "gender-blindness" seems to reflect a more general "dearth of gendered analysis of migration by political scientists" (Donato et al., 2006: 16), and this can be argued to be particularly acute in the area of asylum, where there are few studies which take into account the real gendered impacts of current policies. Analysing in terms of gender means not just studying female refugees and asylum seekers but aiming to assess in what ways the constructed relationships between men and women, male and female have an impact in structuring the whole of their experiences. Thus a gendered analysis of asylum and refugee policies not only will tell us that women flee their countries of origins for different reasons from men, but will try to understand the ways in which constructions of femininity and masculinity in their country or their community or their family have led to persecutions which make them leave their home. Similarly we will not just assert that women have often been refused asylum in Western states, but we will seek to analyse the way that gendered understandings of the political sphere as more "masculine" and the private or home sphere as more "feminine" have led to women's persecutions being rendered either invisible or irrelevant under international and national laws and policies.

Peterson and Runyan suggest that gender analysis can function as a lens through which world politics can be examined "to 'see' how the world is shaped by gendered concepts, practices and institutions" (1993: 1). The lens of gender will be used in this book to try to "see" and understand the way in which gendered structures and relations of power affect the experiences of asylum seekers and refugees and the way in which national and international politics on asylum and refugee protection help to construct and reinforce these gendered relations. It is not only an external lens which is applied from the outside by Western researchers, but also a way in which asylum seekers and refugees may understand their own experiences. Turner's (2004) research on refugees in a Tanzanian refugee camp, for example, shows that gender appears to be the primary perspective through which most refugees seek to understand social changes.

The theoretical and methodological basis of this research is drawn from feminist theories on politics and international relations and by feminist methodologies which, as Tickner argues, seek to make visible, understand and challenge "the often unseen androcentric or masculine biases in the way that knowledge has traditionally been constructed in all the disciplines" (2005: 3). Major contributions of these feminist theories of politics and international relations have been to deconstruct the assumption of a public/private divide in much political theory and analysis and to challenge the supremacy of the state as a unit of analysis, particularly in relation to concepts of security. Deconstructing the division between public and private has shown the ways in which relations of domination exist within the supposedly "private" sphere of the family and has exposed as highly political concerns issues which otherwise may have remained hidden. Feminist critiques of traditional theories of security have also made visible the ways in which women confront security issues in their daily lives and the ways in which these security issues are linked to unequal relations of gender (Youngs, 2004). Moving the focus away from the security of states and on to that of human beings (and gendered human beings), women have thus enabled the theorisation of domestic violence, for example, as a security issue. This type of understanding allows us to make links between the various forms of violence and persecution faced by women and to link these to gendered relations and structures of power.

What research for this book has shown are the ways in which, despite huge differences in their situations, there is a continuity of the experience of women refugees and asylum seekers, a continuity which can be understood by the ways these experiences are shaped by gendered relations of power. These women are made vulnerable by constructions of femininities which assign to women a particular and often subordinate position within many societies and which legitimate or justify violence against women with reference to the symbolic and practical roles assigned to them: roles as biological and cultural producers and reproducers of the nation; roles as principal providers of care; and roles as "modest" wives. Moreover, national and international political systems which extend "protection" to refugees may reinforce gendered inequalities by their representations of these women either as "vulnerable" or as "threatening". We will argue that these two constructions of refugee and asylum-seeking women which may at first seem to be diametrically opposed are in fact part of the same gendered and racialised construction which emphasises difference not only between men and women, but between Western and "other" women. In the following chapter we will begin with an examination of "who are the refugees"; in other words we will try and deconstruct the general assumptions that "the majority of the world's refugees are women" or that "asylum seekers are generally male" to understand why women and men are forced to migrate and how their conditions of migration are shaped by relations of gender and ethnicity.

2
Who are the "Refugee Women"?

How many of the world's refugees and asylum seekers are women? It is very difficult to estimate with any degree of precision what proportion of the twenty one million people "of concern" to the UNHCR are female and impossible to know how many of the "undocumented" refugees are women. Even with regard to women coming to seek asylum in the West, there are relatively few reliable statistics. Many governments do not provide a breakdown of statistics on asylum claimants according to sex and even fewer provide gendered statistics regarding the proportions of asylum seekers granted refugee status or other forms of subsidiary protection. This deficiency in the provision of accurate statistics can in itself be seen as showing a lack of interest on the part of governments in these states in issues concerning gender in the asylum process, and although UNHCR has recommended that more should be done to identify asylum seekers and refugees by gender and age (UNHCR, 1991), there are still few governments who have responded. Recently, in the *Agenda for Protection* (2003), the UNHCR urged all states to provide and share detailed sex and age disaggregated statistics, to enable a quantitative identification of particular groups of refugees and asylum seekers in order to better provide for their needs. However, in their comparative analysis of the treatment of female asylum seekers in Europe, Crawley and Lester (2004) report that less than half of the states surveyed provided gender-differentiated statistics on asylum applications and less than one-fifth provided gender-differentiated statistics on the outcomes of initial asylum claims.

The lack of accurate gender-disaggregated statistics on refugees and asylum seekers leads some people to make exaggerated claims as to the numbers of women amongst the world's refugees. These claims can be seen as in a large part aiming to reverse the "invisibility" of women refugees and asylum seekers which has been a feature of research and policy-making until quite recently (see Chapter 1). In response to the way in which women have been ignored, some have pushed for a much greater recognition of gender-related issues in the protection of refugees and asylum seekers on the basis that women are the majority of the world's refugees. Oosterveld, for example, claims that: "The faces of refugees are overwhelmingly female: women and children represent eighty per cent of the world's twenty seven million refugees and displaced people" (1996: 570). Such figures are often used to claim that women are the "forgotten majority" amongst refugee populations and to make the case for further international and national actions specifically in aid of women refugees. However, a basic problem with these statistics is that they conflate "women and children" into one single category, thus obscuring even further the real nature of the statistical differences between men and women. The amalgamation of "women and children" into one category of "vulnerable" refugees is an important feature of the representations of women refugees in humanitarian actions, representations which can be argued to have major impacts on the way in which gender is treated in issues of refugee protection. We will return to these issues of the representation of "women and children" later in the book (see Chapter 5). What is important here is to note that in any normal population, women and children considered together will make up the majority of that population, so to claim that women and children are the majority of the world's refugees actually tells us very little. In fact, what statistical data do exist show that women make up about half of the global refugee population (UNHCR, 2006a), although they may be the majority in some particular refugee situations. This is particularly true of some of the refugee situations resulting from civil wars or other conflict situations where men will be those principally engaged in fighting and women will be more likely to flee. Although, as Carpenter (2006) argues, the category of women and children should not be used interchangeably with that of civilians, as in contemporary wars many men are also civilians and women may also be combatants. In some refugee camps then there are more women than men, but in terms of those claiming asylum in European and other industrialised countries, women are still in the minority. What these varying accounts about the statistics tell us is that there are many questions that still need to be asked about the exact make up of different refugee populations in terms of their demographic characteristics. It would be a mistake to generalise about the disproportion of men or women refugees as each individual situation of exile entails gender-differentiated conditions which will lead to men and women finding themselves in diverse situations with varying options open to them. Rhetoric which claims that women are the forgotten majority of the world's refugees is clearly produced within an ideological frame that aims to garner sympathy and (more importantly) funds for humanitarian efforts. It does little, however, to uncover the realities of forced migration. In the rest of the chapter we will examine four different aspects of forced migration to analyse more closely the evidence relating to the gendered experiences of men and women in these differing situations. We will start with an investigation of the situation of those seeking asylum in Europe, the United States, Australia and Canada.

Women asylum seekers in the West

One of the major trends in asylum statistics in recent years has been a general fall in the number of asylum claims made in Western states. The UNHCR statistics show that between 2001 and 2005, asylum applications in fifty industralised countries dropped by nearly 50 per cent. The figures showing asylum claims in the top ten countries of reception in 2001 and 2005 are shown in Table 2.1. These figures show massive falls in the number of asylum claims in many of these countries. These reductions in the number of asylum claims received are not, however, an indication of a fall in the number of people in need of protection,

Table 2.1 Asylum claims in the top ten receiving countries in 2005

Country	Number of asylum claims in 2001	Number of asylum claims in 2005	Share of global total of asylum seekers in 2005 (per cent)
Austria	30,140	22,470	6.7
Belgium	24,550	15,960	4.8
Canada	44,040	19,740	5.9
France	54,290	50,050	15.0
Germany	88,290	28,910	8.1
Netherlands	32,580	12,350	3.7
Sweden	23,520	17,530	5.2
Switzerland	20,630	10,060	3.0
UK	91,600	30,460	9.1
USA	104,340	48,770	14.6

Source: UNHCR (2006a).

but more likely a sign of the effectiveness of the barriers put in place by Western States to stop asylum seekers arriving within their borders (see Chapters 1 and 6). Further, given the obstacles that now exist to making an asylum claim in many countries, it is also probable that many of those who would have made such a claim are either prevented from doing so (by refusal of the authorities to register their claim, fast-track procedures to return them directly to their country of origin before they enter national territory etc.) or choose not to claim asylum as they judge that this would expose them to the dangers of detention or deportation, and so remain in a country "illegally" without any kind of papers. It is impossible to know how many undocumented refugees there are in each of these countries or how many of those who would have claimed asylum are now waiting in "neighbour" states hoping for a chance to reach Europe, Canada or the United States. Nor can we determine exactly the effects of these policies on the numbers of women reaching the West to claim asylum. What is apparent, however, is that the specific problems that women already encountered in trying to reach a Western country to claim asylum must only have been exacerbated by the restrictive policies adopted by these countries.

As argued above, the need for detailed statistics on asylum applications and decisions according to sex and age has been recognised by UNHCR for many years. However, many countries still fail to provide gender-disaggregated statistics either on the number of asylum applications received or on the numbers receiving refugee status. Crawley and Lester's (2004) report showed that, of the EU member states only twelve produced gender-disaggregated statistics on asylum applications and six produced gender-differentiated statistics on initial decisions on asylum claims. Although, following pressure from the UNHCR, there are now more states who produce these statistics regarding asylum claims and decisions by sex, there is still a relative dearth of accurate information in this area. The absence of statistics telling us how many women there are amongst asylum claimants in the West and how many of these women will receive refugee status, or subsidiary protection, can be seen as symptomatic of a more general lack of interest in these issues. The research for this book demonstrated this lack of interest on behalf of some states, a response from the migration board in the Netherlands for example indicated that gender-disaggregated statistics did not exist and that the last attempt to undertake this type of analysis had been in 2000.[1] In other cases, statistics may exist but may not be made available to the public or to researchers. One researcher in Spain commented that she had requested statistical information from the director of the immigration office who had informed her that this was "impossible".[2] The "impossib-ility" of producing gender-disaggregated statistics does not seem to stem from a lack of capability, however, but more from a lack of willing. As one UNHCR officer in a European bureau commented, producing these statistics would not be in any way difficult for European States who in general routinely collect demographic data from all asylum applic-ants when they make their initial claim.[3] The UNHCR statistics office provides figures that show that where figures do exist, the proportion of female asylum applicants in European countries is about 30 per cent (Crawley and Lester, 2004). This figure is roughly the same for other industrialised countries such as Australia, Canada and the United States, and it can be generally assumed that in all Western states male asylum applicants outnumber female applicants (Bhabha, 2004).

Why then do fewer women than men make a claim for asylum in the West? It is certainly not because women suffer less from persecutions and violence than men, but because of the social, economic and political obstacles that women may face and which will affect their decision on whether or not to migrate. Gendered relations and structures of power thus play an essential role in the decision of whether or not to migrate (Binder and Tosic, 2005), and although as argued in Chapter 1, it would be wrong to continue to accept the figure of the migrant as male, there are specifically gendered barriers which make it harder in some circumstances for women to leave their countries of origin. The first of these barriers can be seen in the gendered social roles and norms which may exist in a country. In some countries it may be problematic for a woman to live alone or with children without the protection of her husband or another male relative. Prevalent norms may prevent a woman from working outside the home or travelling outside alone. In these circumstances, the idea of leaving her home or community and travelling long distances in order to reach another country to claim asylum may seem almost unimaginable. Nada, a Saudi Arabian woman who sought asylum in Canada explains the situation which makes it so complicated for a woman to leave: "First of all, it's very hard to leave [Saudi Arabia]. Even if a woman thinks about leaving she cannot get permission. It's also not easy for a woman to do things by herself. Women are raised to be incapable of doing anything. One pays a big price to come here and the woman who is willing to do that is rare" (cited in Macklin, 1995: 220). Further problems arise in relation to financial resources necessary for travel. Women may find themselves in a situation of economic dependence which makes it very hard for them to find the necessary resources to pay for their journey. The increased use of smugglers to help asylum seekers reach the West makes this problem even more acute, with the necessity of paying for one's passage adding yet another obstacle in the way of women with few financial resources. Many women asylum seekers interviewed explained the problems that they had encountered in trying to raise money for their journey or the way in which they had swapped services (including sexual relations) in order to bargain with those who would help them reach Europe (see Chapter 7).

Women who travel alone may also expose themselves to dangers of violence or sexual abuse on the journey and this fear may mean that they choose to stay and endure persecutions at home, rather than risking the dangers of a long journey. The danger of becoming a victim of sexual abuse is very high, both within the country of origin, during the journey and also in the host country (Binder and Tosic, 2005). These dangers may be exacerbated by policies designed to prevent asylum seekers reaching countries in the West, which force many to use the service of smugglers, and thus make them more vulnerable to exploitation and extortion as they make their journey. For women this may take the form of sexual exploitation or forced prostitution.

Another key difficulty faced by many women in making their decision to migrate or not is that of care of their children. Without wishing to essentialise women's role as mothers, they are often the primary carers for young children and this makes any idea of flight much harder. Travelling with children under forced migratory circumstances will expose these children also to the dangers of the journey, which some women will be reluctant to do. Others may decide to leave their children in their country of origin with other relatives or friends, but this decision to separate from one's children may also be very painful, as the testimonies of women asylum seekers makes clear (see Chapter 7).

All these issues explain why there are fewer women than men seeking asylum in the West. The latest statistics, where they are available, demonstrate this continuing gap between female and male asylum seekers. Table 2.2 shows the figures for male and female principal applicants in some EU member states and Canada. It is important to note that these figures concern principal applicants, as in some countries women may still be considered in many cases as dependents in the asylum application process, which entails its own difficulties, including dependence on a male relative (see Chapter 4).

In nearly all countries women make up around one-third of all asylum seekers. The figures for Canada are higher, but in Canada asylum seekers constitute only a proportion of the refugees accepted, many of whom

Table 2.2 Women asylum applicants in a selection of receiving countries

Country	Total number of principal applications in 2005	Number of women principal applicants	Percentage of women principal applicants
Belgium	15,461	5,223	33.8
Canada	19,935	9,099	45.6
France	42,578	14,741	34.6
Sweden	31,454	10,962	34.8
UK	25,710	7,365	28.6

Sources: CGRA, Belgium; Ofpra, France; Home Office, UK; Migration Board, Sweden.

come through humanitarian and resettlement programmes. In fact, of the total number of refugees accepted into Canada, women make up only 34.1 per cent, a figure which is more in line with the percentage of female asylum seekers in other Western countries. Whilst the Belgian CGRA note the relative stability of the proportion of women amongst asylum claimants, a proportion that has remained at around 30 per cent despite the rapid fall in the overall number of claims between 2000 and 2005,[4] in France, the Ofpra notes in its annual report that there has been a "feminisation" of asylum claimants between 2001 and 2005. In fact, in France, the percentage of female asylum claimants has grown from 29.6 per cent of the total in 2001 to 34.6 per cent in 2005, a feature that the Ofpra attributes to its new powers to grant subsidiary protection.[5] In its annual report the Ofpra points to a particular growth in the number of women asylum seekers from Guinea and Nigeria who are fleeing from female genital mutilation (FGM), forced marriage or forced prostitution, and women from Algeria claiming asylum on the basis of persecutions suffered because of their Westernised lifestyle. Perhaps worryingly for those who would like to see these types of persecution recognised as legitimate grounds for claiming refugee status under the Geneva Convention, the Ofpra report refers to these types of claims as emerging in "parallel with classic political problematics arising from the Geneva Convention" and makes a very strong link between the emergence of these types of claims and the new practice of granting subsidiary protection (Ofpra, 2006). This type of argument seems to substantiate fears that have been expressed by those campaigning for a more gender-sensitive interpretation of the Geneva Convention that claims involving gender-related persecution will automatically be treated as claims for subsidiary protection rather than full convention refugee status[6] (see Chapters 4 and 6 for a fuller discussion of this issue).

Whilst it is possible to estimate that in most Western countries women make up about one-third of the total of all asylum seekers, significant differences emerge when the figures for asylum claims from different countries of origin are examined. Research carried out in the UK shows that the proportion of women claiming asylum in 2001 varied greatly depending on the country of origin. Women made up approximately 14 per cent of claimants from Iran and Sudan, but over 56 per cent of claimants from Eritrea. The report notes that with the exception of Sudan, "the proportion of women asylum-seekers is higher for countries where civil unrest and/or war are widespread. It is lower in countries where the primary focus on human rights violations is political and civil rights abuses and where women's rights are repressed" (RWRP, 2003: 35). These figures reinforce the arguments outlined above which describe the difficulties that women have in undertaking any kind of forced migration and suggest that it is more likely that they will leave a country only when it absolutely the last choice, such as in times of civil war or conflict where their lives are in immediate danger, and that they will be less likely to flee when persecution is in the form of general violations of their human rights such as discriminatory laws or practices existing in some countries. It may also be more difficult for a woman to flee a country such as Iran where there are such strong laws and norms restricting women's lifestyles and movements.

More recent figures also show major differences in the proportion of female asylum seekers from various countries of origin, with a far larger proportion of women amongst applicants from some African countries, and very few women asylum claimants from Afghanistan, Iran or Iraq. Again, this difference might be explained by the additional hurdles that women face when trying to travel in a country where there are strong norms limiting the way in which women can behave in public and where women may even be afraid to travel outside of their own home. Table 2.3 provides the breakdown of male and female applicants in the top ten countries of origin of asylum seekers to the United Kingdom in 2005.

Similar variations emerge when considering the proportion of women amongst asylum claimants of different nationalities in France. Here it can be noted that there are proportionately fewer female asylum seekers from Algeria and Turkey. Table 2.4 shows the percentage of women amongst asylum seekers from the top ten nationalities claiming asylum in France in 2005.

Table 2.3 Percentage of women amongst asylum applicants to the UK by country of origin, 2005

Country of origin	Total number of asylum applications in UK in 2005	Number of female applicants	Percentage of female applicants
Iran	3,150	335	10.6
Somalia	1,760	780	44.3
Eritrea	1,760	535	30.4
China	1,730	630	36.4
Afghanistan	1,580	135	8.5
Iraq	1,415	165	11.7
Pakistan	1,145	540	47.2
DR Congo	1,080	605	56.0
Zimbabwe	1,075	545	50.7
Nigeria	1,025	395	38.5

Source: UK Home Office, 2006.

Table 2.4 Percentage of women amongst asylum applicants to France by country of origin, 2005

Country of origin	Total number of asylum applications in France in 2005	Number of female applicants	Percentage of female applicants
Haiti	4,953	1,594	32.2
Turkey	3,612	616	17.1
China	2,579	1,434	55.6
Serbia and Montenegro	2,569	1,006	39.2
DR Congo	2,563	1,251	48.8
Russia	1,980	954	48.2
Moldavia	1,964	768	39.1
Sri Lanka	1,894	577	30.5
Algeria	1,777	337	19.0
Bosnia Herzegovina	1,658	672	40.5

Source: Ofpra, 2006.

The variations in the proportion of women asylum seekers coming from different countries of origin to various Western states which are demonstrated in the two examples above illustrate the necessity of avoiding generalising too much about the causes of forced migration or about the conditions under which these migrations take place. Gendered relations of power in different countries will affect women in varying ways and will either encourage them to flee and/or hamper them in this flight. In countries where gendered inequalities are very severe and where discriminations and persecutions against women are widespread, women may have more incentive to migrate, but at the same time this migration may become extremely difficult. In addition, widespread persecution and discrimination and the gendered relations of power upon which they rest may become normalised to such an extent that women do not even perceive that it might be in their interest to leave their country to escape from these persecutions.

There may be a general assumption that given the tendencies to not recognise gender-related persecution as coming within the grounds of the Geneva Convention (see Chapter 4) and also the difficulties women may have during the asylum determination process, women would be less successful in their asylum applications than men. There are even fewer gender-disaggregated statistics available concerning the outcomes of asylum applications than there are concerning the number of claims, but where figures are available they seem to demonstrate that this numerical discrimination against women is not the case. In some cases women even seem to have a higher rate of recognition as refugees than men (Spijkerboer, 2000). Figures for 2005 in the UK show that 6 per cent of male principal applicants were granted asylum at the initial decision stage, compared with 10 per cent of female principal applicants (Home Office, 2006). Roughly the same proportion of male and female principal applicants were granted humanitarian protection or discretionary leave to remain at the initial decision stage (10 and 11 per cent, respectively) (Home Office, 2006). In other countries, women also seem to have been numerically more successful in gaining refugee status. In 2005 in Belgium, for example, 45 per cent of those recognised as refugees under the Geneva Convention were women[7] and in France 40 per cent of recognised refugees were female (Ofpra, 2006).

This quantitative "success" of women in gaining refugee status should not lead us to believe, however, that decision-making processes are untouched by gendered assumptions which are unfavourable to women or that on the contrary women are somehow favourably treated in the asylum process in Western states. Spijkerboer who reveals the same questions concerning differences in statistics and qualitative analysis of decision-making on asylum claims, points to the way in which his research revealed a great discrepancy between the "quantitative data indicating no discrimination of women and the qualitative data indicating clearly negative treatment as a result of gendered assumptions"

(2000: 6). Research carried out for this study also supports the idea that statistics suggesting that women are favourably treated in the asylum decision-making process in the West give a false picture of a system which is underpinned by deeply gendered assumptions and where, qualitatively, women may be negatively affected by these gendered inequalities in the asylum process.

A possible explanation for the discrepancy outlined above may be that as fewer women arrive to claim asylum in the West, their claims may somehow be seen as more "credible" by those immigration officials and judges who take the decision. Or it may be argued that because flight is a real "last resort" option for women, and more difficult than for men in many circumstances, those who do flee have more substantial reasons for claiming asylum. Qualitative research seems to discount both of these linked explanations and instead reveal a system of decision-making in which gendered constructions and representations of female asylum seekers may have both positive and negative impacts depending on the individual case. Van Wetten et al. (2001) tried to assess whether cases involving gender-related persecution were judged differently by male and female immigration officials in the Netherlands and again found no significant difference. This would seem to indicate that the gendered constructions of women asylum seekers and the ways in which gender-related persecutions are represented and understood in national policies are deeply anchored and do not change in function of the sex of the immigration official dealing with the case. Qualitative research carried out for this study also points to the emergence of an institutional culture within immigration bureaucracies and judiciaries which leads to the framing of asylum cases in specific ways with highly gendered constructions of male and female applicants. Whilst it is clear that there is a need for more and better statistics to give a fuller picture of the numbers of women and men who claim asylum and the numbers of these who are granted refugee status, far more qualitative research into the ways in which asylum processes reinforce gendered stereotypes and inequalities is also essential.

Women refugees in the West

The lack of research and data on women seeking asylum is mirrored by a similar void in research on women who are granted refugee status in the West. One problem with an analysis of the experiences of these women refugees is that often, once they have gained refugee status they become for governments and for researchers part of a greater category of "immigrant women", and thus lose any specificity which might relate to their particular status as refugees. Although refugees do have a lot in common with other migrants, and although as has been argued in Chapter 1, it is now more or less impossible to separate refugees from other categories of migrants such as "economic migrants", so closely are their experiences and trajectories interwoven, it might be argued that those who have gone through the process of claiming asylum and being recognised as refugees in a Western State will have some particularities which shape their specific experiences. Again these experiences will be affected by characteristics of class, ethnic or national origins, age as well as gender, and so it is impossible to generalise about the experiences of "women refugees". However, some studies have pointed to significant shifts within the balance of gender relations which may occur for refugee populations within Western States and particular problems or advantages which may arise for women within these populations.

Once an asylum seeker has been recognised as a refugee, or once a refugee has been resettled in a Western state through a humanitarian resettlement programme, a complex process of integration and adaptation will take place which may involve significant shifts in family structures and community relations, as well as complicated interactions with host societies. As Castles et al. (2001) point out, receiving societies are not monolithic entities and thus the process of "integration" will be a matter of different overlapping routes which will have varying outcomes according to the diverse spheres of society in which they take place. Some Western states provide specific programmes targeted at refugees and aimed at facilitating their "integration" within the host society, but in other cases the refugees are more or less left to fend for themselves with little support or intervention from national or local authorities. The presence or absence of such programmes may lead to differing experiences on the part of refugees and their communities. Korac points to the contrast between the lives of Bosnian refugees in the Netherlands where there are structured reception facilities for asylum seekers and refugees, and in Italy where refugees are more or less abandoned to their fate by the authorities as no infrastructure exists to help them with housing, employment or integration into society. Both of these models of "integration" proved problematic for those involved, with the Bosnian refugees in Amsterdam finding that the Dutch system of integration manifested itself as state control over their lives and demands to conform to various policy measures, measures which kept them to a large degree separate from the rest of Dutch society. The refugees in Italy on the other hand had experienced considerable financial insecurity and had had difficulties integrating into the labour market in any meaningful way, with women in particular confined to low-paid domestic jobs. They had, on the other hand, experienced more agency and some felt they had established closer relations with Italian society (Korac, 2003).

A key factor in the possible "integration" of refugees into host societies is their access to the labour market. Studies have pointed to the ways in which refugees have had difficulties in finding jobs in Western societies and in having their qualifications obtained in their country of origin properly recognised (Bloch, 1999). These barriers to access to the labour market may be experienced differently by women and men both because of unequal gender relations that they have experienced in their countries of origin and also because of gendered relations and structures in the host society. Thus many women from countries of the South may have had less access to education and qualifications than men and may have had less work experience. Sales (2002) reports that women in the refugee populations that she has studied have fewer language skills than their male partners and are less likely to be in paid employment. This finding supports previous research in the UK which found that 44 per cent of men said their English language was good, compared to only 28 per cent of women (Carey-Wood et al., 1995). Women refugees may also have difficulties entering the labour market because of lack of provision for child care and the fact that they stay at home with children may in turn compound their social isolation and make it even harder to eventually find a job (Bach and Carolle-Seguin, 1986; Bloch, 1999). Similar results were revealed for refugees in other states. A study of Vietnamese refugees in the United States, for example, revealed that women were less likely to be employed and that when they were employed they earned less than male refugees (Tran and Nguyen, 1994).

The lack of qualifications and language skills on the part of women may be seen as a barrier but at the same time women refugees may find access to the labour market easier than their male counterparts in their new host societies because they are able to find lower paid and lower qualified jobs in cleaning and childcare, for example. Binder and Tosic describe the situation of de facto Bosnian refugees in Austria who were granted temporary permission to work in 1993. Bosnian women found it much easier to find jobs than Bosnian men as they were more readily employed as cleaners and thus more easily integrated into the Austrian job market where this type of low-paid and low-skilled employment was in demand (Binder and Tosic, 2005).

The access of women to paid employment in this way, even if it is in low-paid jobs, might be imagined to have a transformative effect on gender relations within family units, especially if men are at the same time kept out of the labour market. Franz (2003), however, reports that her research on Bosnian women in Vienna and New York showed the way in which women maintained "traditional" gender roles and values even whilst they were in full-time employment, meaning that they often took on all of the domestic chores in addition to their salaried work. Other research points to the way in which changing roles within the labour market and within the family may prove difficult for familial relationships, and the ways that the tensions inherent in the refugee experience may lead to the reassertion of patriarchal values and to increasing domestic violence. If male refugees find it harder to find jobs than their female partners, they may feel that their role as head of the household is being undermined, and these feelings may lead to conflict in relationships between men and women and even domestic violence (Refugee Council, 1996).

Negotiating new forms of gender relations may thus prove complicated, and if the refugees are settled within a community of other refugees from their country of origin there may be strong community pressures which limit the extent to which women and men may change their modes of behaviour from those that they had in their country of origin. Shahidian notes the community pressures which exist on Iranian exiles in Canada and in Europe, particularly relating to issues of sexual politics. One woman was asked whether in her opinion male refugees had changed in their attitudes or behaviour regarding relationships, she replied "not an inch", and went on to explain that "It is the same with all of them: they accept you as long as you don't go 'too far'; when you step beyond what they approve, they will consider you a dangerous 'radical feminist' " (1996: 56). Similarly, research on Eritrean refugees in Canada showed that community pressure concerning gender relationships and gendered norms of behaviour was strong and that "the use of public space by diaspora women continues to be circumscribed by the direct exertion of control by men and by rumour, gossip and innuendo" (Matsuoka and Sorensen, 1999: 227).

Hostility, violence and various forms of control or exclusion may also be experienced from outside of the family and community, from members of the host society in the form of racism and xenophobia. In Chapter 1 it was noted that the framing of asylum policies in terms of a security threat and the appeal to nationalist and xenophobic discourse to justify restrictive policies could have a very negative impact on asylum seekers who would be labelled as "undeserving" or "bad" migrants. These types of discourse will also have an impact on those recognised as refugees as the distinction between asylum seekers and refugees – or between those at different stages of the asylum process – is not evident to many, and in general amalgams are made between all of those who come within the general category of forced migrants. Lentin (2003), for example, describes the attitudes of hostility and racism directed against pregnant asylum seekers in Ireland, which in practice affected all black Irish women. Again it is impossible to generalise about these experiences and as Reed's study in the UK showed, some women found that they had experienced verbal racism from their neighbours whilst others felt that English society was racially tolerant (Reed, 2003). Experiences of racism are thus obviously variable and dependent on context. However, it might be argued that in societies where xenophobic framings of the issue of asylum and refugees have prevailed in public debate, there is likely to be a rise in racist reactions to those accepted as refugees, so that even if they have a legal residence status, their full citizenship rights may be undermined by these relationships of social racism and xeno-phobia. In addition, the ways in which racism is expressed will clearly be gendered and will thus affect women differently from men.

Women in refugee camps

For many, the word "refugee" evokes the images of the displaced camped in temporary and poor housing, dependent on humanitarian aid for food and protection. The reality of the refugee experience is that many people who are displaced or exiled do live in refugee camps of one kind or another, often for many years. The US Committee for Refugees estimates that seven and a half million refugees have been "warehoused" in camps for at least ten years (USCR, 2004). These are the people who do not have the resources or the desire to migrate to a Western state to seek asylum. Those that stay within the borders of their own countries, rather than crossing the border to a neighbouring state to seek protection, are officially classed as "internally displaced persons" rather than "refugees" but often their living conditions are remarkably similar. As remarked earlier in the chapter, women make up around 50 per cent of the refugees housed in camps around the world, and in some cases, especially where these camps are established to receive populations fleeing from civil wars or ethnic conflicts, women may be in the majority as they have made up the majority of non-combatants in these wars.

Refugee camps may be envisaged as zones of protection for the populations within them, places where they will be safe from the conflicts they have fled, but these camps may also be zones of conflict, as Hyndman explains:

> Sanctioned by the governments who host them and governed by UN agencies, they tend to be temporary cities of sanctuary, often dependent on external economies of international aid. Relations between refugees and the local populations they come to join are fraught with competition for resources, feelings of unfair treatment, and questions about political instability where large numbers of refugees settle.
>
> (2004: 193)

Specific problems arise for women within these camps because of both material factors, such as the lack of essential resources, and gendered political and power structures that exist within the camps. Callamard (2002) argues that these political structures, which in effect deny refugee women within camps effective protection, amount to persecution of these women as women and as refugees.

Some of the key difficulties that arise for women living in refugee camps are to do with the ways in which the camps are organised spatially and also the ways in which the camp routine is organised by those in charge. Based on her research in refugee camps in Kenya, Hyndman describes the ways in which women's every day lives in these camps is regulated and framed by tasks such as collecting water and food rations. The spatial organisation of the camp structures the women's management of their time and shapes the social routines and income-earning strategies of refugees and in particular women. Access to health care, food and other services are concentrated within one area in the camp which facilitates the work of the staff of the UNHCR and NGOs, but can be inconvenient and potentially dangerous for refugees, and can exacerbate women's workload (Hyndman, 2000). In comparison with the status of citizens and expatriates working within the camp, for the UNHCR and other humanitarian organisations, refugee women occupy a peripheral status of non-citizens or "sub-citizens". This "sub-citizen" status is clearly visible in the camp layout where the UNHCR housing compound is protected by layers of barbed wire and armed guards, whereas the refugee women, who remain the most vulnerable groups among the camp populations lack these forms of protection and live in unsafe and unprotected spaces (Hyndman, 2000; Abdi, 2006).

A major issue is that refugee camps are designed to facilitate the administrative tasks of the UNHCR and of other aid agencies that run the camps or work in them, rather than to make life easier for the refugees who live there. Sometimes this organisation may put women at risk of violence, for example when they have to go outside of the camp to look for firewood. Gathering firewood is generally designated as a task for women as it is they who are responsible for cooking and they usually have no choice in the type of fuel they can use to light fires to cook with. The need for firewood is reinforced by the types of food provided by humanitarian relief which usually consists of rice or flour as staple items, foodstuffs which require wood and water to prepare, both of which are often in short supply in camps (Hyndman, 2004). The dangers associated with going outside to collect firewood have been documented in relation to a number of different refugee camps in various countries. A Human Rights Watch report on camps in Tanzania highlighted the vulnerability of women when they went outside the camp to gather firewood or collect vegetables (Human Rights Watch, 2000), and this pattern has also been observed in many other situations (Hyndman, 2004).

In addition to the dangers of violence or sexual attacks incurred whilst collecting firewood or water, women are also faced with a lack of resources for their basic needs. Again, as it is women who are principally responsible in these situations for feeding their families, it is they who often bear the brunt of the problems involved in managing with the very scarce resources which they receive (Kreitzer, 2002). Facilities for sanitation and washing may also be inadequate. Drumm et al. (2001) report that in one camp for Kosovan refugees in Albania there were only two bathrooms provided for over three hundred people, whilst in another neighbouring camp there were approximately two thousand refugees and only six toilets. Despite UNHCR's commitment to provide sanitary materials which are viewed as "crucial to the health and dignity of women and girls", they admit in a recent report that budgetary constraints mean that the goal of providing adequate sanitary materials to meet the needs of women and girls has been achieved in less than 20 per cent of refugee camps worldwide (UNHCR, 2006a).

Adjusting to life within a camp and finding strategies of survival faced with the lack of resources can also be a process of re-alignment and redefinition of gender roles and relationships. These processes of change may benefit women as they are empowered to take on roles not previously open to them, but they may also have negative impacts. Some studies have shown that transformations in gendered divisions of labour may be at the expense of women, for example, involving women taking on extra tasks which were not economically rewarding or income generating (Ager et al., 1995; Callamard, 1996). Other studies have pointed to a reinforcement of the gender roles that existed in countries of origin within the new setting of a refugee camp. Thus Light argues that gender relations among Guatemalan refugees in camps in Mexico changed little during the course of eight years of displacement. In fact, the conditions in the camp reinforced women's subordinate position as the social structure of the refugee communities within the camps provided men with an expanded pubic role, but made women both more isolate and dependent (Light, 1992).

Above all, refugee camps are sites of violence and a violence which is clearly gendered in nature. This violence stems from the disruption of family and community structures during forced migration, and from the continuation and reproduction of previously experienced violence whilst in exile. Although UNHCR and NGOs have made commitments towards protection of women within camps, in practice the organisation of camps, the political structures within them and the representations and conceptualisations of women and men within these camps mean that this protection is often not effective.

Although it might be imagined that the situation of common exile might create some kind of feeling of solidarity or community within refugee camps, in practice these concepts of "community" or "solidarity" are not always (even rarely) applicable to the relations between populations in the camps. Families and communities have been separated by the conflicts they were fleeing and during their migration; the communal and familial structures that previously existed are thus disrupted and support structures that may have been in place to protect widows, single women or children may no longer be in existence (Hyndman, 2000; Forbes-Martin, 2004). This disruption to communities and families may engender forms of violence which did not previously exist or which were previously controlled in a community setting. Heightened levels of domestic violence have, for example, been reported in some camp settings (Forbes-Martin, 2004). Szczepanikova also reports increased and frequent incidents of domestic violence in refugee camps for Chechens in the Czech Republic which she interprets as a result of the loss of men's status in the family and consequent frustration. Men are unable to undertake the traditional "breadwinner" role that they had previously occupied and may be unwilling to take on new roles such as helping to look after children or doing housework. Chechen refugees also experience the absence of family and community networks that would denounce domestic violence of this type. Family or community control is replaced by "external control" by camp staff which is perceived as oppressive rather than supportive (Szczepanikova, 2005).

In addition, the experience of violence and conflict which has led to the forced migration may impact on the relationships between refugees and between men and women, again leading to increasing levels of violence. For example, research on Lugufu refugee camp in Tanzania suggests that women and girls in this camp face particular problems of protection, which are often linked to the experiences of rape and sexual violence that they experienced before and during their flight. A report on the camp by Oxfam explains that:

> Domestic violence is most common, often affecting women with polygamous husbands, and survivors of sexual violence. Women who were raped during flight are frequently harassed, even disowned, by their ashamed families once they reach the relative security of the camp. Another widespread problem is forced marriage, particularly for recent widows, who face pressure from their in-laws to remarry within the family. Finally, rape is reported in the camps, particularly when the victim is a minor.
>
> (2005: 63)

Harrell-Bond criticises the assumption of solidarity between refugees in camps, and what she calls an "over-socialised concept of man", in other words a presumption that a group of people sharing the same space will automatically cooperate and find commonalities and shared practices. This assumption ignores the effects of diversity in origins and local customs of the refugees, the effects of post-traumatic stress, the realities of the continuing every day struggles for basic resources and the power relationships which evolve within the camp (Harrell-Bond, 1986). These power relationships clearly involve gendered relations of power which may act to create or reinforce situations of subordination for women.

In a later article, Harrell-Bond summarises her observations about the refugee camps that she has studied thus:

> None of them could be described as "communities". They are better described as places where disparate populations have been lumped together and where at times every sort of anti-social behaviour is manifested, for example, alcohol dependence, rape, theft and domestic violence, even murder – not to mention the cases of suicide, depression and gross psychotic behaviour that can be observed.
>
> (2004: 27)

In a study of Kakuma camp in Kenya, it was found that although legal processes had been set up to try and arrange access to "justice" for refugees within the camp, in practice women had little access to these processes, feeling that they were reserved for men. In addition, women who came forward to tell stories of rape or sexual violence within the camp still feared retribution from those they accused and did not believe that the structures of protection set up by the UNHCR were reliable enough to protect them. The structures promoted by UNCHR for achieving gender equality and justice within the camp were thus clearly not perceived as working by the women in the camp, particularly the women in the protection area who are judged to be most vulnerable (Ratner, 2005). The type of processes established by UNHCR and other agencies and NGOs in refugee camps to try and promote gender justice can also be seen to fail in some instances because they reproduce and normalise cultural differences, ascribing unequal gender relations and violence against women to the product of "traditions" which cannot or should not be challenged (Giles, 1999; Cusimano Love, 2007).

Violence against women is perpetrated not only by men within the camp, but also by men from the local population who may resent the presence of refugees, particularly when there is competition for scarce resources. In this case the refugees are perceived as outsiders and competitors and resentment can increase, disproving what Kibreab refers to as the "myth of African hospitality" (Kibreab, 1985; Abdi, 2006). In Dadaab camp in Northern Kenya, Somali women fear attack by local bandits or *shiftas* who attack women when they go to gather firewood, but also enter the camp and attack women in their houses in the night. Abdi's research in Dadaab revealed the extent of the insecurity faced by women in the camp, one of whom related her experiences as follows:

> Intruders come into your house in the middle of the night. They know the door to your dwelling, search the house, and when they don't find anything, they take you away and rape you. You come back to your house and then tomorrow you are raped again. There is no security whatsoever here. How many times have we been raped now? We have become grateful that it is only rape. Being only raped by this stranger becomes a luxury. When you have to choose between being raped and being killed, you think that it is better to be raped. We go in search of wood in the bushes, since we have no wood. Again, in the outskirts of the camp, we are raped, and we still go fetch firewood. And if you don't go fetch firewood, how will you feed your children? How do you cook the grains for them? If you have no

wood, you have nothing. They say they distribute firewood now at this place. It is once in a blue moon that they distribute these. You can do nothing. And if you go to the outskirts, there is an enemy waiting for you there. The enemy might as well rape you over and over; all that matters is getting firewood to cook for your children.

(cited in Abdi, 2006: 238)

This narrative reveals both the insecurity of women in the camp and the lack of any coherent policy on the part of the UNHCR or other NGOs to act against this insecurity, for example, by providing firewood so that women do not have to go outside the camp to look for wood to cook their children's food. Abdi's research revealed that the insecurity experienced by women in the camp was almost uniform irrespective of their social status. Moreover she points to the way that this experience of insecurity has changed men and women's perspectives on rape in that men have not been able to protect their female partners by going to collect firewood themselves, because in this case men are likely to be killed by the bandits. So whereas Somali men would previously have abandoned their wives if they had been raped, they have now been "tamed" to accept the humiliation of "sharing a woman" with the rapists (2006: 241).

Callamard argues that discrimination and violence against women within refugee camps is politically determined by the actions of or under the influence of international, national and local actors. She points to the way in which militarisation and criminalisation of refugee camps constitute major obstacles to the protection of refugee women in these camps and affirms that these trends have altered the meaning of refugee protection, employing a very reductionist and short-term understanding of what is security (2002: 138). Others have also pointed to failures in attempts to protect women within camp settings despite specific programmes aimed at this end, because of the emphasis on control and management of the camps from a distance (Hyndman, 2000).

In its guidelines on the protection of refugee women, one of the targets of the UNHCR is to involve women equally in camp-planning programmes. However, this target is as yet largely unmet, with women still a minority in management committees in most camps (UNHCR, 2006a), and obstacles still remain to women's participation, based both on their assigned roles as those primarily responsible for domestic tasks and childcare, jobs which lessen their availability for participation in other programmes[8] (Kreitzer, 2002), and through political and power structures which continue to frame women as vulnerable and as less capable of managing economic or planning structures. Light (1992) argues that many Guatemalan women in refugee camps in Mexico were unable to speak Spanish, could not read or write and therefore lacked the ability to participate effectively in decision-making processes within the camps. Callamard's (1996) research on a camp in Malawi concludes that the culture of the camp had reinforced the ideological construction of male domination of economic structures, an ideology which was constructed both by international actors and by male refugees themselves. Turner found a similar resistance by male refugees to UNHCR and NGO programmes to empower refugee women in Tanzanian refugee camps. Male refugees who made up the dominant groups within the camps interpreted these programmes as spreading social and moral decay – the fact that refugee women might be given an opportunity to work for an NGO and thus become the "breadwinner" in the household threatened traditional gender relations and men's perceptions of their own roles and that of their female partners. Male refugees insisted on retaining gendered roles and divisions of labour based upon women's subordinate role within the family, thus undermining any attempt to create more equal gender relations (Turner, 2004). Thus even when women are specifically targeted by humanitarian policies this does not necessarily improve their position or safety within the camps.

Turner points to the importance of changes in gender relations as a lens through which all the social changes experienced by refugees are understood. These changes in gender relations can have far-reaching effects on the lives of both women and men. These possible changes in gender relations will be mediated both by the physical and political circumstances of the camp itself and by the variety of populations within the camp. Whilst Malkki (1995) points to the way in which camps in Tanzania are spaces where identity and tradition are maintained in exile, in other situations camps may be sites of far-reaching change. Mann points to the transformations that have occurred in gender relations and in the roles of Afghan men and women in refugee camps in Pakistan. Afghan men, she argues, have been more resistant to changes in their traditional roles, whereas women, and in particular young women, have been able to benefit from increased access to education and work opportunities within the camps. These changes have in some cases made young women more reluctant to return to their homes in Afghanistan (Mann, 2006).

Despite all the violence and discrimination encountered by women in refugee camps, it is important not to overlook these women's agency and not to paint a picture of them merely as "vulnerable" or "victims".

As Kelly (2000) argues, even in surviving violence, women show a form of agency and resistance. This is not, however, always recognised as such, as it does not conform to male behaviour and male models of agency. Women in camps have often fled situations of extreme violence and have managed to escape with their children. They play a vital role in maintaining the well-being of their children within the camps and also show economic resourcefulness in bargaining and selling merchandise to aid their survival. They continue to provide for their families needs in the face of insecurity, rape and violence (Abdi, 2006). This type of agency and resourcefulness should be recognised.

Gender and internal displacement

The internally displaced, whilst not formally recognised as "refugees" as they have not crossed the borders of their country of origin, may none the less find themselves in situations very similar to those of "real" refugees, either in camps or trying to survive in or on the margins of cities. The internally displaced are the largest category of forced migrants, with a total of 23.7 million IDPs recorded in 2005 (IDMC, 2006). As with other categories of forced migrants, these figures are probably an underestimate, as many IDPs are not registered with any national government or international agency. The countries with the largest populations of IDPs in 2005 were Sudan with 5.4 million and Colombia with 3.7 million (IDMC, 2006).

Many of the problems faced by the internally displaced are similar or identical to those of other refugees, particularly when they are living in camps. Incidences of sexual and gender-based violence, for example, are also prevalent in IDP camps. Other IDPs may be left more to fend for themselves in and around the margins of cities. This is the case for Colombia's huge population of forced migrants who are largely rural dwellers forced to flee the countryside and seek refuge in one of Colombia's cities. In this case, gender relations will also be under pressure to change, as women and men react differently both to their displacement and to the new conditions of survival. Meertens (2004) points to the way in which displaced Colombian women have more readily found a place in the economies of cities, taking up any kind of domestic work, which is a continuation of their previous roles as domestic workers in the countryside. Men, however, who had more agricultural-type skills have found it much harder to find work. In addition, he points out the way in which women who are busy looking after the daily survival of their families have little time to deal with the bureaucracies of government or of aid agencies. Men on the other hand are more likely to become "institutionally dependent". Differences also become apparent in the projects for the future of displaced men and women, with men more nostalgic for their past lives and women more ready to envisage future lives in the city. As Meertens explains:

> Men mostly dream of returning and trying to recover their political discourse. They demand solutions from the state, but paradoxically become sometimes dependent on public institutions. Women often develop more autonomous behaviour and become rooted sooner than men, precisely because of their survival responsibilities. Thus, the *gender balance* of the displacement process refers to traditional dichotomies of the public and the private, the political and the social, but these become redressed with new meaning in the daily construction of the future.
>
> (2004: 80)

Despite the considerable variations in the situations of asylum seekers, refugees and the internally displaced in countries of the Third World or in countries of the West, processes of re-negotiation of gender relations take place in the context of adaptation to the new environment and new political and material situations. Often this re-negotiation involves a shifting of the balance between women's and men's public and private roles, which may lead to conflicts as the balance of power shifts from one group to another. These conflicts may be resolved in a positive manner with a greater equality in gender roles and relationships or may, on the contrary, mean that women's position becomes more difficult as male domination is reasserted in various forms. Whatever the outcome, it is clear that women should not be represented as merely passive victims. Their agency is apparent in a multitude of strategies for survival and resistance which enable them to adapt and continue to live in their new circumstances of exile and displacement.

3
Gender Related Persecutions: Why do Women Flee?

This chapter will examine the reasons for which women may be forced to flee their countries, and the types of persecution which can be labelled as "gender-related" persecutions. The notion of persecution is central to the definition of a refugee in international laws and conventions, but it is a concept which is very ill-defined. As we will see in Chapter 4, women seeking asylum have often been refused refugee status in Western states because the violence and discriminations that they have experienced in their countries of origin are not regarded as "persecution" within the sense of the Geneva Convention. This does not mean, however, that women are not persecuted. In fact, women worldwide are subject to a wide range of violence and persecutory treatments which are related to their social, economic and political status as women. So-called "traditional" practices such as female genital mutilation (FGM), forced marriage or dowry murder continue to harm some women, whilst others are subject to forced abortion or sterilisation, rape (particularly in times of war and conflict) or domestic violence. All of these forms of violence and persecution may force women to flee their homes and countries and seek international protection. However, for many women flight is not an option, either because their material circumstances will not allow it – through lack of money, inability to travel without risk and physical restraint[1] – or because the violence and persecution has been normalised to such an extent that women accept it without questioning whether there is an alternative. This normalisation of violence against women is accompanied by a silence because women do not speak out about what has happened to them, and because the violence or persecution often occurs in what is regarded as the private sphere of the home, family or community, it is not seen as a matter for state intervention, or for national or international politics. The true scale of such violence thus remains unknown and largely unknowable. It is not the intention of this chapter to list all of the various forms of violence and persecution which may cause women to flee their homes, but rather to establish the gendered nature of such violence. We will argue that there is a continuum of violence which links all of these various manifestations of persecution against women and which is connected by the thread of gendered relations of power, relations which ascribe particular roles and behaviour to women. Thus persecutions and violence are not the result of spontaneous individual behaviour but rather part of a larger pattern of violence caused by unequal relations of power. These gendered norms may be enforced through particular practices, such as FGM aimed at controlling women's sexuality, or may be legally enforced through laws requiring certain forms of dress for women. In other cases, women are the subjects of violence when they are seen to infringe the norms of gender and to behave in ways that are not in conformity with how a woman "should" behave. Much of the persecution which women face is directed against their sexual and reproductive capacities, as men seek to control both their sexuality and their capacity to reproduce. This control of reproductive functions is often part of a nationalist schema which seeks to preserve ethnic or cultural identity within a population. Thus the rape of women in times of war, or by men from "opposing" sides of an ethnic conflict, should not be understood merely as a sign of men's uncontrolled "lust" but as part of a strategy of conflict within which women have a particular symbolic role. Moreover, these rapes cannot be divorced from the racialised and gendered constructions which have been employed to normalise the practice of providing women as prostitutes for the military (Enloe, 2000). This chapter will attempt to analyse the gendered relations of power underlying some of these forms of persecution. We will start, however, with a more general discussion of what is meant by "gender-related persecution" and of the significance of this debate for international and national refugee and asylum laws and policies.

What is gender-related persecution?

The concepts of gender-related or gender-specific persecutions are ones which have been discussed at some length within the context of national and international asylum laws. These discussions have taken place largely at the instigation of feminist critics of asylum and refugee law, who have argued that women have been largely excluded from the dominant definitions provided by these laws because persecution relating to gender is not recognised as persecution under the terms of the laws. One of the difficulties involved in this debate has been how exactly gender-specific persecution should be defined, and what its extent is. Can any type of discrimination against women be considered as gender-specific persecution? The Committee on the Elimination of Discrimination against Women (CEDAW) defines gender-based violence as violence that is "directed against a woman because she is a woman or that affects women disproportionately".[2] Should all violence against women be considered as gender-based violence, and as gender-specific persecution for the purposes of refugee and asylum law?

Rather than talk about gender-specific persecution, we will rather refer here to gender-related persecution, a term which encompasses persecution which is done to women because they are women, but also persecution which is carried out for other reasons, but takes a particular form because the victim is a woman. In some instances the two elements may be combined, but this is not necessarily the case. As Macklin explains:

> Gender may explain why a woman was persecuted. Gender may also determine the form that persecution takes. Sometimes, it may even be a risk factor that makes a woman's fear of persecution more well-founded than that of a man in similar circumstances. Though one or more of these links between gender and persecution may be present simultaneously in a given case, they are not synonymous. The idea of women being persecuted *as* women is not the same as women being persecuted *because* they are women.
>
> (1995: 259)

To illustrate these differences between persecution *as* a woman and persecution *because* the victim is a woman, three scenarios can be imagined. In the first scenario, a woman is arrested because of her activities in the opposition political movement, activities including attending protest meetings, making speeches and writing articles condemning the government's actions. Following her arrest, she is imprisoned and raped by military forces supporting the government. In this case, the form of persecution (rape) might be argued to be gender-related as rape is used against women as a way of inflicting pain and humiliation. The use of rape is an exercise of power over women, and may be used to reinforce nationalist aims in times of conflicts (see below). Rape is also used against men as a form of persecution (although it is more rare than that against women, particularly in times of war when men are more likely to be the combatants) and this too is a gendered form of persecution. When men are raped, it is also to prove gendered relations of power, to show that their masculinity is not the hegemonic masculinity of the persecutors, but an inferior one. The message of rape of male opponents may be to show them that they are inferior like women, and that therefore they will be treated like women.

A second scenario in which the motive rather than the form of persecution is gendered could be that of a woman subject to persecution for not wearing a veil or hijab when she went outside in a Muslim country where this form of dress was legally obligatory for women. In this case, the woman may be persecuted through police harassment and threats, but the form of persecution may not be explicitly "gendered". In this case, it is the grounds of persecution rather than the actual form that the persecution takes which might be considered as gendered. The woman is being persecuted because she is not behaving like a "proper" woman in accordance with the definition of proper feminine behaviour and codes of dress prevalent in social norms in her society, and in national legislation. But the punishment for the infringement of these gendered norms of behaviour might itself not necessarily be specifically gendered – the woman might be imprisoned, lose her job, be harassed in the street. Similarly, in the case of honour crimes – where women are the victims of acts of violence and even murder because they are perceived as having infringed the norms of acceptable behaviour for women and have thus harmed the honour of their family and their society – women are persecuted because they have not conformed to the required behaviour in a particular society, but the form of the attack might not be specifically gendered.

In a third scenario, we can imagine persecution that is gendered both in its cause and its form. A woman who undergoes FGM, for example, is persecuted because she is a woman, and because the norms of femininity prevalent in her community or society deem that all young women should undergo this practice in order to become "proper" women. The form of the persecution is also highly gendered, involving cutting of a woman's genitals, supposedly to control her sexuality. The persecution is carried out on women because they are women, and it is a type of persecution which can only physically happen to women.

Having described these three scenarios, it must be added that these are ideal type situations, and that as with other attempts at categorisation, it is very hard, or perhaps impossible to establish firm boundaries between these different causes and forms of persecution. What is clear, however, is that these types of persecution occur because of gendered relations of power within different societies, and they are not merely the result of individual acts of violence or "private" matters, but part of larger structures and ideologies within which women have unequal shares of political, economic and social power.

It would be impossible in the limited space of this chapter to analyse all of the gender-related forms of persecution and violence to which women are subject. However, in the analyses of particular forms of violence and persecution which follow, the aim is to uncover the ways in which these forms of violence are not isolated from each other, but form part of a more general continuum of violence against women, violence which is structured by gendered and racialised relations of power. Rather than examining each of these types of persecution as separate, they need to be seen as part of a more general phenomenon. Further, we need to avoid the trap of describing what happens to women in other countries merely as a result of their "cultures" which are different from our "Western" cultures. To ascribe persecutions or violence merely to the result of "other" cultures is to miss the extent to which these persecutions are a product of gendered relations of power which underlie all cultures and societies, manifesting themselves in differing ways at different times and in different places. Often in analysis of violent incidents, on whatever scale, gender as a relation of power remains overlooked (Cockburn, 2004), but it is clear that what makes the link between the different forms of violence described is the relation of gender, which are "like a linking thread, a kind of fuse, along which violence runs" (Cockburn, 2004: 43). The linkages between different forms of gendered violence are illustrated by the increase in domestic violence that occurs when societies are militarised (Enloe, 1993), and this type of violence often continues after the immediate war of conflict ceases. Violence and conflict also construct and reproduce particular gendered identities and representations, propagating specific conceptions of femininity and proper feminine behaviour, which are often centred on women's bodies and their reproductive functions. Feminist authors have demonstrated the ways in which nationalist discourse constructs women's role as that of biological reproducers of the nation, and cultural guardians of the boundaries of ethnic or national collectivities (Anthias and Yuval-Davis, 1992; Yuval-Davis, 1997). These constructions of femininity and of women's roles have an impact on the way in which women will become victims of precise forms of persecution and violence in times of conflict. Women's bodies become sites of symbolic struggle between opposing sides, and also sites of repression, both in times of war, and also during periods of "peace". Various authors have pointed to the way in which militarised violence occurs before, during and after conflicts, during times of peacemaking and reconstruction (Enloe, 1989, 1993, 2000; Cockburn, 2004). This gendered violence can also occur in societies which are supposedly "peaceful" or "democratic" and which have been labelled "safe" by those national and international authorities who make asylum policies (see Chapter 6). The fact that women are seen as bearers of national identity, producers and reproducers of national boundaries, identities and cultures explains why the control of their bodies and their sexuality is deemed so important in many instances (Pettman, 2002). This control will take different forms, and will affect women from different classes and ethnic groups in different ways. All, however, will be in some way positioned in relation to the dominant constructions of masculinity and femininity which prevail in any society.

Cockburn makes three very relevant points in her analysis of the gendered continuum of violence which exists and connects different forms of gender-related persecution. First, she argues, gender links violence at different points on a scale "reaching from the personal to the international, from the home and the back street to the manoeuvres of the tank column and the sortie of the stealth bomber"; secondly, a gendered analysis emphasises continuity between relations and events, thus making sharp distinctions between war and peace, prewar and postwar, meaningless; and thirdly, the continuum of violence runs through the social, the economic and the political with gender relations penetrating all of these relations from the "personal" to the "international" (Cockburn, 2004). It is with this framework in mind that we will discuss some of the forms of gender-related persecution and violence which have been debated in relation to refugee and asylum politics and the international protection of women.

Persecution as a "traditional practice": female genital mutilation

Some forms of persecution encountered by women can be classified under the heading of "harmful traditional practices". This is the way in which UN organisations have sought to understand these types of practice and ritual, such as FGM, dowry murder or forced marriage, in order to try and organise against them. However, it can be argued that despite international attention which has been drawn to these practices and international conventions (such as CEDAW) which have encouraged action against them, they are still very much a feature of gender relations in many countries. Those practices named as "harmful" to women vary from one country and one society to another, and each carries its own different political context and practice. But as Pettman argues, all of these practices "stem from devaluation of women, and masculinist power to define abuses against women as cultural, natural or private, not political" (2002: 210).

One of those harmful practices which has been put onto the international agenda through the activism of women's groups is FGM. FGM is a type of persecution which has recently been the subject of much legal debate, in terms of its relevance as a justification for claiming asylum (see Chapter 4), and also debate amongst feminists who have argued for or against the merits of multiculturalism and have disputed the dichotomy between culturalist and universalist understandings of women's rights (Moller-Okin, 1999; Freedman, 2007a). FGM is still a common practice in many countries in Africa and Asia (as well as amongst immigrant communities in the West[3]). The World Health Organisation suggests that between one hundred million and one hundred and forty million women worldwide have been victims of FGM, and two million girls are subject to the practice every year (WHO, 2000). Although FGM has been the object of international campaigns aimed at ending this practice, evidence shows that it is firmly anchored within the customs of many societies and that in some cases it is even spreading more widely. Ferhati, for example, affirms that in Sudan, around 90 per cent of young girls in Khartoum undergo FGM, and the practice is spreading as girls from the Southern area of Sudan who would not previously have been submitted to FGM, undergo the ritual when they arrive in Khartoum as migrants (Ferhati, 2006).

The practice of FGM is sometimes named female circumcision in order to make a parallel with male circumcision, but this labelling and this parallel may both be considered erroneous in that "the degree of cutting in female circumcision is anatomically much more extensive" (Toubia, 1995: 226).[4] FGM is a term which covers a variety of practices ranging from clitoridectomy (the removal of the clitoris) to infibulation (the removal of the clitoris, some or all of the labia minora, and the stitching of the labia majora to create a small opening, just large enough for menstrual blood and urine). Women and girls who are subjected to FGM experience physical pain and trauma, there is a great risk of medical complications which may be life-threatening, and many women will experience long-term physical and psychological effects.

FGM is sometimes viewed as stemming from Islamic religious practices, but in fact it has no direct link with Islam, even though this may be given as a justification for the continuation of the practice in some geographical areas. Instead, FGM stems from social and cultural norms which portray the practice as one that is necessary to ensure the correct development of young women and girls into "proper" female members of the community. Bellas Cabane's research in Mali suggests that the principal justification and explanation given for the continuing practice of FGM is to control women's sexual desire and to ensure that they conform to the norms of good behaviour prescribed for them by society including chastity, reserve and fidelity (Bellas Cabane, 2006). Similarly, Toubia argues that research on the reasons for practicing FGM in different geographical locations and amongst different cultures, has shown a clear and open underpinning of patriarchal desire for male control of women. Both women and men interviewed for such research seem to accept the constantly reiterated belief that women were inferior, and that FGM was necessary for reasons of beauty and cleanliness, male protection and approval for women, health and morality (Toubia, 1995: 231). As well as invoking gendered discourses of the inferiority of women and the need to control their morality/sexuality, the discourse justifying FGM also incorporates racialised views concerning black women's sexuality and the physical appearance of their genitals. These perceptions were evident in colonialist descriptions of black women's sexuality (Dorlin, 2006), but seem to some extent to have been interiorised by men and women in contemporary societies. Bellas Cabane points out that during her research in Mali, she was struck by Malian women's devalued images of their own bodies (Bellas Cabane, 2006).

Some of the reasons for the lack of success of international and national organisations in stopping the practice of FGM can be traced back to a lack of understanding of the reasons for the deep-rootedness of the practice in local cultures, and of the ways in which outside intervention to try and stop FGM can be seen as colonialist interference with local practices. Discourses which point to the "barbaric" nature of this practice and highlight the differences between Western societies where such practices do not exist and "other" societies which oppress women through primitive beliefs and rituals, only serve to reinforce this impression that Western organisations have not really understood the reasons that FGM is carried out (Toubia, 1995). Winter et al. (2002) criticise the UN's approach to harmful traditional practices precisely for this inability or unwillingness to include harmful practices carried out in the West in the spectrum of different forms of violence against women which are justified with recourse to "culture". The problems of intervention deemed to be coming from "outsiders" may also be encountered by national NGOs which might be perceived as belonging to part of a dominant elite, detached from the real concerns of the population. Ferhati argues that despite the best efforts of national and international NGOs to stop the practice of FGM in Sudan, their arguments are not persuasive because either they are perceived as foreigners who do not understand local practices, and whose intervention may be regarded as patronising and colonial, or in the case of locally based NGOs, because they are perceived as emanating from the dominant elite of Central Sudan, and are thus not seen as valid judges of what is and is not an appropriate practice for local populations (Ferhati, 2006).

For these reasons, it seems unlikely that FGM is a practice which will disappear in the near future. The growing opposition of some women to this practice, however, and their refusal to submit to FGM or to let their daughters be exposed to the practice, has led women to seek protection as refugees. Whilst FGM has been recognised as grounds for granting refugee status in many Western countries, this protection is still, however, not reliable and there is no generally established precedent for granting asylum to women fleeing FGM as will be discussed in Chapters 4 and 7. The reasons why FGM is not always recognised as grounds for asylum can be traced back to the same causes as the lack of success of international programmes to combat FGM, in other words, a construction of the issue in terms which ascribe this practice to different cultures and which build barriers between Western and non-Western women. Moreover, even when asylum is granted to women on the ground of FGM, the discourse of immigration and other authorities still reverts to the framing of the issue as one of the victimisation of these "other" women, using racialised and colonialist images and representations which help to enclose women fleeing this persecution in a state of alterity, and also to reinforce the divisions between different groups of women: white Western women and their African or Asian counterparts.

Forced pregnancy or abortion – controlling women's fertility

Attempts to control women's sexuality are also often accompanied by norms, practices and laws which aim to control their fertility. These attempts at control of women's biological reproductive capacities can be understood as part of the same logic as that which justifies practices such as FGM – the control of women's bodies to ensure that their social roles and behaviour conform to the patterns of gender domination established in societies. Women's role as biological reproducers of the nation, and thus of the particular role ascribed to them by nationalist movements has been analysed in feminist research (Yuval-Davis, 1997), and it is clearly this type of nationalist and gendered understanding which imposes forced pregnancy on women in times of ethnic or national conflicts. For example, during the mass rapes that occurred in the wars in the ex-Yugoslavia, it was noted that one aim of these attacks on women (and not merely an unwanted side effect) was the forced pregnancy of women from opposing ethnic groups, pregnancy which would result in them bearing the children of their enemies.

Attempts to control women's fertility do not only occur during times of conflict. They may be institutionalised outside of conflict in the forms of policies which either limit women's access to contraception and abortion, thus forcing them to undergo unwanted pregnancy, or else restrict the number of pregnancies and children that they are legally allowed. Perhaps one of the most noted instances of the restriction of pregnancy is that of the Chinese one child policy, which forbids women from having more than one child. Women who become pregnant more than once may be subjected to forced abortion, even at very late stages of pregnancy, and to forced sterilisation. Forced sterilisation also takes places in other countries, and may particularly be used against women from ethnic minorities deemed to be "undesirable" or to have too many children. A report on the forced sterilisation of Romani women in Slovakia, for example, points to the way in which medical staff and government officials justify the way these women are sterilised without consent through racialised constructions of Romani women as being unable to control their own sexuality or their own fertility, and as being inadequate mothers who cannot look after their many children (Center for Reproductive Rights, 2006). This type of eugenicist argument may be evoked to ensure that some groups of women are prevented from having as many children as they wish. Despite the evidence of discrimination and violence against these Romani women, Slovakia was declared a "safe" country of origin, thus denying those women who fled from there to full access to asylum procedures in some other European countries. Slovakia is now a member of the European Union, and as such considered as a de facto safe country, although the violence and human rights abuses against some groups of women still continue.

Women from China who have fled because of persecution related to the one child policy have also encountered serious difficulties when seeking asylum in the West. Spijkerboer (2000) describes an asylum claim made by a Chinese woman who he names "Betty". When she was eight months pregnant with her third child, officials from the Bureau for family planning came to her home for an inspection, following which Betty was forcibly brought to a hospital where her baby was aborted and she was sterilised. Asylum official in the Netherlands refused her claim for asylum because her persecution was not deemed to be on grounds that were "political".

Persecutory laws

As well as cultural and social structures and relations which underlie persecutions against women, these discriminations and persecutions may be specifically enshrined in the legislation of a country. In Iran for example, women are legally constrained to dress in a particular way, and a failure to conform to these standards of dress can result in a punishment of seventy five lashes.

Concern has also been expressed about the legally enshrined persecution of women within Pakistani law. The *Hudood* laws in Pakistan have been subject of much debate, both within Pakistan itself and internationally. The laws, introduced in 1979, state that a woman who alleges rape needs to have the testimony of four male witnesses to corroborate her story. Without these witnesses, the charge of rape will be dismissed and the woman may then herself be accused of adultery or fornication. A Human Rights Watch (HRW) report condemned these laws arguing that:

> In effect, the *Hudood* laws have given legal sanction to biased social attitudes towards women, thus not only legitimating the oppression of women in the eyes of the state but also intensifying it: women who seek to deviate from prescribed social norms now may not only be subject to societal censure, but also to criminal penalties. It is this enforcement of religion and its use as a tool to legitimate abusive state power, rather than religion itself, that is at issue here. Although acquittal rates for women in *Hudood* cases are estimated at over 30 per cent, by the time a woman has been vindicated she will have spent months, and in many cases years, in prison and, in all likelihood, been subjected to police abuse while in custody.
>
> (Human Rights Watch, 1992)

Women in Pakistan were rarely imprisoned before the introduction of the laws, but following the adoption of the legislation the numbers of women in prison soared. HRW estimated that between 50 and 80 per cent of all women in prison in Pakistan were there on account of supposed contraventions of *Hudood* laws.

Internal and international criticism of the laws resulted in an attempt to reform them in 2006, but in the face of massive opposition this reform left in place the most discriminatory aspects of the legislation. Notably the criminalisation of sex outside of marriage, the consideration of women's testimony as worth only half that of a man, and the failure to recognise marital rape remain in force. Islamic Shari'a punishments, including possible stoning to death, lashing and amputation for various offences, will also remain.

Similar concerns have been expressed about the adoption of Shari'a law in some states of Northern Nigeria, which can have the same discriminatory and persecutory effects against women as the *Hudood* laws in Pakistan, particularly relating to charges of adultery which are taken as proved by a woman's pregnancy (although for a man to be convicted of adultery, there has to be at least one witness to the act). The implementation of these new Shari'a laws can be seen to reinforce the discrimination that was already existent against women in this area of Nigeria, and to create a political climate within which discriminatory behaviour is encouraged and given a legislative framework. A HRW report argues that "the reintroduction or politicization of Shari'a in Northern Nigeria has contributed in reinforcing traditional, religious and cultural prejudices against women" (Human Rights Watch, 2004a).

Domestic violence

One of the most widespread forms of violence against women is domestic violence, in other words violence committed by a male partner or relative against a woman in her home. Amnesty International estimates that one in three women has been "beaten, coerced into sex or otherwise abused in her lifetime" (Amnesty International, 2004a). Although domestic violence is widespread it is relatively under-documented, both because of a reluctance on the part of women to speak about this type of violence, and because it is often not taken seriously by police or other state authorities and so is not recorded as a crime, and does not appear in crime statistics. The normalisation of domestic violence takes place through the perpetuation of an ideology which treats it as an individual act of violence between two partners, and not as a form of violence which is shaped by social relations of inequality between men and women. Domestic violence takes place in all countries and all societies. Even in countries where domestic violence is illegal, it is often implicitly condoned by the lack of punishment against perpetrators. In Jordan, for example, "honour killings" of women who have been deemed to shame their family, have resulted in prison sentences of six months or less for the perpetrators (Human Rights Watch, 2004b). Whilst in the Russian Federation, complaints of domestic violence are rarely taken seriously or investigated by the police, and men who perpetrate this violence thus hardly ever face prosecution or punishment (Amnesty International, 2004b).

Domestic violence forms part of the continuum of violence structured by unequal relations of power between men and women, and by dominant constructions of masculinity and femininity. The reasons for which men commit acts of violence against women, and the reasons why this violence is frequently dismissed by police and other official institutions, are linked to the way in which proper or normal behaviours for men and for women are constructed and represented. Violence can thus be linked to the constructions of hegemonic masculinities which may entail a proof of a man's virility or power through domination of women. In Jamaica, for example, where high levels of sexual violence against women exist, there is a culture of hegemonic masculinity where status is achieved by the level of "badness" or criminal or violent acts committed, particularly against women. In addition, derogatory attitudes to women are pervasive and highly visible within Jamaican culture – through the lyrics of popular songs, for example (Amnesty International, 2006).

Violence may also be justified by its perpetrators as a means of punishing or controlling women who have crossed the boundaries of expected behaviour, or who have failed to live up to male expectations. Domestic violence in Pakistan is widespread, and is often linked to men's disappointment with the dowry they receive, or displeasure with the way in which their wife behaves. A HRW report on Pakistan concludes that:

> Women in Pakistan face the threat of multiple forms of violence, including sexual violence by family members, strangers, and state agents; domestic abuse, including spousal murder and being burned, disfigured with acid, beaten, and threatened; ritual honor killings; and custodial abuse and torture.
>
> (Human Right Watch, 1999)

This report estimates that the number of women who experience domestic violence in Pakistan is between 70 and 90 per cent of all women. At its most extreme form, this violence results in forced suicide of a woman, or an engineered accident in the home with the aim of killing her – usually the blowing up of an old gas stove. These "gas stove" murders are often carried out when a husband or his family feels that he has not gained enough from his dowry or when he wants to marry again to try and get another or better dowry. The local press in Lahore reported that in 1997 in their local area, an average of four women were burned by these type of "accidents" weekly, three of them fatally. But the Pakistani government and legal and judicial authorities do little or nothing to combat this violence.

> The state's response to domestic violence in Pakistan is so minimal and cases of intrafamily violence are so rarely addressed in any way by the criminal justice system that it was not possible for us to achieve one of our research goals for this report: that is, to track specific domestic violence criminal suits in order to identify larger patterns in the prosecution of domestic violence. We found that despite the staggering levels of intrafamily violence against women, it is widely perceived by the law enforcement system and society at large as a private family matter, not subject to government intervention let alone criminal sanction. At present there is virtually no prosecution of crimes of assault and battery when perpetrated by male family members against women; even intrafamily murder and attempted murder rarely are prosecuted.
>
> (Human Rights Watch, 1999)

Domestic violence is considered as a private or family matter in many countries, and frequently remains invisible or if it is reported to the police, no action is taken. Many women do not therefore even contemplate seeking protection from their own national authorities, let alone fleeing to seek international protection in another state. But for those that do try and claim asylum on the grounds of domestic violence, there are many obstacles. These are exacerbated by the fact that in many of the states which grant asylum, domestic violence is also widespread; and in these states as well, there may be a lack of effective action to protect women nationals from this type of violence. The normalisation of domestic violence is thus so pervasive that it is often not registered as being a proper ground for claiming asylum. One of the most famous cases in which a woman attempted to claim asylum on the grounds of domestic violence was that of Rodi Alvarado, a Guatemalan women who sought asylum in the US to escape brutal beatings and violence from her husband. The immigration authorities in the US admitted that the violence she had suffered was "heinous", and acknowledged that although she had sought protection from the Guatemalan police she had received no help from them. They found, however, that because her husband's actions were "private" and "independent", her treatment could not be qualified as persecution under the terms of the Geneva Convention (Heyman, 2005).[5] The continuing disqualification of domestic violence as grounds for asylum will be discussed further in the next chapter.

Persecution on the grounds of sexual orientation

Persecution against women and men on the grounds of their sexual orientation or homosexuality is a clear case of violence justified on the grounds of non-conformity to the dominant or hegemonic norms of masculinity or femininity. As Dorf and Careaga Perez argue: "Homosexuals are subjected to the vigilance of a heterosexist society that stigmatizes that which it perceives as questioning, exceeding, or subverting social limitations" (Dorf and Careaga Perez, 1995: 325). There are eighty countries worldwide where homosexuality is considered a crime, and many others where persecutions and violence against gay men and lesbians are either tolerated or even encouraged by official institutions. Frequently, the non-assistance of police to homosexuals who are attacked because of their sexuality can be seen as complicity in this persecution (Al'Rassace and Falquet, 2006). Al'Rassace and Falquet (2006) establish a typology of persecutions which are carried out against gay men and lesbians including official persecutions sanctioned by law and committed by state agents, violence linked to the socio-cultural structure of society, community or family, and sporadic violence linked to a specific political context such as civil wars or conflicts in which those outside of the hegemonic definitions of masculinity or femininity may be targeted,[6] or political campaigns aimed specifically against homosexuals.

The persecutions that take place against lesbians may parallel those which are endured by gay men through, for example, laws against homosexuality. However, violence and persecutions against lesbians are often also deeply gendered, resulting in rape and sexual abuse or assault (sometimes with the stated goal of returning them to "normal" models of sexuality). There are far more laws that criminalise gay men's sexual activity, but this should not be seen as evidence of greater tolerance of lesbianism, but rather of its "invisibiliation". Al'Rassace and Falquet (2006) point to the fact that much of the persecution that is carried out against lesbians cannot be easily separated from the violence and persecution experienced by all women who are considered to be "bad" and to contravene the dominant norms of femininity. Thus lesbians may be persecuted through forced marriages, forced heterosexual relationships, rape and sexual assault, which are also the punishments or means of control used against other women who are deemed to have transgressed dominant social norms. Hence it is often hard to distinguish or categorise the reasons for forced migration which depend solely on a woman's homosexuality.

Several countries have now recognised that homosexuals fleeing persecution because of their sexual orientation should be granted the right to asylum, although as with other cases involving the definition of "particular social groups" this is not always guaranteed.[7] In 2006, the Dutch government recognised that gay men and lesbians from Iran should be granted asylum as they could be considered a particular social group facing execution if they were returned to Iran. This decision overturned an earlier policy statement by the Dutch Immigration Minister who announced that these men and women could be returned to Iran as "It appears that there are no cases of an execution on the basis of the sole fact that someone is homosexual.... For homosexual men and women it is not totally impossible to function in society, although they should be wary of coming out of the closet too openly" (cited in Human Rights Watch, 2006a,b). This attitude that homosexuals should not expect to be protected as refugees because they can escape persecution if they do not "come out" publicly in their country of origin is one that has been employed frequently to deny their asylum claims. This type of claim can be seen to reinforce the dominant assumptions that homosexual behaviour is some kind of deviance from a norm which should be hidden to avoid violence or persecution.

Rape and wartime sexual violence

Sexual and gender-based violence can occur at every stage of the refugee cycle: during flight, while in the country of asylum and during repatriation. For example, in Darfur (Sudan) where civil war has displaced more than a million people, gender-based violence has been rampant. In 2004, Amnesty International conducted interviews with hundreds of internally displaced and refugee women from Darfur, who had suffered rape, abduction, sexual slavery and torture. With the majority of displaced people still trapped across the border, and the widespread stigma of rape keeping many women silent, those interviewed comprised but a small fraction of the total number of victims.

(UNHCR, 2006a)

Enloe tells us that whilst prostitution seems "routine" and even "comforting" as part of a tradition around military camps, rape "shocks":

> It shocks, but then it loses its distinctiveness. Typically, when rape happens in the midst of war, no individual soldier-rapists are identified by the victims, by their senior command, or by the media (if there). The women who suffer rape in wartime usually remain faceless as well. They merge with the pockmarked landscape; they are put on the list of war damage along with gutted houses and mangled rail lines. Rape evokes the nightmarishness of war, but it becomes just an indistinguishable part of a poisonous wartime stew called "lootpillageandrape".
>
> (2000: 108)

Wartime rape was made highly visible in the international media and in international politics in the 1990s through the incidences of mass rape during the conflicts in the ex-Yugoslavia and in Rwanda. Rape and sexual violence against women during times of war is not a new phenomenon, but as Copelon (1995) explains, the mass rapes that took place in Bosnia-Herzegovina appeared to be a new and unique occurrence because historically the rape of women during times of conflict has been rendered invisible. Enloe points to the fact that there are a multitude of varieties of militarised rape and that rape perpetrated by men as soldiers has been experienced by women in a wide variety of forms (Enloe, 2000), so that the mass rapes which were so publicised in Bosnia and Rwanda should not be seen as the paradigm of these forms of violence against women. This variety, however, should not hide the fact that wartime rape is not just a produce of individual soldier's misogyny or lust, but part of strategies of conflict and of systems of domination.

Although wartime rape and sexual violence are certainly not new phenomena, it might be argued that since the start of the twentieth century this type of violence against women has been perpetrated on an unprecedented scale. In fact, increasing violence against civilians can be seen as one of the key changes in war in the last one hundred years or so. Whereas conflicts in general used to involve opposing armies fighting on battlefields, now increasingly conflicts are internal to states rather than between two opposing states, and involve the type of fighting and violence which impacts heavily on civilians – conflicts between government forces and rebel militias, for example, in which civilians in towns and villages are targeted for their supposed allegiance to one side or the other. As Giles and Hyndman argue:

Throughout much of the world, war is increasingly waged on the bodies of unarmed civilians. Where it was once the purview of male soldiers who fought enemy forces on the battlefields quite separate from people's homes, contemporary conflict blurs such distinctions, rendering civilian women, men and children its main casualties.

(2004: 3)

Carpenter (2006) warns us against the assumption that the civilians who are increasingly the victims of such conflicts will be female, and argues that gendered constructions of the non-combatant civilian as a woman can discriminate against male civilians who may also be targets of violence but will not be recognised as in need of protection in the same way as women and children. However, although we must be careful to avoid the assumption that all civilians are women and children, it is clear that women, although they may also be combatants, are often among the civilian populations affected by conflict, and that the violence they endure during such conflicts will take on particular gendered forms including rape and sexual violence. As rape, genocide and ethnic cleansing have now become some of the primary aims of wars and conflicts (Kennedy-Pipe, 2000), women are more likely to suffer wartime rape which has been "recognised as a means to demoralize and destroy the enemy" (Niarchos, 1995: 662). Rape is used strategically to terrorise civilian populations and to promote "ethnic cleansing".

Rape and sexual violence during conflict is thus becoming more and more widespread. In an interview with the *New York Times* in June 2005, one of the UN's officials, Warren Hodge, argued that although sexual violence is repeatedly condemned, it persists virtually unchallenged: "Far from making progress, we have regressed. More and more women are being attacked, younger and yet younger children are victims of these atrocities". In Africa, he said, organized, premeditated sexual attack has become a preferred weapon of war, with rapists going unpunished and victims of rape shunned by their communities. Local governments, he added, were resisting international efforts to intervene, suppressing evidence of the violence and sometimes charging the victims with crimes related to becoming pregnant outside of marriage.[8]

Rape in wartime should not be seen as merely a "by-product" of generalised violence, but as a specific consequence of gendered, racialised and nationalist constructions of gender and ethnic relations. As Alison (2007) argues, women and girls are the principal targets of sexual violence and rape during wartime because of the ways in which the opposing constructions of "our" women and "enemy" women create a climate conducive to rape. These constructions bring into play both gendered inequalities and constructions of ethnicity and ethnic difference. The perception that women play a vital role in creating and reproducing ethnic or national groups is an important element of these constructions (Yuval-Davis, 1997), and these ethnic/national uses of women as symbols will vary in form from conflict to conflict. The rape camps in Bosnia were thus used to forcibly impregnate Bosnian women so that they would be compelled to carry the enemies' children as a way of denying their genetic inheritance. The symbolic construction of women's role in this case sees women as vehicles for transmitting the genetic inheritance of the male. In the case of Rwanda, the ethnic differences between Hutu and Tutsi had been shaped and reinforced by colonial processes which amongst other things saw Tutsi women as more "beautiful" and "desirable" than Hutu women. The rapes carried out by Hutu men against Tutsi women can thus be seen as both a form of punishment and retribution, but also as a form of violence imbued with male erotic fantasies about ethnically different women (Alison, 2007).

Rape may also be used as a means of "dehumanising" women and of denying their femininity, and this can be a specific tactic designed to undermine the "enemy" and to reinforce the power of state or opposing forces. Women raped by the military during the Pinochet regime in Chile bear witness to the use of rape as a form of torture and humiliation of women deemed not be acting as "respectable" women (Enloe, 2000). The story of one woman imprisoned and raped by government forces in Iran also supports this story. The woman in question had the courage to ask her torturer how he as a Muslim man could rape a woman. The answer she received was that she was not a woman, but a "piece of shit" (Montazami, 2007).

The consequences of sexual violence and rape can also be highly traumatic and can be made worse by constructions of femininity and of "proper" female behaviour which assign blame for any form of sexual relationship, whether forced or not to the woman involved. Thus many women who have been raped during conflicts then find themselves rejected by their families or their communities because of the sexual contact they have had with "the enemy", and because of behaviour which is seen as improper for a woman. Women who have been raped are frequently seen as bringing "shame" onto themselves and onto their households and communities. Male relatives of these women may also react by rejecting them because of this "shame" and because of feelings of inadequacy or guilt that they have not been able to protect their wives or daughters. A Congolese woman described how her husband reacted to her rape by opposing soldiers: "When the soldiers came into the house they said to my husband, 'we want to rape your wife', at first he said 'no', but they threatened to kill him. After they had raped me, my husband shouted bad words at me and blamed me for bringing this shame. He then threw me out of the house" (quoted in Oxfam, 2005: 52). Another Congolese man interviewed explained that rape was a "curse", and added that: "In our tribe a woman who has been raped is like a prostitute" (quoted in Oxfam, 2005: 52).

Andric-Ruzicic describes the consequences for the survivors of rape in Bosnia as threefold. First, these women often felt that they should assume the responsibility for what had happened to them, they were made to feel that they had somehow provoked the rape and that if they had behaved differently it might not have happened. Secondly, because sexuality is in many ways taboo, the rape or sexual violence experienced is often not discussed, so women are forced to keep quiet about their experiences. And finally, the victim is sometimes forced to bear further responsibility when those in her community are dissatisfied with the mere fact that she has survived. In these cases "the survivor is considered permanently marked, degraded and ostracised" (Andric-Ruzicic, 2003: 105). These feelings of responsibility for what has happened to them, and of fear of talking about their experiences pose additional difficulties for those women who make a claim for asylum in another state. In many cases, there are few resources to support these women or to enable them to talk about their experiences in a friendly environment. As the experiences of asylum seekers interviewed for this study shows, there is still a lack of sensitivity to the particular effects of rape on survivors and this may lead to their experiences being either ignored or discounted.

International reaction to the evidence of mass systematic rape in ex-Yugoslavia and in Rwanda led to the International Criminal Tribunal for the former Yugoslavia (ICTY) and the International Criminal Tribunal for Rwanda (ICTR) both prosecuting for sexual assault and rape as distinct war crimes. Rape is also recognised as a war crime in the treaty establishing the new International Criminal Court. International organisations and international laws have thus made progress in recognising rape as a war crime, but this recognition still seems to have little impact on the thousands of women who are still being raped in conflicts around the world. Moreover, when these women seek international protection under asylum and refugee laws, their claims may still be denied as will be discussed in Chapter 4.

Rape and sexual exploitation by the "protectors"

Gendered relations of power are so deeply entrenched in many situations, that even those who are supposedly "protecting" refugees or civilian populations may become involved in sexual exploitation or violence against women. Members of the UN's Mission in the Democratic Republic of Congo (MONUC), for example, have been accused of exploiting and abusing women whom they are mandated to protect in the area of Bunia. A report in the British newspaper, *The Independent*, claimed that young women, who had often already been victims of rape by Congolese militiamen, were being forced to have sex with Moroccan and Uruguayan soldiers guarding the Bunia IDP camp in order to gain enough food to survive.[9] Many of these young women had babies as a result of their repeated rapes by militiamen and were stigmatised by their own communities as a result. They had no other choice but to become involved in prostitution with the UN forces in order to gain enough food for them and their children. One woman was reported to be so desperate for food that she would have sex with the UN soldiers in return for a couple of bananas or a piece of cake for her baby.

When the UN started investigating these allegations, it became clear that there was a widespread problem. One hundred and fifty cases were brought against MONUC soldiers and UN civilians working in Bunia, including abduction and rape of women and children. In January 2005, the UN's Office of Internal Oversight Services (OIOS) published a report into the allegations which found that at least seven cases of under-age sexual abuse were fully substantiated, and that exploitation and abuse were continuing.

In a further report published in *The Independent* in January 2005, reporters described a typical story of a young Congolese girl, Nadia, who makes a living through prostitution, particularly with clients from the UN forces:

Nadia is 13 years old. She sits on the mud floor of a damp wooden hut in Goma, her eyes cast down and her voice hesitant. "I came from Gisenyi in Rwanda to work in Goma," she says. "My mother died from malaria when I was eight and my father was killed during the war here. When I first came here I worked as a servant to a lady but she didn't pay me so I started to work for a Congolese man who paid me more money to go with him. I have two sisters and a brother and I needed to send money to my uncle for them so I decided to become a prostitute. I have been sleeping with UN men for three months now." Nadia's days and nights are spent standing outside the Oxygen Bar in Goma. She says that her best customers come from the UN. "Sometimes the UN men will take me with them in their cars to a hotel for an hour or two – if that happens I can have a shower which is good because we don't have them where I live," she explains. To the rest of the world, the forces of Monuc have served as shorthand for the good intentions of the international community. Yet girls such as Nadia tell another, more brutal, story: a tale of forces sent to maintain peace who instead abuse their power and act not as peacekeepers but as predators. "The UN men always tell me not to say anything about who I go with," Nadia says, her voice barely audible. "They tell me that they will hurt me if I tell anyone." She stops and then shrugs, looking momentarily as young as any other girl of 13. "They are not always bad," she concludes. "They give me good money. Sometimes one dollar, sometimes five – it depends."[10]

Similar allegations of sexual exploitation and abuse have been brought against UN peacekeeping troops in Bosnia, Kosovo and other zones of conflict. How can we understand this seeming turnaround whereby those who are sent to protect populations including women and children end up exploiting and abusing them? Giles and Hyndman highlight the case of a US soldier posted to Kosovo on a peacekeeping mission who was found guilty of the sexual assault and murder of an eleven-year old girl, and argue that this case brings into brutal contrast "contradictions between the militarised masculinity of soldiers trained to kill or maim and their frequent assignment to UN peacekeeping duties, where their roles involve the protection of a local population" (2003: 12).

It is not only the masculinities of the peacekeeping soldiers which is at question, but also the ways in which the femininity of those "victims" of the peacekeepers have been constructed. Constructions of femininity and of the relations between men and women, have normalised phenomena such as those of prostitution around military bases. However, Enloe argues that while military bases and prostitution have been assumed to "go together" in fact it has taken "calculated policies to sustain that fit" (Enloe, 1989: 81). These policies have constructed hegemonic versions of militarised masculinities which affirm that soldiers "need" the services of prostitutes.

The idea that male soldiers need to be "entertained" emerges in reports in the most recent allegations against UN troops and official in Southern Sudan. *The Daily Telegraph* quotes the local judge who says that there has certainly been an increase in prostitution, and child prostitution since the

UN arrived. He explains this phenomenon with reference to the "needs" of the mainly male staff of the UN: " 'The majority of people working for the UN and NGOs are men and need to be entertained. But no cases have come to court,' he said" (*The Daily Telegraph*, 3 January 2007).

In the case of DRC, young women who have entered prostitution have in many instances already been condemned by the gendered assumptions of their own communities. They have behaved in a manner "not fitting" to the norms of femininity and thus are outcasts, who become vulnerable both economically and socially.

UN troops, although they are "peacekeeping" troops have been militarised, their sexuality and their visions of proper "manliness" have been shaped through the processes of militarisation. These processes of militarisation and of the creation of hegemonic masculinities have profound effects which can be hard to escape. Enloe points out that we know "amazingly little about what happens to a male soldier's sense of masculine licence when he dons the blue helmet or armband of the United Nations peacekeeper" (Enloe, 1993: 33). How easily can these soldiers shake off the militarised hegemonic masculinities which are the norms, and which represent women as being sexual objects for their gratification? Enloe argues that:

> There is nothing inherent in international peacekeeping operations as currently structured that makes their soldiers immune to the sort of sexism that has fuelled military prostitution in wartime and peacetime.
>
> (2000: 101)

In addition to these constructions of femininity and masculinity which make it seem "normal" that male soldiers and officials would need to find "entertainment" with young women and girls who have themselves often previously been the victims of rape of sexual violence, we need to add an understanding of why it is that no other alternatives are being offered to these women and children? The UN and other international organisations have made it their priority to target protection at "vulnerable" women (see Chapter 5), so why is no one making more fuss about the exploitation of these "vulnerable" women and offering them alternative means of survival? Perhaps it is just this representation and labelling of women as "vulnerable" or "victims" which in fact limits their possibilities, in some ways denying their agency, and thus translating in real terms into restricted opportunities for them. Vulnerable women are often placed in special sections of refugee camps but this separation in itself can be problematic, acting to isolate them and erect barriers to their participation in educational or social activities (see Chapter 2). Finally, we need to reflect on the effectiveness of the goals of gender equality put in place by the UNHCR and in particular their relations with other UN organisations, such as those involved in peace-keeping operations. How effective are these policies, and how far have these goals of gender-sensitivity and equality been transferred between different parts of UN operations?

This chapter has not set out to provide a catalogue of all the forms of violence and persecution against women which exist in the world, nor to explain all of the reasons why women are forced to migrate, and why they may seek asylum in the West. Rather it has attempted to describe just a few of the instances of persecution against women which exist and to relate these particular instances to a more general continuum of violence which is exercised against women when they fail to conform to their "proper" feminine roles, and to maintain structures and relations of male domination within various communities and societies. The fact that countries in the West are seen as "asylum-granting" countries, rather than countries which create refugees should not lead to the impression that persecution of women does not take place within these states as well. In effect, as the example of domestic violence shows very clearly, violence against women occurs everywhere in the world, and all of this violence can be considered in the same analytical terms, not as the expression of an aberrant individual act, but rather as part of a larger system of social relations. Although most women faced with such persecutions remain in their countries of origin, some of them do migrate to seek protection in the West. In the following chapter, we will discuss the ways in which gender-related persecutions have been considered under national and international laws and conventions on asylum and refugees.

4
Gender and Asylum in International Law – The Geneva Convention Revisited

The system of international laws and conventions which offer protection to asylum seekers and refugees supposedly offers protection to all on a gender-neutral basis. Many critics, however, have pointed to the fact that these laws and conventions were drafted on the basis of the situation of male refugees, and that moreover, their application is often undermined by deeply gendered practices which fail to offer protection to women because their persecution is not recognised as such. These interpretations of refugee law through the bias of the experiences of male refugees and asylum applicants and their activities has both reflected and reinforced existing gender biases within states. The continuing gendered division of labour within most societies, as well as an underlying assumption of a "public–private" division, undermines the gender neutrality of refugee law and practice by creating situations in which women's experience of political activity or of persecution is not seen as relevant to the law. This means that issues such as the threat of forced marriage, or of female genital mutilation (FGM), for example, are often not considered seriously as grounds for granting of asylum, or may be assigned to "cultural differences" which are part of the order of things. Another consequence of this public–private division is that forms of persecution related to women's "private" behaviour – for example their refusal to adhere to certain dress codes – or to violence that takes place within the "private" sphere of the family – violence committed by a husband, father or another family member – may not be recognised as grounds for the granting of refugee status. The rest of this chapter will examine in more detail these criticisms of international refugee law, and its application in national contexts. We will argue that despite recent advances in jurisprudence which have meant, for example, that some forms of persecution such as FGM are now much more widely recognised under international and national laws as grounds for refugee status, the consideration of gender-related claims is still a relatively arbitrary matter, and that women asylum seekers are still constructed in specific gendered ways which may mean that their claims will not be considered as "serious". We will then go on to consider the claims by some that women should be considered as a particular social group under the terms of international refugee law and in particular the Geneva Convention in order to enable particular gender-related forms of persecution to be fully considered. This solution which is favoured by some international organisations such as the UNHCR is, however, considered inappropriately comprehensive for others, and the chapter will argue that this possibility runs the risk of essentialising gender differences and ignoring variations within the situation of women refugees. All of the arguments about whether or not gender should be included as a separate "ground" of persecution in the Geneva Convention and whether or not women should be considered as a particular social group revolve around the issue of how exactly to define gender-related persecution, and how to make sure that this type of persecution is taken seriously without setting up a separate category which pushes this type of persecution into a position of exclusion from international law frameworks. In other words, how can gender-related persecution and the needs of women asylum seekers be taken seriously without "ghettoising" this persecution and essentialising women's experiences of persecution as fundamentally and unalterably different from men's? We will start though with a brief discussion of the origins and contents of the international Refugee Convention (Geneva Convention).

The Refugee/Geneva Convention

The 1951 Convention Relating to the Status of Refugees (the Geneva Convention), and its protocol of 1967, is the international convention which underpins the currently existing refugee and asylum regimes in most countries of the world. It is the only universal treaty that provides for the protection of refugees[1] and in those countries in which the Convention has not been ratified and adopted into national legislation as the basis of asylum law, the UNHCR uses the Convention as the basis for deciding refugee claims. Recently, the appropriateness of the Convention for governing refugee protection in the current global circumstances has been a matter for debate, with some arguing that given the current "crisis" of asylum in Western countries the Convention should either be abandoned or else re-written. However, politicians and judiciaries as well as NGOs and associations supporting asylum seekers and refugees continue to make reference to the Convention as the "gold standard" of refugee protection.

However, despite the continued use of the Geneva Convention as a point of reference in legislation and jurisprudence on refugees and asylum, it can be described as a "narrow and partisan" approach to the issue of refugees (Marfleet, 2006: 146), a treaty whose vague definitions has opened the way for the reign of the arbitrary in decisions on asylum applications and the granting of refugee status. As Noiriel remarks: "The whole history of international discussions about the legal definition of a refugee demonstrates that there have never been unanimous and just criteria necessary to avoid the arbitrary" (1991: 152). In many ways, the Convention can be seen as a product of its time, the outcome of various international debates and discourses which emerged at the end of the Second World War, and in the context of the start of the Cold War. The Convention is first the product of the Second World War, following which there were about forty million displaced across Europe. The need to deal with these displaced people, together with feelings of guilt and regret by the Allied Powers over the events of the 1930s and the failures to come to the aid of European Jews fleeing from the Nazi regimes, led to the creation of a succession of refugee agencies and the negotiation of treaties relating to refugees and international human rights. Together with these feelings of guilt, however, remained strong sentiments of suspicion towards "foreigners" or "others", and a reluctance to create treaties which would allow too many people to cross international borders. As Marfleet argues, the resulting treaties "did not set out means of assuring the entitlements of those affected en masse by repression or war; rather they were narrow formulae which focused upon the specific rights of certain individuals" (2006: 144).

The United Nations Relief and Rehabilitation Agency (UNRRA) was created by the Allies in 1943, and from 1945 onwards this Agency set out to repatriate the displaced people across Europe, working closely with the Allied armies (Loescher, 1993). This operation was carried out with the interests and wishes of the Allies as a priority, and often the preferences of the refugees were ignored, or took second place. By 1947 UNRRA had repatriated almost 75 per cent of those displaced by the war (Loescher, 1993), and its mandate was only brought to an end when the United States decided that its continued efforts of repatriation to the new Eastern bloc would help the Soviet authorities (Marfleet, 2006). The

UNRRA was replaced by the International Refugee Organisation (IRO) whose objective was to resettle those who had not yet been repatriated. The IRO was in turn replaced in 1949 by a United Nations High Commissioner for Refugees (UNHCR), a dedicated body with responsibilities for refugees.

The Geneva Convention was negotiated primarily by the United States and its European allies, as most of the states of the new Eastern bloc boycotted the negotiations (with the exception of Yugoslavia). As a result of this dominance of the United States, the resulting treaty was highly limited in its application, and aimed at dealing with the cases of those arriving in the West from one of the Soviet bloc countries. As Loescher argues: "The Convention was intended to be used by the Western states in dealing with arrivals from the East, and largely reflected the international politics of the early Cold War era" (2001: 44). The refugee as perceived by the Convention was thus an individual persecuted by a totalitarian regime because of his political views or activism. Large groups of displaced people fleeing from international conflicts or from civil wars were not envisaged. These limitations on the definition of a refugee continue to have important applications today, and mean that is has been difficult for many women to gain refugee status. It can be argued that the Geneva Convention, like other international human rights conventions, was written from a male perspective and that the situations and interests of women were ignored. Spijkerboer notes that during the negotiations which led to the drafting of the Convention the relevance of gender was discussed only once when the Yugoslav delegate proposed that the words "or sex" should be included in article 3 which stipulates that the Convention shall be applied "without discrimination as to race, religion or country of origin". The suggestion was quickly rejected as it was considered that the equality of the sexes was a matter for national legislation, and the then UN High Commissioner for Refugees, Van Heuven Goedhart remarked that he doubted strongly "whether there would be any cases of persecution on account of sex" (Spijkerboer, 2000: 1). These views may be seen as typical of the time at which the Convention was written, when the questions of sex equality and women's rights were far from the centre stage of politics, and particularly of international politics. More seriously, the High Commissioner's remark that he could not envisage persecution on the grounds of sex seems to have endured in many interpretations of the Convention, and the male model of rights on which it was based has in many cases not been challenged in its implementation. As Bunch maintains, "the dominant definition of human rights and the mechanisms to enforce them in the world today are ones that pertain primarily to the types of violations that the men who first articulated the concept most feared" (1995: 13). Thus violations and persecutions pertinent primarily to women are often left out of the spectrum of those that are considered valid as reasons for granting refugee status.

Who is a refugee?

The article of the Geneva Convention which is most often cited is article 1(A)2 which provides a definition of who can be classified as a refugee. This definition of a refugee is of a person who "owing to a well-founded fear of being persecuted for reasons of race, religion, nationality, membership of a particular social group or political opinion, is outside the country of his nationality and is unable, or owing to such fear is unwilling to avail himself of the protection of that country; or who, not having a nationality or being outside the country of his former habitual residence as a result of such events, is unable, or owing to such fear is unwilling to return to it". As argued above, this is an individualistic definition of a refugee, designed to offer protection to a select few, and therefore excludes many people who are commonly referred to as "refugees", for example, those who have fled their homes as a result of natural catastrophes, and the millions of people who flee within their own country, who are considered in a specific category of Internally Displaced Persons. And even within the category of those who might be afforded refugee status under the terms of the Convention, the vagueness of the definition of a refugee has meant a political instrument-alisation which poses extreme limits to those who are actually granted asylum in Western states.

Thus a serious problem with the Convention is the way in which it defines a refugee in very vague terms, which leave everything open to interpretation by legislators and judiciaries within each state. In fact, this problem of definition leads to what Valluy describes as "the judicial fiction of asylum". He argues that:

> The majority of politicians, supported by the media, give credit to the idea that between seventy per cent and ninety nine per cent of the refugees knocking on the doors of European states are in face "false" refugees. And the whole edifice of asylum law – rules, decisions, juris-prudence – built up by judicial experts, lets us believe that there is a clear definition of a refugee and an efficient procedure which enables us to identify a real refugee. In fact this is completely false. The right

to asylum is a void, the concept of a refugee is a judicially undefined notion, and the whole area is left open to political interpretations.

(Valluy, 2004)

The problem with the definition of a refugee found within the Convention is that it is very vague in terms of the criteria for defining who is or is not a refugee. Those who make a claim for asylum have to prove that they have a "well-founded fear" of being persecuted. But what is a well-founded fear? This seems a very subjective notion, which depends on the psychological make up of the person concerned rather than on any objective criteria concerning the type of persecution they have experienced or may be likely to experience in their country of origin. In effect, the vague nature of this term means that it is up to the state deciding the asylum claim, and specifically the immigration officials and judges of that state to determine whether or not they believe the asylum claimant to have a "well-founded fear" of being persecuted. In his study of refugee law, Hathaway (1991) argues that taking into account a subjective emotion of fear when assessing requests for asylum has no practical meaning, and that instead fear should be used to emphasise a future risk in a country or origin, thus making it into a more "objective" criteria. In practice this has meant that states attempt to make "objective" assessments of the political situation in different countries of origin, particularly with regard to respect of human rights, in order to determine whether or not an asylum claimant does really have a well-founded fear of persecution. The difficulty with this situation is that in many cases, these judgements on the political situation in one country or another may not take into account the way in which certain groups of people or individuals suffer from persecution. These generalised judgements about the human rights situation in different countries of origin thus often overlook specific types of persecution, and in particular gender-related persecution.

Another problem of definition is that of what exactly constitutes "persecution"? Again, this is a vague notion which has been interpreted differently in varying contexts, and the practice of different states has been neither coherent nor consistent (Goodwin-Gill, 1996). And as Valluy (2004) remarks: "We can look in vain for a consensus around the notion of persecution: what treatment are we talking about? An intimidating look? A few threats? Someone keeping watch on you from the other side of the street? Daily harassment? The corpse of someone close to you? Scars resulting from torture? Each administrator or judge has his own opinion". Legal experts have come up with varying attempts to define what persecution means in context of the Geneva Convention, and many of these definitions revolve around the notion of basic or universal human rights. The problem with these definitions is that, as argued above feminist critiques of human rights law have demonstrated the ways in which human rights have historically been defined from a male perspective which ignores the experiences of women. Moreover, as Charlesworth and others have pointed out, the human rights laws and conventions upon which definition of persecution may be based, have been elaborated in terms of the violation of existing rights and offer only limited redress in cases where there is pervasive and structural denial of rights, such as those cases where rights are denied because of pervasive and structural gender inequalities (Charlesworth et al., 1991; Crawley, 2001). Thus many of the definitions of persecution that have emerged in the implementation of the Convention by different states have tended to reinforce the gendered inequalities already existing in various countries by failing to acknowledge breaches of women's rights and resulting persecutions.

Gender in the Convention

The Geneva Convention makes no explicit reference to a fear of persecution on the grounds of gender, indeed, the whole question of gendered inequalities was far from the minds of those who drafted the Convention, and there have been no subsequent modifications to remedy this absence. Some theorists concerned with this absence of gender have argued that it should be added as a sixth ground of persecution in addition to the five already defined in Article 1(A)2. They point out that not naming gender-related persecution as such trivialises this type of persecution and demonstrates that it is taken less seriously than other forms of persecution based on race, religion or political opinion. In addition, if gender is not enumerated as a Convention ground, then this adds to the process of "invisibilisation" of victims of gender-related persecution, even though their claims might eventually be admitted under another Convention ground (Stevens, 1993). Others however, have argued that in fact gender-related claims can be made under the existing Convention grounds if states are willing to interpret these in a gender sensitive manner. They have argued that adding a separate ground of gender might cause confusion between persecution because of gender and persecution which takes a gendered form (see Chapter 3 for more details on this distinction), and that this confusion might result in all persecution done to women being subsumed into one category. This would in turn lead to perceptions that women's persecution was always fundamentally different (and perhaps less serious) than that of men.

The UNHCR has concluded that the refugee definition contained in the Convention if "properly interpreted" should cover claims concerning gender-related persecution, and thus that there is no need to modify the Convention to add a further persecution ground (UNHCR, 2002). However, this conclusion seems rather premature when the actual interpretation of the Convention by nation states is considered. Although in theory there might be strong argument against adding a further ground for persecution to those already in the Convention, in practice, many studies have shown that women's claims for asylum when they have suffered gender-related persecution are rejected by national immigration officers or judges. The UNHCR for its part has little or no control over the way in which the Convention is implemented at national level in different countries and although it may offer advice and legal interpretive guidance (Goodwin-Gill, 1996), and may in some instances participate in procedures for the determination of refugee status, this is not sufficient to ensure a standard or uniform interpretation. In fact, one of the areas in which different national interpretations of the Convention have differed widely is that concerned with gender-related persecution. In particular, the issues of whether or not women can be considered as a "particular social group" under the terms of the Convention, and of whether or not persecution by non-state actors (including many of the forms of persecution suffered by women) should be considered as entering with the remit of the Convention, have provoked many different answers from various national legislators and judiciaries.

It can thus be argued that whilst the Geneva Convention and other international agreements on refugees and asylum supposedly offer protection to all on a gender neutral basis, the procedures for granting protection have often been undermined by deeply gendered practices which fail to offer protection to women because their persecution is not recognised as such. Women may also fail to receive protection because of the failure to take into account barriers such as the difficulty in recounting their experiences before immigration officials and judges, but these issues will be discussed further in the next section. As argued above the definitions of persecution which has been adopted by national authorities when interpreting the Geneva Convention have been diverse, but many of these definitions have been based on traditional definitions of human rights which have been defined from a male perspective. As Crawley argues, the interpretation of refugee law has evolved through an examination of male asylum applicants and their activities which has both reflected and reinforced existing gender biases within states: "It is men who have been considered the principal agents of political resistance and therefore the legitimate beneficiaries of protection from resulting persecution" (1999: 309). Thus when considering the practical implementation of the Convention in national legislation and procedures, it is clear that gender bias still remains. Although there has been some limited progress in different countries towards the recognition of gender-related persecution and measures have been put in place in some contexts to provide specific assistance and support to women seeking asylum, this progress remains piecemeal and rather arbitrary, with decisions still depending to a great extent on the discretionary power of immigration officials and judges, and on the views and actions of a number of other actors including NGOs and associations supporting asylum seekers (the role of such NGOs will be discussed further in the next chapter). The progress represented by such individual decisions does not correspond to a real shift away from much of the gender bias present in the application of asylum laws and processes, as will be discussed in the following sections.

The public – private division and the denial of persecution

One of the major effects of this transposition of liberal definitions of human rights into the interpretation of the Geneva Convention been to reinforce the division between public and private found in much of liberal rights discourse. Historically, as many feminist theorists have already pointed out, liberal rights discourse reinforced the division between the public and the private spheres – where the public sphere referred to non-domestic life and the private to domestic and family matters – thus ignoring discriminations and harm to women that took place within the private setting of home and family. Thus huge areas of women's lives are left outside of the scope of legal protection and redress. Whilst demands from women's movements that the scope of rights be extended to include issues like violence against women has led to a re-framing and re-development of the criteria for advancing women's rights across a number of spheres (Charlesworth and Chinkin, 2000), this issue of the demarcation of public from private still remains. The underlying assumption of the public–private division thus undermines refugee law and practice by creating situations within much of what women do and what is done to them may be seen as irrelevant to refugee and asylum law. The threat of forced marriage, or of FGM, for example, may be considered as threats of a "private" nature as they take place within the sphere of the family or home, and therefore it may be considered that they do not come under the scope of the Geneva Convention and they are not grounds for granting asylum to women. Similarly, forms of persecution related to women's "private" behaviour – for example, their refusal to adhere to certain dress codes – or to violence that takes place within the "private" sphere of the family – violence committed by a husband, father or another family member – may not be recognised as grounds for the granting of refugee status.

This public–private division might be argued to be particularly acute in cases of domestic violence which is a type of violence often dismissed as "irrelevant" to asylum claims, even when the women who experience this type of violence can expect no help or protection from the police or state authorities in their country of origin. Because this type of violence takes place within the family, and is indeed perpetrated by family members, it is somehow perceived as less severe than other types of violence which are experienced in the public sphere (Copelon, 1994). A woman who is severely beaten by her husband or father can thus expect less recognition from immigration officials and judges than one who is beaten by the police in her country of origin. Crawley, for example, recounts the experience of two women from Ghana who had both suffered severe domestic violence at the hands of their husbands. One of the women recounts the violence thus:

> My husband started chasing girls after my son was born. He wouldn't come home. If I said something about it he would beat me, with his hands, his belt. I had a very swollen face. He beat me for three years. He said if I tried to stop him he would cut me with knives and kill me. He didn't want me to divorce and his family has to divorce me.
>
> (Ghanaian woman, cited in Crawley, 1999: 318)

Although the abuse this woman and her compatriot suffered was so severe that they both fled the country without their children, their asylum claims were described as "frivolous". The adjudicator at the appeal hearing of one of the women claimed that as far as he understood the law "being beaten up by your husband is not a ground for asylum however deplorable it might be" (cited in Crawley, 1999: 319). This type of official reaction shows the way in which violence which takes place within the home is considered less "serious" and less worthy of official attention by immigration officials than other forms of violence, even though a woman who is beaten in her home every day by her husband may under other criteria of judgement be considered just as much a victim of "persecution" as a political prisoner who is beaten by a guard in his prison cell.

Similarly, sexual violence and rape may not be considered on the same level as other types of violence as they are deemed "personal" or "private", a result of private feelings of lust or desire, and not a form of persecution or torture. As discussed in Chapter 3, rape and sexual violence are often effectively normalised, and considered as part of the universal relations between men and women. This normalisation or relegation of rape to a "private" affair between individuals means that it might not be taken seriously when women make claims for asylum. Although many studies have pointed to the extensive use of sexual violence against women, particularly in conflict situations (Pearce, 2003), this type of violence is still not always recognised as a form of "persecution" that can justify the granting of refugee status. The true scale of this sexual violence is probably unknown, since as the UNHCR concludes, numerous incidents are never reported, often because of the shame of the women involved (UNHCR, 1995a); however, is it estimated that over 50 per cent of refugee women have been raped (Pearce, 2003). Sexual violence may be an explicit tool of political oppression, or may be part of generalised violence in situations of civil war. Its effects on women are both physical and psychological harm. Women who have experienced such violence may also be rejected by their communities and their families as they are perceived to have dishonoured them by engaging in sexual intercourse even if this was forced. However, despite the prevalence of rape and sexual violence and the clear harmful effects on women, often it is not recognised as a form of "serious harm" under the terms of the Geneva Convention, and so women who have suffered from these types of violence do not receive refugee status. As Macklin argues:

> Some decision makers have proven unable to grasp the nature of rape by state actors as an integral and tactical part of the arsenal of weapons deployed to brutalize, dehumanize and humiliate women and demoralize their kin and community.
>
> (1995: 226)

In Germany, for example, women have been refused asylum on the grounds of rape during times of ethnic conflict, because "widespread rape by hostile militia has been dismissed as the common fate of women caught in a war zone and not recognised as persecution" (Ankenbrand, 2002: 48). A report by the Black Women's Rape Action Project and Women Against Rape in the United Kingdom describes a similar phenomenon of the rejection of asylum claims by women who have been raped, as the political nature of this type of violence is not acknowledged and rape is not recognised as persecution. The report provides an example of a Ugandan woman who was raped by soldiers during an interrogation about her alleged support for rebels in the country. The Asylum Appeal Adjudicator rejected her claim, dismissing the rape as an act of "sexual gratification" and not persecution under the terms of the Geneva Convention. This judgement was upheld in the High Court where the judges argued that the woman was not a victim of persecution but merely of "dreadful lust" (BWRAP and WAR, 2006). And in another case in the United States, an immigration judge told a woman from El Salvador that the fact she was raped by a soldier who accused her of being a guerrilla was not a political or state sanctioned act, part of a regime of repression and persecution by the government against supposed guerrillas, but more "because she was a female convenient to a brutal soldier acting only in his own self-interest" (cited in Macklin, 1995: 225). Further, the conditions under which female asylum seekers are interviewed about their experiences often makes it almost impossible to talk about the sexual violence of which they have been the victim (see discussion below).

Are women's activities "political"?

The underlying presence of this public–private division also has an impact on the way that what is "political" is defined, and this in turn means that women's activities may not be considered as "political" in the same way as men's and that their asylum claims will be denied for this reason. Persecution on grounds of political opinion is one of the least disputed grounds included in the Geneva Convention (Crawley, 2001), and in fact, asylum is often referred to in common usage as "political asylum". The importance of the political as a criteria for granting refugee status can be seen as a result of the way in which the Geneva Convention was interpreted historically, and in particular of its development through the Cold War period (see above). However, although engaging in political activity for which one is persecuted seems clearly to enter within the terms of the Convention as a justification for granting refugee status, a gendered interpretation of what counts as "political activity" invalidates many claims by women. As Indra argues:

> The key criteria for being a refugee are drawn primarily from the realm of public sphere activities dominated by men. Where women's presence is more strongly felt, there is primarily silence – silence compounded by an unconscious calculus that assigns the critical quality "political" to many public activities but few private ones.
>
> (1987: 3)

The question of what is "political" and what type of activity should be considered as "political activism" has been largely debated by feminists who have been critical of the traditional narrow definitions of the political sphere. Political action, they argue, is not defined merely by belonging to a political party, by standing for election to a representative body or by taking a role in a political executive. All of these activities have traditionally been dominated by men, and women have in most states been excluded from this formal sphere of political power. However, there are many different ways of being involved in political action which are not always recognised as such, including activism in grassroots and non-governmental organisations, providing alternative networks for food, shelter and medical provision. A recognition that these types of activities are related to power relations and structures, means a widening of the definition of what is political to include a wide range of activities. The gendered division of labour and gendered roles adopted within most cultures and most societies, mean that women's activities within any given society will often be different from those of men. They may indeed participate more "indirectly" in political activity, becoming involved in "supporting" roles such as hiding people, passing messages or providing food or medical care. But because they have been largely absent from political elites they are often considered as non-political (Waylen, 1996). When considering asylum claims under the Geneva Convention, often the different types of political activity undertaken by women are overlooked or dismissed, so that their claims for asylum on the grounds of persecution based on political opinion are not accepted. A further argument for taking women's political activity seriously, and for considering women's claims for refugee status on the basis of this political activity, relates to women who refuse to comply with discriminatory laws or norms in their countries of origins. Rather than viewing this refusal as a private matter which has no political relevance, it might be considered that women who choose to disobey rules and laws in this way are committing a highly political act. Women who refuse, for example, to comply with laws which impose particular modes of dress, such as the veil or chador, might be seen to be undertaking a highly political act of opposition. A similar analysis could be made of Chinese women's opposition to the one-child policy imposed by their government which exposes those who contravene the regulations to the risk of forced abortions and sterilisations. Again, however, the issues of pregnancy and childbirth involved in this type of opposition are often not constructed as "political" and so fall outside of the interpretation of who is a refugee. This type of analysis of women's activities has often been missing, however, in the rather limited interpretations of the Geneva Convention that have been prevalent in Western states.

Cultural difference and non-recognition of persecution

A further barrier to the recognition of gender-related persecution within current definitions and interpretations of the Geneva Convention, is the way in which persecutory practices which may be common in "Third World" Countries are assigned to "cultural difference" and are thus viewed as part of the order of things. This normalisation of persecutions through their ascription to cultural differences which should not be challenged by Western states feeds into the debates over the possibility of defining universal women's rights, or whether these rights should be culturally sensitive. Liberal rights discourse has been criticised for its "false universalism" and its inability to accommodate cultural diversity. In international arenas, some of the resistance to universal standards for women's rights has in fact been led by conservative states and religious NGOs (Sen and Correa, 1999; Molyneux and Razavi, 2002) but this universal rights discourse has also been criticised by some feminists who have argued that it does not take account of differences amongst women, and reproduces an ethnocentric and Western model of rights which supports the idea of Western cultural superiority (Mohanty, 1991). The difficulty is thus to determine how far any defence of "cultural difference" is actually a defence of practices which amount to an attack on women's rights and to persecution of women. As Rao points out, the arguments against universal rights based on the need to maintain cultural difference, actually serve a variety of interests and may in fact be employed by regimes which are unfavourable to women's emancipation (Rao, 1995). Claims to defend "traditional" cultures often involve control of areas such as family life which lead to the subjugation of women within the domestic sphere and as Molyneux and Razavi argue:

> The fact that the roles and symbolism associated with femininity together with patriarchal authority and masculine privilege are often made into cultural signifiers, places women's individual rights in conflict with those seeking to impose "traditional", "authentic", or "national" customs on their people.
>
> (2002: 15)

These conflicts between women's individual rights and those who seek to impose "traditional" or "cultural" practices upon them can easily lead to persecutions of women, but claims for asylum based on these persecutions may not be recognised as legitimate if the imperative of recognising cultural difference prevails. For example, in a recent decision, the British Court of Appeal rejected an asylum claim from a Sierra Leonean woman who feared forced genital mutilation if she were returned to her country. One of the judges argued that the practice of FGM was clearly accepted by the majority of the population of Sierra Leone and was not in those circumstances discriminatory (RWRP, 2005). This decision was later overturned by the House of Lords who ruled that the claimant could be considered as part of a "particular social group" of women from Sierra Leone who were at risk of FGM; however, despite the positive outcome for this woman, the earlier ruling by the appeal court judges shows a worrying trend of cultural relativism which is present among many of those involved in processing and judging asylum claims. This cultural relativism goes hand in hand with the fears mentioned above of a "flood" of female asylum seekers if Western states were to admit that what these women were experiencing was indeed persecution and not merely a local custom which was widely practiced and therefore acceptable.

Persecution by non-state agents and non-protection by the state authorities

A further barrier to the recognition of gender-related persecution as justifying refugee status is the fact that often this persecution is carried out by private individuals and not agents of the state in the applicant's country of origin. Some states have refused to grant refugee status under the Geneva Convention when the persecution that has been suffered has been from a non-state agent (Bouteillet-Pacquet, 2002), thus ruling out many forms of gender-related persecution as grounds for granting refugee status. The new qualifications directive of the EU (see Chapter 6) has removed this restrictive possibility, directing national governments to consider persecutions by private or non-state agents as coming under the terms of the Geneva Convention. However, there are fears that national authorities may continue to use a restrictive interpretation regarding the author of the persecution, and in particular a restrictive definition of whether or not the victim of the persecution could expect any protection from their state. In order to prove that he or she should be granted refugee status, an asylum seeker must not only prove a well-founded fear of persecution but must also show that he or she cannot expect any protection from their own governments or authorities. Some NGOs interviewed for this research expressed a fear that this clause would be used by governments and immigration authorities to refuse asylum claims, in a similar way as the dismissal of claims of persecution by non-state agents was used in the past.

Another fear expressed about the evolution of asylum policies was that immigration officials and judges would move towards the granting of temporary or subsidiary forms of protection for cases involving gender-related persecution, rather than offering full refugee status to those claiming asylum on this basis (see Chapter 6 for a fuller discussion). This relegation of gender-related persecution to a sub-category which justifies a lesser form of protection for those claiming on this basis has already been experienced in some countries such as Sweden (see below).

Should women be considered as a "particular social group"

Much of the legal debate over the best way to ensure that gender-specific forms of persecution are brought within the remit of the terms of the Geneva Convention has revolved around the notion of a "particular social group". One of the grounds for persecution that is included within the Convention as a basis for granting refugee status is that of membership of a particular social group. Although many cases of gender-related persecution might be thought to enter into this category, with women in a particular country being considered as members of a particular social group when gender-based persecution is widespread within this country, there has been a reluctance to admit that women can be recognised as a particular social group in this way.

The recognition of women as a particular social group is a solution favoured by the European Parliament, which adopted a resolution in 1984 calling upon states to consider women who had been the victims of persecution because of their sex, as a particular social group, under the terms of the Geneva Convention. The UNHCR also supports this line of action, its *Guidelines on the Protection of Refugee Women* (1991), also calling for women who face persecution for violating social norms to be considered for refugee status as members of a particular social group. However, although there have been cases where women have been offered refugee status under this ground of the Convention, the limits to the particular social group constituted are always very precise, in order to avoid setting a precedent of a wide category which could be open to many women asylum seekers. It seems unlikely that most Western states will move towards a more general recognition of gender as a characteristic of a particular social group because of the perception that this recognition would lead to a "flood" of asylum claims by women. In an interview, for example, the head of the French Commission de Recours des Réfugiés (Refugee Appeal Commission), expressed the opinion that the recognition of the principle that women formed a particular social group would lead to the risk of receiving asylum claims from "half of humanity".[2] This fear of a "flood" of women refugees is, as we have discussed earlier in the book, clearly unfounded when the barriers to women leaving their countries of origin and arriving in the West to claim asylum are considered (see Chapter 2).

Further, the issue of whether or not it would be beneficial for women asylum seekers to be classified as a particular social group in this general way, with the notion of particular social group being based on the idea of a shared gender, is a matter for debate, with some arguing that this would be inappropriately comprehensive (Kofman et al., 2000; Crawley, 2001). As many feminists have previously argued, "women" do not constitute a cohesive social group, and within any country there will be numerous differences between the status and situation of various women. With reference to asylum claims therefore, "the very assumption that women have common experiences which can be explained by reference to their gender alone can itself undermine the argument" (Crawley, 2001: 73). Attempting to define women as a particular social group may also fall into the trap of essentialising gender differences, and portraying refugee women as victims of "barbaric" third world cultures (Oswin, 2001). The problems with these types of representations which portray women from Third World countries as "victims" is that it fixes an opposition between "them" and "us", between "Western women" and "Other women" which might obscure the real structures of gender inequalities in different societies and the reasons for the persecutions that women suffer as a result. We will discuss further in the next chapter some of the problematic issues concerning the representations of refugee and asylum seeking women, the next section will discuss more practical barriers that women face when making an asylum claim.

Practical barriers to making asylum claims

The UNCHR's dialogue with refugee women in 2001 revealed that these women still felt there were many gender-related inequalities and discriminations present within asylum determination processes in Western countries:

> When seeking asylum, participants reported that refugee women are often not aware of their right to file a claim separately from their husbands. Thus, even when they have an asylum claim of their own, their fate depends on the outcome of their husband's claims. Also, refugee women argued that often judges or immigration officials lack awareness of the status of women within the culture from which female asylum seekers come, which impacts negatively on their ability to claim and be granted asylum. In the regional consultation in Montreal, Canada, refugee women spoke of the need to sensitise and inform male immigration officials, border guards, police and security officers about gender-related issues. Participants at the Montreal regional consultation described the "second trauma" of asylum procedures, where sensitive gender issues are often misunderstood, ignored and at times, ridiculed. "All the women gathered agreed that immigration judges are insensitive to asylum seekers, especially female applicants. Most adjudicators are uninformed about issues affecting women... [they] did not have much knowledge regarding the country of origin" (Montreal, Canada, 3 May 2001) Refugee women stated that long processing times for asylum procedures increased psychological stress, and requested UNHCR to advocate with governments to shorten time periods. They also stated that decision-making of asylum cases must be made more transparent.
>
> (UNHCR, 2001: 26)

The various legal and judicial barriers to recognition of women's claims regarding gender-related persecution have been exacerbated by the way in which claims are heard in many countries. In the asylum procedures in some countries, married couples are encouraged or forced to make a joint claim for asylum. This means that the man will in almost all cases be the primary claimant, and the woman will be considered as his dependent. Being reduced to the status of dependent, rather than making a claim in her own right may have serious consequences for a woman, who will be reliant on her male partner for any legal status that she has, and may thus be forced to stay with a violent or abusive partner in order not to lose her right to stay in a host country. As Valji explains:

> The omission of any clarification on the rights of a spouse has led most states to practice what is termed derivative status. In essence, a man is granted the category of asylum, and his wife is then given asylum status (or in many countries, a lower protection category such as residency), which is derived solely from her position as the wife...the practice leaves women at the complete mercy of their partners.
>
> (2001: 28)

Moreover, the joint hearing of couples' claims has the effect of reinforcing the idea that it is the man who has a legitimate justification for claiming asylum – it is he who has experienced real persecution – and on the contrary of invalidating any independent claim the woman might have had due to her own persecutions. This understanding that it is the male partner whose claim to have been persecuted is that which counts means that any evidence the wife might have put forward as to her own experiences of persecution could be dismissed. Asylum claims which may have succeeded if the evidence of persecution of both partners were considered may thus fail as the woman's testimony will not be heard.

More practical issues arise in that joint interviews for couples may lead to a woman being unable or unwilling to express what has happened to her in her country of origin, particularly if this story of persecution involves any kind of sexual abuse or rape which she may not want to mention in front of her husband. Karola Paul, explains the difficulties that arise from Canada's procedure of hearing husband and wife asylum claimants at the same time:

> Persecution as well as the kind of mistreatment a woman suffers generally concerns her honour and thus the honour of her family. A woman coming from such a culture who admits during the hearing that she has been sexually mistreated or even raped during detention would normally have to take her own life in accordance with

the traditions of her home country in order to restore the honour of her family. There are examples of women being beaten by husbands who suspected they had been sexually mistreated while tortured. Men are ashamed because they feel that they have failed as protectors and their aggressions turn against those they were expected to protect.

(cited in Oosterveld, 1996: 587)

For women making an asylum claim on the basis of gender-related persecution, it may also be very difficult to explain their histories to male immigration officials. Many countries have in theory admitted that women in this case should have the possibility of being interviewed by female immigration officials with female interpreters present if necessary. However in practice, this recommendation is often not followed, either because there are not female immigration officers available to carry out the interview, or because women are not informed of their right to ask for a female official, or are too scared to do so (Liedtke, 2002). In Spain, for example, female asylum seekers have the right to file independent applications and to be interviewed by female staff, but they are not always informed of this right. Further "legal representatives dealing with cases involving sexual violence, rape or forced sterilisation are not sufficiently trained for interviewing such cases", which creates a disadvantage based on gender and "accentuates the differentiation among asylum seekers" (Jaubany-Baucells, 2002: 422).

The fact of having her asylum claim examined by a male official can thus exacerbate the tendencies noted in previous research of cultural or psychological misunderstandings which occur frequently during the examination of asylum claims, and in asylum adjudication hearings (Kälin, 1986; Barsky, 1994; Pelosi, 1996). Women who have experienced particularly traumatic incidences of violence may manifest their trauma in a variety of ways, some of which may be misinterpreted by immigration officials or judges (Pelosi, 1996; Rousseau et al., 2002). These cultural and psychological misunderstandings are also gendered, a point highlighted by research showing the differences in the ways that men and women react to trauma and tell their stories. Daniel, for example, points to the fact that men are more likely to present coherent narratives of violence while women may find it much more difficult to speak about violence and in particular, sexual violence (Daniel, 1996). This factor is often overlooked by immigration officials, however, who may take silence or a lack of emotion as a sign that the asylum seeker is not credible (Spijkerboer, 2000).

The burden of proof and credibility

Even when women are heard independently from their husbands and have the opportunity to explain their case to a female immigration official, they come up against a barrier of proving their case in front of immigration officials and judges who are more often than not sceptical about their claims. The climate of disbelief surrounding asylum seekers means that the level of "proof" needed to substantiate their claim has risen continually. Noiriel refers to the "absence of proof" as the "leitmotif which justifies all the rejections" of asylum seekers (Noiriel, 1991: 237), and as rejection rates continue to rise, so too does the level of proof required to avoid rejection. Often the form of proof required is that of physical evidence of violence or torture in the form of a medical certificate certifying the scars of such violence. Again this demand for proof may be particularly difficult for women who have suffered sexual violence or rape and are reluctant to talk about it or to submit to medical examinations which will heighten their feelings of humiliation or shame. And as Valji argues "sexual violence is by nature difficult to prove, compromising women's evidentiary assessments" (2001: 30). Women and NGOs interviewed for this research commonly pointed to a lack of proof as the reason for which women's asylum claims had been rejected.

Ironically, a move towards greater recognition of some forms of gender-related persecution has also resulted in some instances in greater barriers to proving these cases. This results from assumptions among some immigration officials that once they have created a judicial precedent, many other asylum seekers will be tempted to "jump on the bandwagon". Thus, French NGOs report that in cases where a woman is claiming asylum on the grounds of feared FGM, the level of proof required in terms of medical certificates and expert witness statements has become very stringent, and that any claimant who does not have all of these certificates will be sure to have her claim rejected.[3]

The rising number of women who claim asylum on the grounds of rape or sexual violence has also led to a problem of credibility as some decision-makers seem to assume that "all women say they've been raped".[4] As Schottes and Schuckar point out, asylum seekers coming from civil war regions quite often tell very similar stories about sexual abuse and rape. They are then accused of making up their story in the hope of being granted asylum (Schottes and Schuckar, cited in Binder and Tosic, 2005: 616). This presumption that asylum seekers copy their stories off one another was taken to the extreme in one case in the

United States where a Nigerian woman who had spent time in detention had her asylum claim prejudiced by the fact of this detention. In effect, the judge rejected her claim on the basis that her story of gang rape by Nigerian militia had been embellished by other asylum seekers during the time that she was in detention (WCRWC, 1997: 38). Women's accounts may also be less likely to be believed if they fail to give details of rape or sexual violence when they first make their claim, although there are often compelling psychological or social reasons not to do so (Rousseau et al., 2002; BWRAP and WAR, 2006). Rousseau et al. describe the case of a Congolese woman claiming asylum in Canada who had not reported her rape when she made her claim at the border. Members of the Immigration and Refugee Board did not understand this non-disclosure "even though her previous disclosure of this event had had devastating consequences for her: her husband had abandoned her, and her father had been assassinated because he intended to ask for her aggressors...to be brought to justice" (Rousseau et al., 2002: 58).

Many other women recount stories of how their credibility is undermined by failure to remember exact dates and place names in their stories. Often these errors or contradictions will concern only minor details, but they are enough to falsify the whole of the claim in the eyes of the decision-makers.

Gender guidelines

In order to respond to some of the above criticisms of the operation of international laws and policies regarding female asylum seekers and refugees, a few countries have introduced so-called "gender guidelines" which aim to ensure that issues related to gender are taken into account in the determination of asylum claims. The adoption of such guidelines is a solution favoured by the UNHCR who have produced a range of guidelines over the years in order to try and encourage states to incorporate a gender-sensitive approach into their processes of determining asylum claims. Crawley and Lester highlight the positive value of such guidelines, arguing that: "They are an important policy mechanism for ensuring a gender-sensitive perspective on the 1951 Convention and for ensuring that the gender-related and gender-specific aspects of asylum claims are properly assessed and taken into account in procedures for refugee status determination" (2004: 22). However, evidence from most Western states suggests firstly that there is little uniform acceptance for the need to incorporate such guidelines into their national policies or legislation, and secondly, that even where guidelines have been adopted their implementation rests patchy at best.

It can be argued that the first international acknowledgement from an international body of the need for a gender-aware interpretation of the Geneva Convention, came from the European Parliament which in 1984 passed a resolution calling upon states to recognise women who "face harsh or inhumane treatment because they are considered to have transgressed the social mores of the country" as a particular social group under the terms of the Convention.[5] This initiative was taken up by the UNHCR Executive Committee which in 1985 adopted a conclusion echoing the resolution of the European Parliament.[6] This conclusion encouraged all member states to adopt an interpretation of the 1951 Convention under which women who faced inhumane treatment because of their failure to conform to the social mores of their country should be considered as a particular social group. However, it was not until 1991 that the UNHCR sought to effectively implement their recommendation of 1985, by issuing a set of guidelines on the protection of refugee women (UNHCR, 1991) outlining actions to be taken to increase international protection for these women, and advocating improvements in the standards of asylum and refugee determination procedures to improve the access of women to refugee status (Forbes-Martin, 2004). In 1995, additional guidelines were issued to deal specifically with the problem of sexual violence, a question closely related to gender-specific persecutions (UNHCR, 1995b), and in 2002, further guidelines on international protection and gender-related persecution were published (UNHCR, 2002).

These latest guidelines from the UNHCR point to the need to understand the wide-ranging nature of gender-related persecution and to recognise that these gender-related forms of persecution may be considered as coming within the remit of the Geneva Convention. However, they also underline the individualised nature of persecution and the need to prove in each case a well-founded fear of persecution, limitations of the refugee definition which have been previously criticised (see above) The guidelines state:

> What amounts to a well-founded fear of persecution will depend on the particular circumstances of each individual case. While female and male applicants may be subjected to the same forms of harm, they may also face forms of persecution specific to their sex. International human rights law and international criminal law clearly identify certain acts as violations of these laws, such as sexual violence, and

support their characterisation as serious abuses, amounting to persecution. In this sense, international law can assist decision-makers to
determine the persecutory nature of a particular act. There is no doubt
that rape and other forms of gender-related violence, such as dowry-
related violence, are acts which inflict severe pain and suffering –
both mental and physical – and which have been used as forms of
persecution, whether perpetrated by State or private actors.

(UNHCR, 2002: 3)

Feminist NGOs and transnational networks clearly had an important
influence in placing these issues on the UN agenda and in lobbying
for specific policies to respond to the situation of refugee and asylum
seeking women. In particular, during the late 1980s and early 1990s,
the Working Group on Refugee Women, a coalition of different NGOs
with an interest in the subject put pressure on the UNHCR to address
the situation of women refugees and asylum seekers, convening meetings to coincide with the Executive Committee meetings at the UNHCR
and lobbying these meetings to ensure that the position of refugee
women and gender issues were taken into account (Forbes-Martin,
2004). Transnational action has also had an impact at the level of
the European Union, starting from the European Parliament resolution of 1984. During 2000–2001, for example, the European Women's
Lobby (EWL) undertook a campaign entitled "Persecution is not gender
blind: women demand refugee status in their own right",[7] attempting
to highlight the specific forms of persecution faced by women and the
difficulties that they encounter in making asylum claims based on these
persecutions. Most recently the EWL has launched a campaign based on
the adoption of the new "qualification" directive (Directive 2004/83/CE)
that all EU member states should transpose into their national law by 10
October 2006. The campaign is aimed at ensuring the potential benefits
of this directive for women asylum seekers – the recommendation that
states take into account acts of sexual violence and discriminatory acts
directed against a person because of their sex when considering who
should qualify for refugee status, and the recognition that persecution
committed by non-state actors should be considered as entering under
the terms of the Geneva Convention – are fully achieved when the
directive is transposed into national legislations.

It can thus be argued that the recognition of the need to address
specifically the question of women refugees and asylum seekers and to
adopt gender-specific policies has taken place, at least to some extent, at
international level, and that norms of gender specific action have been

adopted in international policy and directives on refugees. These norms, however, have had an uneven transition into national policy arenas, especially concerning the recognition of gender-specific persecution and the protection of female asylum seeker and refugees. Few countries have officially integrated such directives into their legislation on asylum, and even where the directives have been transposed into national policies and legislations, they are not always adhered to in the asylum decision-making process. The first country to integrate gender guidelines into their national asylum policies and legislation was Canada. In 1993, the Canadian Immigration and Refugee Board issued *Guidelines on Women Refugee Claimants Fearing Gender-Related Persecution.* These guidelines affirmed that the definition of a refugee should be interpreted so as to protect women who demonstrate a well-founded fear of gender-related persecution, and sought to provide principles which would lead those making decisions on asylum claims to more fully account for the partic-ularities of women's experiences of persecution. The adoption of these guidelines in Canada was followed by similar policies in the United States and in Australia. In 1995, the US Department of Justice issued a memorandum which directed immigration officers to consider that women may face specific types of persecution, and to treat these perse-cutions seriously when adjudicating asylum claims.[8] And in 1996, the Australian Department of Immigration and Multicultural Affairs issued their own *Guidelines on Gender Issues for Decision Makers.* Macklin points to the resemblance between the guidelines of the three countries and argues that the Canadian adoption of international norms in this area provided an example for the other two states, so that "demonstrating what could be achieved – politically and legally – in one jurisdiction, made it politically feasible to follow suit" (1998: 68). However, this model of "cross-border shopping" whereby the fact that one state adopts and validates international norms provides an example for other states who are persuaded to follow suit and to undertake a similar integration of international norms into their own national policies, seems not to be fully supported by the evidence of policy transfer. Although the United States and Australia were quick to follow Canada and adopt directives based on the UNHCR guidelines, other countries have reacted much more slowly, or not at all. In particular, it is noteworthy that despite the early initiative taken by the European Parliament, and further directives issued by European institutions following lobbying on the subject at the supra-national European level, the only countries amongst the EU members to have adopted any kind of gender directives or guidelines into their asylum procedures are Sweden and the United Kingdom.

Sweden integrated a clause into their reformed Aliens Act of 1997, which details categories of persons in need of protection and includes those who have a well-founded fear of persecution on account of their sex (Folkelius and Noll, 1998), and have further reformed their legislation regarding gender-related asylum claims with effect from 1 January 2007 (see below). Whilst in March 2004, the UK Home Office introduced gender guidance to its Asylum Policy Instructions (APIs) in a document entitled *Gender Issues in the Asylum Claim*[9] (see below). This guidance sets out a number of instructions and considerations with regard to gender issues that the Home Office caseworkers should take into account, "when looking at the persecution experienced and whether there has been a failure of state protection". It also covers procedural issues such as the need for female interviewers and interpreters for female asylum claimants. Although these initiatives in Sweden and the United Kingdom fall short of a full transposition of UNHCR guidelines into national legislation (Crawley and Lester, 2004), and although there has been evidence that the guidelines that have been adopted are not always utilised when processing asylum claims (Wallace and Holliday, 2005), they go some way towards integrating international norms into national policies and legislation. Other European countries have been far less ready to take any action to adopt the international directives and guidelines into their own national legislation, and thus although there may be some partial acknowledgement of the specific needs of female asylum seekers and refugees, and of the particular nature of gender-specific persecution, this is not officially recognised or integrated into policy.

To explain these divergences in the ways in which the international directives on female asylum seekers and gender-specific forms of persecution have been incorporated into national contexts, it is necessary to interrogate more generally the processes through which global norms are created and implemented. Global norms have to be understood as intertwined international, national, subnational and transnational normative discourses, and within this framework, global norm creation and enforcement is dependent on specific institutional contexts and opportunities and on the particular mobilisation strategies of actors at national and transnational levels. Finnemore and Sikkink's three-stage model of global norm creation and implementation (Finnemore and Sikkink, 1998) has been widely discussed within social science debate. The model proposes a process whereby norm entrepreneurs create a new norm and try through transnational advocacy networks to convince the major international actors, that is, influential states and international organisations to adopt this norm. At a certain point, when enough support has been gained for the new norm, it "cascades" and attracts ever increasing numbers of norm supporters. Finally, in the norm implement- ation stage, the norm which is now basically uncontested, is adopted and implemented within national policies and legislation. Whilst this model can serve as a useful starting point to analyse the way in which global norms on the protection of female asylum seekers and refugees are trans- lated into national political arenas, it is also open to some criticisms. Two criticisms in particular are apposite in the case in question. The first of these is aimed at the final part of the model in which norms which have been adopted and are basically uncontested at global level are taken up by national institutions and bureaucracies to be implemented within national contexts. This conceptualisation seems too simple an inter- pretation of a more complex process, a top down perspective whereby normative standards are seem to trickle down to national level, and are accepted without any real active debate or discourse. In fact, it might be argued that the process of implementation at national level is a much more active process whereby norms are either actively appropriated or refused, and where the institutional context and political oppor- tunity structures, and the mobilisation strategies of actors are important factors. Secondly, the model can be criticised for its lack of attention to relationships of power in the process of global norm creation and imple- mentation, and in particular in this context, gendered relationships of power enmeshed in the construction and naturalisation of gendered identities. It can be argued in the case under consideration that the neglect of the ways in which the construction of gendered identities and gendered relations of power lead to persecutions specific to women mean that the experience of women refugees and asylum seekers is not always considered in its entirety, but rather that representations of women asylum seekers and refugees either as "vulnerable victims" or as "bogus" asylum seekers using their supposed vulnerability to try and get around the immigration and asylum legislation of Western coun- tries. These representations mean that some forms of gender-related persecutions are more likely to be recognised as such because they conform to dominant Western norms and values on human rights and what constitutes an infringement of these rights. Thus the idea of the universality of rights practices is confronted with the context of existing social relations and values. This problem of the definition of what should constitute women's rights from the perspective of Western women, and of the neglect of the norms, values and processses involved in the construction of gendered relations of power in other locations,

will be discussed further below, but first we will turn our consideration to the uneven adoption and implementation of global norms on
gender-related persecution and asylum in different national contexts.

The uneven adoption of international norms in different national
contexts has been analysed by Zwingel (2005) with regard to the implementation of CEDAW[10] at national level. This analysis leads her to
argue that there are three major factors which influence the degree to
which the international norms contained in CEDAW are implemented
in national contexts, these being, the degree to which political institutions enable the representation of women's interests within public
policy formation, the existence of transnational governmental or non-
governmental activism that supports the appropriation and implementation of international norms, and the level of cultural affinity with
the Convention. These factors all seem highly relevant to the case of
norms relative to asylum and gender-specific persecution, albeit in a
slightly differing configuration related to the location of the issue at the
intersection of national and international debates on the prevention of
persecutions specific to women and on asylum policy and legislation. In
particular, what seems to "make a difference" in terms of the adoption
of international norms in this area, is the degree of non-governmental
activism within a particular country, and the extent to which there exists
a cultural affinity with the goals of women's equality and an acceptance
of gender-specific approaches to diverse political questions. It must also
be assumed that norms relative to asylum, and sites and processes of
policy making on asylum are important factors in whether or not these
international norms are adopted into national policy arenas. However,
there is less diversity in these cases as in all Western countries the norms
on asylum can be argued to have become much more restrictive in the
past two decades (Boswell, 2000). Asylum policy is a contentious area of
policy making which has become the object of much tougher regulatory
policies deployed by state officials and institutions and justified by the
rhetoric of security (Geddes, 2000b; Bigo, 2001). Within this context, the
framing of asylum seekers as "threats" to national security has become
prevalent in almost all Western countries, and the political opportunity
structures for those mobilising in favour of asylum seekers have become
more limited. Thus those mobilising for the adoption of specific policies,
legislation or guidelines relative to gender-specific persecution and the
treatment of female asylum seekers have had to employ strategies which
maximise the potential opportunities which exist. The most successful
mobilisations have been those which have been able to bring together a

wide-ranging coalition of actors and associations to lobby for the introduction of gender guidelines or directives within asylum policies. In
these circumstances, it has been possible for these coalitions to work
with government institutions and officials to define and draft such
guidelines and to assist with the transposition of international directives into national policy. In analysing the variations in the degree
and success of mobilisations on these issues across different national
contexts, it is thus important to compare both the degree and nature of
mobilisations and the opportunity structures that are available for these
mobilisations. In particular in this case, what seems important are the
discursive opportunity structures (Koopmans and Statham, 1999) that
exist in each national context. The concept of discursive opportunity
structures enables the mapping of symbolic, cultural and ideational
resources available to political entrepreneurs and activists in any given
international, national or local context (Adamson, 2005). As Adamson
points out: "Individual entrepreneurs do not exist in a vacuum, but
are rather embedded within structures of meaning. The structures of
meaning within which individual entrepreneurs operate can influence
the content and type of claims that are made by agents within any
particular political space" (Adamson, 2005: 553). In the case of norms
related to gender-specific persecution and female asylum seekers and
refugees, the discursive opportunities available for framing claims in
terms of gender inequality and women's rights in any national context
are vital for the transposition of international norms into national
policies.

National and local activism produces appropriate strategies for change
including contextualised interpretations of international norms. The
degree of national action and mobilisation around the issue of gender-
specific persecution and the right to asylum has clearly had a major
impact on persuading national authorities to adopt and implement
international norms and conventions, as do the discursive opportunity
structures which exist in each different national context.

Canada

As mentioned above, Canada was the first country to react to the
UNHCR's directives and to introduce gender guidelines into their
asylum process. The Canadian guidelines on gender-related persecution aimed to deal with four major questions relating to the ways in
which gender has an impact in the asylum process and in judgements
relating to the granting of refugee status. These questions were first,

to what extent can women who are victims of gender-related persecution rely on being granted refugee status on one of the five grounds mentioned in the Geneva Convention; secondly, under what circumstances does sexual violence or other prejudicial treatment of women constitute persecution; thirdly, what specific kinds of evidence might be used by women to support their claims of gender-related persecution; and finally, what are the particular problems that women face when making an asylum claim and during hearings to determine refugee status.

The early implementation of the UNHCR guidelines in Canada was directly influenced by the lobbying of women's groups who managed to target their action effectively and to work closely with the immigration authorities. The Canadian guidelines were in fact developed by the Immigration and Refugee Board (IRB) in consultation both with refugee advocacy groups and women's groups such as the National Action Committee on the Status of Women, and the IRB organised its own working group on the issue from 1991 onwards (Erdman and Sanche, 2004). The issue was also taken up by the National Action Committee on the Status of Women which organised, amongst other events, a big demonstration in favour of the adoption of the guidelines. As Macklin argues in relation to the adoption of the Canadian guidelines, the role of feminist and human rights activists was a vital element in the transposition of global norms into a national political framework:

> Without doubt, the Guidelines would not exist but for the concerted efforts of a coalition of feminist, human rights, refugee, and immigration activists, as well as the personal commitment and leadership of a committee and leadership of a committee of members working under the Chairperson of the IRB.... In addition, an international framework within which the Guidelines could emerge had already begun to crystallize in the late 1980s through the assiduous efforts of the UNHCR Executive Committee.
>
> (1995: 215)

The context for the adoption of the guidelines was also one of public interest in the issue, as several well-publicised incidents of women being refused asylum had been diffused in the media (Oosterveld, 1996). Perhaps the most well-known of these cases was that of a woman called Nada from Saudi Arabia who had defied the law in her country of origin by refusing to wear a veil and travelling alone without a male relative, and had been threatened with arrest and publicly harassed as a result of this decision. The Convention Refugee Determination Division (CRDD) in Canada judged that she should have conformed to the laws of her country like other Saudi women and worn her veil at all times.[11] This decision caused such a huge public outcry that the Immigration Minister eventually granted Nada leave to remain in Canada on humanitarian grounds. The public attention to the case also highlighted the difficulties faced by women seeking asylum and pushed the IRB to take further action.

The Canadian guidelines, like others introduced in different national contexts, do not alter the statutory definition of a refugee. In other words, they do not add gender to the Convention definitions of grounds of persecution. However, they have gone further than other guidelines in answering the concern that a particular social group defined by gender would be too large, and have argued that the size of the group is irrelevant as long as it can be proved that the members of the group suffer harsh or inhumane treatment that is distinguished from the situation of the general population. The major criticism that has been levelled at these guidelines is that they are not binding on members of the IRB, but if the members do not follow the guidelines they must provide a written decision explaining their decision.

The United States and Australia

The gender guidelines adopted in the United States and Australia were both directly and explicitly modelled on those previously adopted in Canada, with a similar process of involvement of NGOs and women's groups in drafting the guidelines in consultation with immigration authorities. Indeed the US guidelines include a self-description as a "collaborative effort" between immigration officials, NGOs and academics (Macklin, 1999). In the United States, the mobilisation around this issue was led by the Women's Commission for Refugee Women and Children, who together with other activists in the area drafted a document in 1994 related to women's asylum claims and submitted it to the Immigration and Nationality Service (INS). The INS used this document as well as the Canadian guidelines as a basis for their 1995 guidelines, *Considerations for Asylum Officers Adjudicating Asylum Claims from Women*. These guidelines give specific instructions that rape and other forms of sexual violence should be recognised as persecution, and also emphasise that asylum officers should attempt to create a "customer-friendly" interview environment so that women feel able to talk about their experiences of such persecutions (Crawley, 2001). A major difficulty that has been highlighted in relation to the US guidelines is that they only apply at one stage of the asylum determination process. There are two routes for applying for asylum in the United States: affirmative applications require the applicant to initiate the process through the asylum officer level, whereas defensive applications occur when the asylum seeker has been arrested by the US government and must file an appeal at the level of an immigration judge. The gender guidelines only apply to the level of the asylum officer, which means that many women will not benefit, particularly given the increase in the arrest and detention of asylum seekers in the United States (see Chapter 6).

The Australian *Guidelines on Gender Issues for Decision Makers* were introduced the following year in 1996. They are more comprehensive than the Canadian guidelines in that they apply not only to inland asylum applications, but also to the overseas humanitarian selection programme, but in other respects they are very similar to those adopted by Canada and the United States. Kneebone argues that a noteworthy feature of the Australian guidelines is that they "appear to recognise that the claims of women refugees, whilst special, need not be confined to the 'social group' category" (Kneebone, 2005: 17). In other words, the guidelines seem to recognise that women persecuted for infringing discriminatory laws or social norms may be expressing a political opinion and so could be protected under this Convention ground. However, Kneebone also argues that the rest of Australian asylum policy and legislation does not conform to this point of view put forward in the guidelines, leading to a "dissonance between the guidelines and the current policy of the Australian government, and between the latter and the jurisprudence, which is arguably narrower than the guidelines" (Kneebone, 2005: 18).

Moreover, the adoption of these guidelines in Canada, the United States and Australia may be seen as positive steps in recognising gender-related persecution, but at the same time optimism needs to be framed within the current context of rejection of asylum seekers in all three countries. Even Canada which has been reputed as one of the most welcoming states for asylum seekers and refugees has recently seen more repressive legislation in this area. And in Australia the policy of mandatory detention of all asylum seekers (discussed further in Chapter 6) might be seen to negate any benefits accrued to women by the introduction of gender guidelines.

The United Kingdom

The United Kingdom has, in theory at least, one of the most explicitly gender-sensitive approaches to determining asylum claims in Europe (Crawley and Lester, 2004). However, in practice the extent to which the existing gender guidelines are actually implemented is open to question (Wallace and Holliday, 2005; Refugee Women's Resources Project, 2006) and the ways in which women's asylum claims are determined seems, as in other European countries, to be highly dependent on discretionary powers of Home Office officials, asylum adjudicators and judges. The UK's guidelines were first drafted by the Refugee Women's Legal Group (RWLG). This group was formed in 1996 by individuals and organisations who were concerned about the impact of changes in immigration and asylum laws on women applying for asylum in the United Kingdom. The guidelines drawn up by the RWLG were based on those already in force in Canada, Australia and the United States, as well on the UNHCR's 1991 Guidelines.

The RWLG both targeted its guidelines at asylum caseworkers within the immigration services of the UK Home Office in order to try to sensitise them to gender issues during the asylum procedure, and at the same time lobbied Members of Parliament to try and make the case for an official adoption of these guidelines by the Home Office. The RWLG worked closely with a network of other refugee and asylum associations such as the Refugee Council to make this lobbying work more effective. For many NGOs and associations campaigning in this area, the issue of gender was one which could not be ignored, and in addition the question could be seen as strategically beneficial in creating alliances between various NGOs which was not always easy in other areas relating to asylum, and in providing a "winnable" battle to fight with the Home Office.[12] Asylum Aid, a leading NGO in the United Kingdom in this field, set up its own internal "department", the Refugee Women's Resources Project (RWRP)[13] to deal with the question of gender and to work with the RWLG in lobbying the government.

In 2002, the Immigration Appellate Authority produced its own Asylum Gender Guidelines and finally the Home Office bowed to pressure from this lobby and worked with the RWLG and with the UNHCR's representative in the United Kingdom to draw up its own guidelines which were adopted in 2004. These Asylum Policy Instructions (APIs) should in practice give guidance on the gender-specific considerations caseworkers ought to bear in mind whilst assessing asylum claims, as well as giving practical advice on means of taking gender issues into account while interviewing asylum claimants. As in the Canadian case, the international norms have been adopted into national policy through an active appropriation and mobilisation at national level, a mobilisation which was possible both through the availability of political opportunities for cooperation with government bodies and through discursive opportunities for talking about gender in the associational sector. As Crawley and Lester comment: "This is a strong illustration of the potential for the voluntary sector to catalyse positive change at official level" (Crawley and Lester, 2004: 30). Indeed, the question of gender was seen not only as one which was important to talk about by British NGOs and associations, but one which would provide a new focus of campaigning and would enable the sector to have an impact on a government which otherwise seemed firm in its intentions to introduce more and more restrictive legislation in this area.[14] The RWRP which was set up by Asylum Aid has become one of the major foci of this NGO and has made itself a role in leading campaigns, in conjunction with the EWL, for the introduction of gender guidelines across the EU.

Despite the promise of the Home Office APIs, the early research on the application of the guidance shows that it has so far had little impact on the way that asylum cases are processed or judged. A study by the RWRP found that despite a few examples of good practice, the overwhelming impression was of a lack of gender sensitivity and awareness of gender issues, and of the gender guidelines not being followed by those making decisions on asylum applications (Refugee Women's Resources Project, 2006). Morevoer, recently the UK's Asylum and Immigration Tribunal removed the copy of the gender guidelines from its website.

Sweden

Sweden was the first country in Europe to react to the UNHCR's gender guidelines and to put in place their own legislative provisions for taking account of gender in asylum claims. In 1996, a new Aliens Act was passed by parliament in Sweden. This Act, which was effective from 1 January 1997, changed the categories of people to whom asylum could be granted and extended the possibilities of granting temporary protection (Abiri, 2000). Previous to this law, Sweden granted asylum to four categories of person, Convention refugees (who qualified under the terms of the Geneva Convention), de facto refugees (those who did not qualify under the Convention, but could provide strong grounds for not returning to their country of origin), war resisters and those qualifying on humanitarian grounds. Under the new Aliens Act of 1997, the

Convention refugee category was retained, but the other three categories were replaced by a new general category of "persons otherwise in need of protection". Within this second category was a clause offering protection to a person who "has a well-founded fear of persecution on account of his sex or homosexuality".[15] Regarding this inclusion of sex/gender specifically as a category deserving of protection, it might be argued that the separation of this category from that of Convention refugee status sets a dangerous precedent of considering gender-related persecution as something separate from other more "serious" forms of persecution. In an assessment of this legislation, Folkelius and Noll argued that Sweden had set a dangerous international precedent because, "the introduction of a special category for cases with a gender aspect is too easily misunderstood as their exclusion from the framework of international law by other countries" (1997: 634). They argue that this precedent is particularly dangerous with respect to countries of Central and Eastern Europe which have no alternative protection categories to those of the Geneva Convention, meaning that gender-related claims for asylum in those countries would run the risk of receiving no protection whatsoever, and conclude that "it is hoped that other States avoid the Swedish model in their quest for national solutions on issues of gender and persecution" (Folkelius and Noll, 1998: 636).

In 2001, the Swedish government provided further directives on the issue of gender-related persecution, issuing *Guidelines for the Investigation and Evaluation of the Needs of Women for Protection*. These guidelines were intended as a guide to the assessment of women's asylum claims, but they specifically rejected the possibility of considering gender as a defining characteristic of a particular social group. A study examining the implications of the 1997 Aliens Act with regard to gender-based claims found that the only cases which succeeded under the new gender clause were those relating to fear of FGM and that these women were granted complementary protection (Bexelius, 2001). Bexelius points to a lack of transparency in the gender-related cases that she analysed, and argues that it is still very difficult for a woman fearing gender-based violence to obtain convention refugee status or subsidiary protection. She claims that "the assessment of whether a woman's fear is well-founded is made without enough knowledge of the often complex human rights situation for women of different contexts and experiences, in the countries of origin and the difficulty to substantiate their claims with documentary evidence" (Bexelius, 2006: 8). Lyth argues that considering these cases under the gender clause means that the women concerned cannot be granted full refugee status but only complementary protection which does not provide the same absolute protection from removal and so is a lesser form of protection from these acts of gender-specific persecution. Further the definition of gender-related persecution contained within the Aliens Act and the accompanying guidelines, reduces this type of persecution to physically specific types of persecution carried out on women – FGM and forced abortion, thus implying a very narrow view of gender limited only to biological sex and not taking into account socially constructed gender inequalities (Lyth, 2002).

In November 2005, the Swedish Parliament voted in favour of a reform of the Aliens Act which would remove the article of the 1997 law relating to gender-based persecution and would instead include gender-related persecution within the remit of the definition provided in the Geneva Convention and transposed into Swedish law. The new law thus defines a refugee as someone who is outside of his or her country of nationality because he or she feels a "well-founded fear of persecution on grounds of race, nationality, religious or political belief, or on grounds of gender, sexual orientation or other membership of a particular social group".[16] The definition goes on to further specify that this applies irrespective of whether the persecution is committed by the state authorities in the country of origin, or whether these authorities cannot be assumed to offer any protection against persecution by private, non-state agents. This law means that the Swedish Parliament has acknowledged that a risk or fear of gender-related persecution should lead to refugee status, and not just subsidiary protection, and thus the new legislation answers many of the criticisms that were made with regard to the previous Aliens Act. It is as yet too early to judge the results of this new law, but as with other laws and guidelines in other States, any real changes will depend on interpretation and implementation of officials and judges. One fear which has been expressed by NGOs, however, is that the preparatory work for the new legislation incorporates a need to take into account the motives for the failure of state protection in the asylum seekers' country of origin. This may adversely affect women as if it can be shown that the motives for lack of state protection were merely a lack of resources, then the asylum claim will fail. If then, for example, a woman was fleeing domestic violence and had not been protected by the police forces in her country of origin, it could be explained by the immigration board that this lack of protection was just due to a lack of funding for the police and not any persecutory intention on the part of the state. Again the relationship between the public and the private and between state and non-state agents of persecution may come into play to the detriment of women's asylum claims.

Europe

Although other European countries have not adopted official gender guidelines as in Sweden and the United Kingdom, some countries have taken different measures to try and ensure that women who have suffered from gender-related persecution receive fair treatment under asylum laws and processes. The Netherlands and Germany both have advice on interviewing female asylum seekers within their asylum guidelines, and in Germany, a handbook has been produced on the definition of gender-related persecution, whilst in the Netherlands a gender-inclusive approach is incorporated into immigration officers' training (RWRP, 2005). Germany has also introduced a procedural framework for nominating and training special adjudicators to deal with victims of gender-related persecution (Crawley and Lester, 2004). In Belgium, the Commissariat Général aux Réfugiés et aux Apatrides (CGRA) has recently appointed an officer to coordinate actions with regard to gender-related persecution. Recent reforms introduced to facilitate women's access to the asylum process include a guarantee that in any cases where a claim contains reference to persecution linked to sexual violence or rape, the asylum interview will be carried out by a woman official. In addition women will always be heard separately from their husbands or any other male members of their family, and crèche facilities will be provided to ensure that women can be heard without their young children being present. Further, an internal directive has been circulated within the CGRA suggesting that officers examining asylum claims should adopt the UNCHR's guidance on definition of a particular social group with respect to gender-related asylum claims.[17]

The difficulties with these different measures, as with the implementation of gender guidelines described above, is that the measures introduced are not always (and in some cases rarely) applied in practice, and that often immigration officials and judges, and others involved in the asylum process are not fully aware of the existence of specific measures or of their relevance to asylum claims. Another reason for caution when talking about the positive effects of these measures on gender-related asylum claims, is that often they are taken at the discretion of one or more individuals, and will rely on the continuing presence of those individuals to remain in practice. This is clearly the case with the reforms introduced in Belgium (described above), which were put into place on the initiative of the current head of the Francophone section of the CGRA, an individual whom one of the employees of the CGRA described as "much more positive than previous directors, and really interested in helping women".[18] The same individual, however, pointed to discrepancies between judgements emanating from the Francophone and the Flemish speaking sections of CGRA, thus highlighting the very haphazard nature of decision-making.[19] Measures vary across European states, with some, such as France, having taken no action regarding this question. The non-appearance of this issue on the agenda in France can be explained by a latent anti-feminism within the NGO sector (see Chapter 7), as well as a continuing insistence on universalism which prevents a discussion of separate categories of refugees. Thus NGOs and official institutions have been wary of any discussion of the "category" of female asylum applicants. In addition, the UNHCR representative in Paris points to a reluctance of the French authorities to accept directives they believe to be imposed from "outside", and thus to adopt guidelines coming from the UNHCR.[20] Even in countries where there is assumed to be a general receptiveness to gender-equality issues, this does not always translate into policies which are favourable to gender equality in the asylum determination process. Sweden, for example, a country which is generally reputed to have a relatively high level of gender equality in other areas of society has adopted legislation which until very recently could be seen to be unfavourable in terms of recognition of gender-related asylum claims as discussed above. In addition, one member of the Swedish Migration Board described the way in which a presumption that Sweden was a gender-equal society could actually get in the way of actions taken in favour of women asylum seekers because male immigration official did not want to accept that it would in some cases be better for a female claimant to be assisted and interviewed by a female official. The male immigration officials believed that because they were sensitive to gender issues there was no reason why they should not interview women. This point illustrates how questions of gender can become confused with those of specific actions for women – sometimes the two will coincide, but this is not always the case. As Cockburn argues, it is a question of knowing when an emphasis on difference is "more productive of equal outcomes" (2004: 29).

Conclusions

There is often still little transparency in the process for granting asylum in Western countries, and the idea that any kind of logical or "scientific" process has been established to distinguish between "real" and "false" refugees is highly misleading. Decisions often rely on the personal intuitions of an immigration official or a judge. In this sense, whilst some decisions favourable to a more gender-sensitive asylum policy and process may be highlighted, a general trend of structural gender inequality still underlies the asylum process. In a study in Denmark amongst recent asylum applicants from the Middle East, for example, it was found that single mothers had the lowest probability of gaining refugee status, irrespective of whether or not they had been subject to human rights violations. The authors conclude that is it is socio-economic and cultural factors which are the greatest predictor of the granting or not of refugee status in Denmark (Montgomery and Foldspang, 2005). Whilst much of the discussion relating to gender in the asylum process has centred on legal discussions about whether women can be defined as a particular social group, and how gender-related persecution should be brought under the terms of the Geneva Convention, much less attention has been paid to the utility of this Convention itself. Perhaps a more wide-ranging analysis which brings into focus the particular circumstances in which the Convention was elaborated and the very political nature of its implementation in various national contexts can help us to better understand why it is that women fleeing persecution in their countries of origin have found it so difficult to have this persecution recognised as such in Western states. Moreover, a gendered analysis of the way that asylum seekers are constructed through the procedures of asylum determination procedures shows that although in some circumstances it may now be easier for a woman to be granted refugee status on the basis of gender-related persecution, this is dependent on her ability to conform both to an appropriate image of the "convention refugee" (Barsky, 1994; Rousseau et al., 2002), and to representations of proper modes of "female" behaviour.

5
Supporting Women Refugees and Asylum Seekers

The issue of gender-related persecution and violence against women have been put onto the international agenda, largely thanks to lobbying by feminist NGOs and transnational networks. There is a question, however, of how successfully this agenda setting has translated into effective policy-making and policies that will increase the protection of women who are victims of gender-related persecution. One of the problems with policies to support women refugees and asylum seekers lies in a failure of transmission of the goals of gender sensitivity through all the various bureaux and representatives of a large bureaucratic organisation such as the UNHCR. There is thus a gap in many cases between adoption of policies and their implementation. The process of diffusion of international norms relating to protection of women asylum seekers and refugees into national policy domains and national legislation is also problematic. Thus, as outlined in Chapter 4, whilst the UNHCR adopted gender guidelines in 1991, few states have adopted these guidelines into their national asylum policies or legislations. In this chapter we will examine various responses to the particular situation of female refugees and asylum seekers, both from international organisations and from NGOs in order to try to analyse to what extent international and national responses to refugees and asylum seekers have taken into account gender-related persecutions and gendered differences in the situations of women and men forced migrants. We will argue that although there have been attempts to respond to the particular needs of women refugees and asylum seekers, by the UN and by other national and international organisations, these have not always had the intended effect and that efforts to include a gendered perspective in refugee and asylum policy often remains at the level of discourse rather than action. An underlying problem with many of the attempts to "help" women asylum seekers and refugees often lies in the representations of these women as primarily "victims" with no real agency, representations which fail to appreciate the evolving nature of gendered relations and of women's part in reinforcing or in challenging these relations. This chapter will argue that in effect the most effective and real advances in recognising the specific needs of women refugees and asylum seekers have come from grassroots organisations which work closely with these women themselves and give them an active role in expressing and formulating policies. We will start, however, with an examination of the evolution of UN policies with regard to women refugees and to gender-related persecution.

The UN and action for women refugees

For nearly twenty years, since the early 1990s, the UNHCR has identified "refugee women" as a policy priority, and yet despite this prioritisation of concerns with women refugees and gender issues in the asylum and refugee process, "implementation continues to be slow and ad hoc" (Baines, 2004: 1). The seeming inability to put into practice much of the discourse on gender and women refugees must be seen in part as a result of internal difficulties and crises with the UNHCR's own organisation. It is an agency which is dependent on donor funding, with up to 98 per cent of funds coming directly from national governments (Vayrynen, 2001). These funds are renewed annually creating a particular dependence on donor states.[1] This means that donor states can have a large degree of control over the UNHCR's agenda and that in some cases the agency might be seen to prioritise these state's interests over those of asylum seekers and refugees (Crépeau, 1995; Hammerstad, 2000).[2] In particular the contribution of the European Commission and individual European states make up nearly half of the UNHCR's budget, thus placing Europe in the position of a "majority shareholder" in the agency (Agier and Valluy, 2007). These pressures from states have led to what some have argued is a change of direction from the UNHCR, moving from a function of protecting refugees to one of controlling them in the interests of donor states. One sign of this has been the promotion of the policy of "voluntary returns" which might be argued to be more "forced" than "voluntary" (Preston, 1999). Thus a function of "containment" of humanitarian emergencies can be seen to have been added on to or indeed replaced UNCHR's primary functions of protecting refugees. Whilst some see this new function of containment as an unwitting complicity of the UNHCR with donor states

(Barnett, 2001), others have been more critical and have seen a strategic positioning of the UNCHR to align its concerns with those of donor states, particularly with regard to policies of "externalisation"[3] of asylum processes (Agier and Valluy, 2007).

In addition, Vayrynen highlights the problem of "earmarking" of UNHCR's funds:

> In UNHCR problems have not concerned only the voluntary nature of funds, but also the tendency of donors to earmark them. This means simply that conditions are imposed on the use of funds... These conditions have usually required that monies should be used for particular country programs. Such earmarking tends to create inequities in the refugee regime as the main donors seem to favour crisis areas that are geographically close to them and/or politically more important due to the potential of cross-border instability or competition for influence with other powers.
>
> (2001: 156).

This earmarking of funds has had notable impacts in relation to the comparative availability of funds for projects in Africa and in Eastern Europe, with African countries often falling to the bottom of the lists of priorities for donor states (Vayrynen, 2001). These particular motives for distribution of funding may have impacts on UNHCR's ability to adequately fund activities and programmes which aim at promoting gender equality or extending adequate protection to women refugees. This is both because many of the women who are most in need of protection find themselves in geographical regions which are not considered a priority by donor states and so do not receive much funding and because gender equality programmes which are seen as long-term investments with often intangible or only marginal results are not favoured by the UNHCR staff who have to decide how the scarce budgets should be spent.

UNHCR must also be viewed as a huge bureaucracy[4] and one that holds tremendous discursive and institutional power over refugees. This power can be seen to take away possibilities of agency from refugees and displaced people, limiting their participation in any form of planning, implementation or management of operations (Baines, 2004). This critique might be particularly relevant to operations designed to overcome gender inequalities, which are often designed and implemented without any input from women themselves as to what their needs or desires might be and which can be criticised for their framing of women merely in terms of their vulnerability. The bureaucratic structure of UNHCR and the number of people it employs also means that policies designed to promote gender sensitivity and the enhanced protection of women refugees and asylum seekers may not be adopted or implemented by some of its own staff. Some UNCHR employees interviewed for this study pointed to the continued need to persuade and remind their colleagues (and in particular their male colleagues) of the needs for integrating a gendered approach into their work. They also highlighted the problem that in much of UNCHR's work in the field, and particular in situations of extreme conflict and crisis, the majority of the protection officers are male and thus may not always be sensitive to gendered needs.[5] Without wishing to advocate a position which implies that only women can be sensitive to gendered aspects of policy-making and implementation, it does seem that the balance of men and women working within an organisation will have some impact on the way in which gender is considered, and that in the case of the UNHCR women are still under-represented both at higher levels of the bureaucracy and in field operations.

A further characteristic of the UNHCR's organisation which impacts on the way in which gender issues are considered is the very hierarchical nature of the organisation, with a mistrust for anyone "parachuted" in from outside to senior levels of management (Loescher, 2001). Baines points to the way that this hierarchy has disadvantaged some of the women appointed in the role of Senior Coordinator for Refugee Women, who have been perceived as "outsiders" and have thus had less authority within the organisation (Baines, 2004).

Baines traces the way in which the issue of women refugees was placed on the international agenda through the campaigns of a transnational advocacy network of women's organisations. One of the first signs of the issues of gender in refugee crises becoming visible was, she argues, during the massive forced migrations from South East Asia in the early 1980s. The plight of the "boat people" was reported worldwide, and particular attention was paid to the vulnerability of women on the boats, who were at risk of sexual violence and rape if the boats were attacked by pirates. The international media transmitted eyewitness reports and accounts of the experiences of those fleeing, many of which were similar to the one below:

> While all the men were confined to the hold of the refugee boat ... some, if not all of approximately fifteen to twenty women and young girls, who were kept in the cabin of the boat were raped. The

youngest of these girls was around twelve years old. Soon afterwards, the pirates set the boat on fire with all the Vietnamese on board. In the ensuing panic, the Vietnamese grabbed buoys, cans, and floats and plunged into the sea. The crews of the pirate boats then used sticks to prevent them from clinging to floating objects...Women and children were the first to perish

(quoted in Forbes-Martin, 2004: 46).

Other reports claimed that the boat people were being forced by the pirates to choose young girls to offer to them in return for the lives of the rest of the passengers on board (Forbes-Martin, 2004). These types of reports highlighted the vulnerability of women and girls and the prevalence of rape and sexual violence used against those fleeing, putting pressure on the UNHCR to react by providing added protection for these women.

At the same time, it became more and more difficult to ignore women in refugee camps because of their sheer numbers. The number of women-headed households within these camps, for example, made models of resource distribution that targeted men with the idea that this would then be distributed to the rest of their household, unworkable. Various issues like these gradually entered the international consciousness and coalesced to provide a focal point for the start of transnational activism, which gained momentum at the World Conference on Women, held in Nairobi in 1985. At this conference, which marked the end of the UN Decade for Women, hundreds of representatives from refugee women's associations attended the parallel NGO forum. Following this conference an International Working Group for Refugee Women was set up, creating a network of national groups aiming to push the UNHCR to take action.

The UNHCR responded to this international pressure by appointing a Senior Coordinator for Refugee Women in 1989. Baines recounts that when the first woman to take up this post, Anne Howarth-Wiles, arrived in Geneva she had a rather cold welcome with few resources at her disposal and "little enthusiasm amongst her co-workers" (Baines, 2004: 44). In an interview with Baines, Howarth-Wiles describes her initial experiences:

As soon as she arrived, it became obvious to her than most UNHCR staff were reluctant to embrace a gender perspective. Most believed that international refugee instruments and practices applied equally to men and women and were therefore non-discriminatory. A policy on refugee women was considered unnecessary.

(Baines, 2004: 45)

Despite this initial reluctance to engage with issues of gender, the Senior Coordinator managed to impose a campaign involving the development of a policy on refugee women, together with training programmes to raise awareness of the issues involved both inside and outside of the UNHCR. In the following years several key policy documents on refugee women were produced, notably the *Policy on Refugee Women* (UNHCR, 1990), the *Guidelines on the Protection of Refugee Women* (UNHCR, 1991) and the *Guidelines on Prevention and Response to Sexual Violence against Refugees* (UNHCR, 1995b). Initial policies and programmes focused on women refugees, rather than on the relational issues of gender in refugee programmes. This focus on women as a special or separate group could be argued in some contexts to further marginalise women by targeting them as a "separate" group and so essentialising their difference and ignoring the relational aspects of gender which affects both women and men. By the end of the 1990s, the focus within the UNHCR was moving away from one that was specifically on women and more towards gender-based policies and programmes. This coincided with efforts to incorporate gender mainstreaming in all UN operations. Main-streaming is, however, a notoriously difficult concept to implement, and as research for this study suggests, it may in fact lead to gender slipping off the agenda, as it becomes dissolved within other concerns. Interviewees pointed to the fact that although mainstreaming could have advantages in that it reminded UNHCR employees of the need to consider gender in all aspects of their work and not merely to relegate it to a separate "women's issue", in effect without the dedicated effort of an individual or group devoted to bringing gender issues to the forefront of policies and programmes these issues might easily be ignored.[6]

So what have been the substantial changes that have resulted from the UNHCR's attempts to take more account of specific needs of refugee women and to integrate and mainstream gender in its policy-making and activities in the last two decades? In 2001, the Women's Commission for Refugee Women and Children carried out an assessment of the results of ten years of implementation of the 1991 *Guidelines on the Protection of Refugee Women* (UNHCR, 1991). This assessment concluded that the *Guidelines* had succeeded in raising awareness among UNHCR staff and partners of women's specific needs and interests, but that overall the implementation of the *Guidelines* was "uneven and incom-plete, occurring on an ad hoc basis in certain sites rather than in a globally consistent and systematic way" (WCRWC, 2002: 2). The report cites barriers to implementation including a lack of female UNHCR staff which is a serious obstacle both to obtaining information from refugee women and to addressing the specific protection issues they face. It argues further that insufficient participation of refugee women themselves in decision-making is also a serious barrier to the full implementation of the *Guidelines* (WCRWC, 2002). A consultation exercise that the UNHCR organised with some refugee women came to similar conclusions that despite progress in some areas, women refugees often still lacked access to food and other basic resources, and that they were not adequately protected against sexual and gender-based violence. One issue which was raised was the continuing failure to provide refugee women with their own personal documentation, such as their own food ration cards. The distribution of these cards to male "heads" of families led to particular problems as explained in the report:

> Participants of the Dialogue and the local and regional consultations identified the lack of personal documentation as a major problem facing displaced women. Even when such documentation is provided, the refugee women reported that it is usually only given to male heads of household. The distribution of food ration cards to men only is a continued practice, despite the fact that dependence on male family members often increases the protection problems women face. In the Pakistani regional consultation, UNHCR staff was informed of this problem, and its severe impact on the family, in a case where a ration card belonging to a deceased refugee man was recalled, leaving his remaining four widows and twenty-five children without access to food. Fortunately, refugee women eventually successfully lobbied to have the ration card reinstated to the widows. Also, in places such as Guinea, where individual ration cards were not provided, some refugee women and girls were forced to exchange sex for food. Most refugee women participants agreed that food would be distributed more evenly within families if ration cards were distributed to refugee women and they were equal partners in the development and implementation of food distribution strategies.
>
> (UNHCR, 2001: 19)

The consultation also highlighted the way that women seeking asylum in Western states did not feel that their specifically gendered experiences were taken into account by decision-makers and judges. Finally the consultation exercise criticised the way in which refugee women were often left out of camp planning and decision-making processes.

Women in Guinea, for example, "felt they were left out of planning, designing, implementing and even evaluating programmes for refugee assistance" (UNHCR, 2001: 26). This exclusion of women from planning and implementation was a contributing factor in lack of access to basic resources.

These criticisms of the implementation of UNHCR policies on refugee women and on gender are consistent with other analyses of UNHCR's actions in particular refugee situations in which they intervene. Many of the criticisms stem from an underlying understanding and construction of the relationship between the refugee and the UNHCR/NGO bringing aid as one between "helper" and "victim", with no possibility of collaboration as equals being envisaged. Relations of power which start off as highly unequal may be made even more so by the way in which aid is administered. In the context of management of refugee camps, for example, UNHCR and other aid agencies have been criticised for promoting unequal power relations between aid workers and refugees and for encouraging types of dependent behaviour on the part of refugees (Hyndman, 2000; Harrell-Bond, 2002). It is argued that the nature of aid given out develops a patron–client relationship within which powerful and competent aid workers distribute aid to the "helpless" refugees. Even the conditions in which refugees tell their stories and register their claims for protection with the UNHCR authorities in a camp can be seen as reinforcing power inequalities. Often they may be forced to wait hours in a queue in the sun before gaining access to a UNHCR official. And when they do get access to a UNHCR official to relate their stories, they are themselves frequently forced into a re-affirmation of their "victim" status. As Ratner (2005) comments, refugees often feel the need to tell stories about their own "powerlessness" in order to gain certain advantages from UNHCR officials or from other aid agencies, benefits such as extra food rations, child support or even third country resettlement. This re-appropriation of stories of "powerlessness" and "victim" status can be seen as a form of agency on the part of refugees who adapt their strategies for survival to the dominant representations created by those providing aid to them.

> The refugees have to tell stories of "powerlessness" to invest in their future and ironically, the disempowering experiences that got them in their hopeless situations in the first place, become a strategic tool for survival in the form of a utilitarian narrative that is far from a powerless act.
>
> (Ratner, 2005: 19)

These unequal power relationships within which refugees are constructed as "vulnerable" or "helpless" victims may have particular resonance in the case of women refugees, reinforcing gendered constructions of women's powerlessness and lack of agency in certain societies. We will discuss below the way in which representations of "refugee women" have perpetuated particular understandings and constructions of the specificities of these women's situations, which may serve to essentialise women's experiences and to diminish the understanding of the differences in their positioning dependent on class, ethnicity, age and other factors. As with other refugees, however, women may in fact exercise a very particular kind of agency in re-appropriating and mobilising these representations for their own benefit. Thus the way in which they are treated as "victims" may be used to help their own personal survival strategies. In some camps, for example, women may actively use the stories of sexual violence which they have experienced as a pragmatic strategy for improving their own situation (Ratner, 2005).

However, despite these possibilities of re-appropriation of the discourse of "victimisation" to further personal survival strategies, the overall effect of the highly unequal relationships between UNHCR and refugees has been that of removing refugees from the decision-making and planning processes concerning the organisation of their lives and their protection. This is in many cases particularly problematic for women (as discussed in Chapter 2) as they are generally already positioned in a subordinate position with relation to these processes in their own societies, and so relationships with UNHCR and other aid agencies can act to reinforce local gender inequalities and mechanisms of domination. Further, important physical and material barriers may exist to women's participation in planning such as lack of childcare facilities to enable them to participate in meetings. Unless all these factors are taken into consideration by UNHCR staff, then gender equality in any camp planning programmes will remain illusory.

Another explanation for the difficulties in implementation of UNCHR's gender policies and programmes in refugee camp situations is highlighted by Baines and Harrell-Bond who point to the way in which goals of cultural sensitivity may undermine efforts to implement gender equality policies. Harrell-Bond points particularly to the way in which the aim of cultural sensitivity has led humanitarian agencies to encourage "traditional" methods of solving disputes within refugee camps. This method of favouring "traditional" methods of negotiation and arbitration can reinforce the power of those already dominant in any society or population and can give license to many kinds of oppression by the camp "elders" (Harrell-Bond, 1999). As these "elders" are generally older men, then their judgements may well reinforce unequal gender relations among refugee populations. Baines also points to the way in which resistance to gender equality policies within the UNHCR has sometimes stemmed from the ideal of universalism which is used to deny the validity of treating women as a separate category. This type of recognition can be "associated with privileging one group over another in a zero-sum game" (Baines, 2004: 63). In parallel with this claim to universalism, however, exists a discourse which locates the roots of gender inequality and practices of domination or oppression within the realm of cultural values and norms of the country of origin or of the host society:

> Gender equality then, is regarded by some staff as a cultural imposition, undermining the principle of non-intervention embedded in UNHCR culture. That gender equality is perceived to be a Western-feminist imposition is defended by staff who maintain a certain cultural relativism in their belief systems, despite their loyalty to principles of universality.
>
> (Baines, 2004: 63)

This sometimes paradoxical parallel belief, both in the value of universalism and in the need to respect "other" cultures, is repeated in other areas of refugee protection, notably in asylum determination procedures which at the same time often refuse to treat women as a specific category because the theoretically gender-neutral laws and policies should apply to all equally, and at the same time attribute much of the persecution suffered by women to "cultural difference" which is not a matter for intervention by Western authorities.

The mixed results of UNHCR's attempts to integrate a gender dimension into its policies and programmes can thus be traced back to a variety of causes, including the structure of the organisation itself and its institutional culture, the policies of donor governments, and the dominant representations of refugees which have been created by UNHCR and other humanitarian aid agencies. Within these constraints there are certainly individuals who are working hard to try and ensure that the goals of gender equality are met, but these efforts may go unrewarded faced with the difficulties of implementing policies and programmes to promote gender equality within different contexts of refugee protection.

In the following section we will discuss in more detail one humanitarian programme designed to extend greater protection to "vulnerable" women, before going on to examine more closely the transnational campaigns that have emerged around the issue of gender and refugee protection and the representations of women refugees and asylum seekers that have been promoted by these campaigns.

The "Women at Risk" programme

The "Women at Risk" programme is one of the ways in which the UNHCR has sought to respond to the needs of women refugees, and particularly those in refugee camps around the world. The programme was introduced in 1988 following recommendations emanating from the third World Conference on Women in Nairobi in 1985. It is a programme which aims to identify women in refugee camps who are at extreme risk of harassment, physical or sexual violence or refoulement and to fast track their removal and resettlement in one of the seven Western countries that have agreed to take part in the programme. The criteria state that exiled or displaced women who have been identified as being at extreme risk should be eligible for immediate resettlement whether they have formally been recognised as refugees or not. The problem, however, is how to identify those women "at risk". This is a term which is open to varied interpretation and is subject to the personal biases of those involved in selecting women for the programme. The problem of definition and selection is particularly acute when a large number of women can be identified as potentially at risk. Pittaway and Bartolomei quote one director of a refugee camp in Africa who comments that: "Every woman in this camp has been raped. Do you want to resettle them all?" (2003: 91). In addition to the criteria established by the UNHCR to qualify for this programme, the countries which accept these refugees for resettlement may also have their own criteria for selection. In Australia, for example, to qualify for resettlement under the women at risk programme, a woman must be living without the protection of a male relative and be in danger of victimisation, harassment or serious abuse because of her sex, and she must be able to pass medical and character checking procedures (Manderson et al., 1998). Similarly, Canadian criteria for the selection of refugees for resettlement insist that the person must have been recognised as a refugee by UNHCR, and that in addition they must meet the standard of "admissibility", which generally means that they should demonstrate the potential for successful integration and settlement in Canada. But as Boyd argues the characteristics used to evaluate such potential are largely of a socio-economic nature such as education, job skills or knowledge of English or French. And since gender inequalities in many countries mean that women have fewer educational opportunities and less job skills, these criteria may discriminate against them (Boyd, 1993). This critique of the women at risk programme also highlights a more general problem with resettlement programmes in general, namely that the refugees who are chosen for resettlement are often those who are most "desirable" in terms of a set of criteria set out by the host country, and these criteria can discriminate against women who have had fewer educational or employment opportunities in their countries of origin. This perception of discrimination in selection for resettlement is widespread in countries with large refugee populations. A Tanzanian official in the Ministry for Home Affairs thus explained to an Oxfam researcher that Western states only want to resettle the "healthy, brainy refugees who are more likely to integrate easily" (Oxfam, 2005: 51).

In fact, the total number of women who have been resettled under the women at risk programme has remained minimal for the reasons explained above. Canada, for example, accepted a total of five hundred and eighty six women and children through the Women at Risk programme between 1988 and 1993, which comprised only 0.8 per cent of the total number of refugees accepted into the country. "In other words, the Women at Risk programme, laudable in its conception, has in practice scarcely touched the numbers and proportion of women refugees resettled in Canada" (Macklin, 1995: 220). Figures for 2005 show that a total of 2777 women were resettled worldwide. The main countries of destination for these women were Australia (921), United States (918), Canada (360) and Sweden (168) (UNHCR, 2006b). Again these numbers represent a tiny percentage of those women who are living in refugee camps in Africa, Asia or the Middle East, and more importantly of those women who continue to run daily risks of sexual attacks or other violence. Moreover, evidence from Australia shows that the women who are most likely to be resettled originate in Europe or the Middle East rather than from Africa, and that as a consequence "the Women at Risk programme seems to have barely touched the problem of the high proportion of immobile refugee women, mainly in camp situations in countries of first asylum or refuge" (Kneebone, 2005: 12).

In addition to this confusion about which women are "at risk" and the limited numbers actually chosen for resettlement, it can also be argued that the programme is weakened by its failure to address the wider issues of protection of women by focusing only on resettlement of these women to third countries. Finally it can be argued that resettling women to a Western country is not sufficient to achieve effective protection. As Pittaway and Bartolomei argue: "The response to the special needs of women at risk in receiving countries...is often sadly lacking. Many countries do not understand, nor are equipped to deal with the high levels of trauma which can be the result of protracted refugee situations, endemic sexual and gender based violence, and torture" (Pittaway and Bartolomei, 2006). The fact that once they have been accepted for resettlement and have received legal status in their host country, these women cease to receive any special support or help can thus be a barrier to their integration into a host society or to the fulfilment of their continuing needs for protection and assistance. Single women with children as those resettled under the programme usually have, may have particular needs and continuing vulnerabilities when they arrive in the host country which may thus remain unmet, and so the value of assisting women in resettlement can be limited "if the conditions which led to their classification as 'at risk' during the assessment period cease to be recognised during the period of resettlement" (Manderson et al., 1998: 282).

The ambivalent role of NGOs

The high political profile of the debate over asylum seekers and refugees, and the politics of "new humanitarianism" has led to a proliferation of NGOs and voluntary associations working with forced migrants, both nationally and transnationally. The UNHCR increasingly relies on NGOs to administer its programmes on the ground, or to help with running of refugee camps and aid distribution, leading to a sometimes problematic symbiosis between the UNCHR and NGOs (Vayrynen, 2001). Donor governments have also shown a tendency to work directly through NGOs rather than through the intermediary of the UNHCR, as the NGOs are often viewed as more flexible and a cheaper alternative than donating more to the UNHCR. In addition, NGOs may have easier access to refugee populations in the case where the UNHCR is not authorised to work in a certain country's national territory (Raper, 2003; Cusimano Love, 2007). The proliferation of NGOs working with forced migrants is not unproblematic, however. At a most basic level, the sheer number of NGOs both national and international, all working in the same area, has led to a competition between these different organisations. This competition can be conceptualised as a "market" within which NGOs bid for funding and contracts, and could be seen in some instances to lead to the neglect of the best interests of the refugees themselves. In the rush to provide humanitarian relief in emergencies, local NGOs which have better knowledge of and contacts with the population may be pushed aside by larger and better-funded international NGOs, which may also seek to take over these smaller local organisations and recruit their personnel (Zetter, 1996; Cusimano Love, 2007). It is precisely these locally based NGOs, with their better understanding of the barriers to women's participation and of gender relations in any particular context, who may be able to make a difference in "empowering" women. This is particularly the case if the NGOs are founded by or in collaboration with women refugees themselves. Blue describes the success of the Mamá Maquín organisation, founded by Guatemalan refugee women in Mexico in raising the consciousness of women refugees. She cites one of the founders of the organisation who points to the way in which it changed her and other women's understanding of their own situation:

> Before we had the organization, we were discriminated against, because the women only worked in the house and cared for the children. It is the women, said the men, who have the children. It's fate that women get screwed. That's what they said to us. And a woman, because she doesn't know how she is going to protest for her rights, accepts that it is her duty. But when we organized ourselves in the organization, then we began to recognize the rights that women have, that women have equal rights to men. Women can also participate in any activity, not just the men. We have achieved literacy through the organization . . . It has been a pure struggle to have achieved what we have.
>
> (Francisca, leader of Mamá Maquín, cited in Blue, 2005: 107)

Mamá Maquín was able to organise literacy classes for women in the camps which focused specifically on issues of concern to women, they also raised funds to provide women with gas stoves and corn mills which made their cooking tasks much easier and quicker, thus allowing them time for other activities. Blue argues that the success of this initiative was due precisely to its grassroots organisation and focus on issues of immediate concern to women. Because the organisation's founders were refugee women themselves they were able to better understand the needs of other women, and to help them to overcome the gendered barriers to participation without being seen as importing "foreign" models of gender equality (Blue, 2005: 110). Sadly, this type of initiative seems to be relatively scarce in refugee camp situations, and bigger and better-funded Western NGOs are often able to crowd out smaller local initiatives that might in fact have a better understanding of the populations they are serving. This is particularly damaging in the case of initiatives aimed at empowering women, where intimate knowledge of local gender relations, and ideas about ways to empower women without trying to radically reconstruct these relations (which would be seen as a source of outside interference), will be more likely to be provided by local NGOs founded by or closely involving women themselves.

Similar problems exist for NGOs working with asylum seekers in the West. In Europe, the process of Europeanisation and harmonisation of asylum policies (even though this harmonisation has not been complete because of the various obstacles to a unified policy in this area) have led to the emergence of new actors in the NGO sector who have developed actions at a transnational European level (Favell and Geddes, 2000). However, these transnational activities have not replaced those of national NGOs and associations who have often built up privileged relations with governments and immigration officials in their own country and who therefore have a greater experience in the area than some of the newer European organisations. Moreover, the continuing dominance of inter-governmental (rather than supranational) policy making in the area of immigration and asylum means that it is often more rational for NGOs to lobby at a national level if they want to have an effect on policy outcomes (Gray and Statham, 2005). National NGOs have thus retained their place in the policy networks around asylum and immigration, but have in some senses been forced to reconfigure their actions to take account of the new multi-level politics of asylum in Europe.

The NGO sector has traditionally been weak in areas of asylum and immigration policy with little power to influence policy-making (Gray and Statham, 2005). This weakness has been exacerbated by the increasingly restrictive policies of national governments and by the framing of asylum seekers as a "threat" to Western States, a framing which leaves few discursive opportunities for defence of asylum seekers or their rights. Frequently it is very difficult even for those working within NGOs which aim to "defend" the rights of asylum, to escape from the dichotomies established in dominant discourses between "genuine" and "false", or "good" and "bad" asylum seekers. Especially when faced with a heavy work load, the NGOs may thus justify their failure to help some asylum seekers by the claim that they were not "real" asylum seekers anyway, and that some kind of sorting process needs to be carried out in order to ensure that the "genuine" cases get the help that they deserve.[7] The weakness of the NGO sector over asylum issues may also be attributed to a fragmentation resulting amongst other things from a competition to secure a place in an increasingly competitive "market". As argued above in relation to NGOs which cooperate with the UNHCR in administering humanitarian aid in refugee camps, the multiplicity of actors involved can act merely to create a confusion as to the supposed goals of the NGOs, and their relation to their clients. Fragmentation may also be caused by the dilemma facing NGOs in the West of deciding to what extent they will cooperate with governments in the administration of their restrictive asylum policies. Whilst some, mainly smaller NGOs have deliberately avoided any government funding in order to retain their independence, others have entered into cooperation with government agencies in order to implement various programmes, for example, concerning the housing of asylum seekers. The impacts of this collaboration can seem perverse. For example, the cooperation of several large NGOs with the British Government in implementing their dispersal and accommodation programmes led to cases of asylum seekers being expelled from their accommodation centres by NGOs because they have not fulfilled the conditions for assistance demanded by legislation. Legal Action for Women, for example cites the case of an Eritrean woman in the UK who was evicted from her accommodation when she refused to sign a document saying that she would return to Eritrea. A spokesperson for the Refugee Arrivals Project who ran the accommodation centre argued that as the NGO was partly funded by the National Asylum Support Service (NASS), it had to adhere to legislation in the 1999 Immigration and Asylum Act: "One of the requirements is you have to co-operate with removal. If the claimant refuses to fill out the form, we are unable to help" (cited in Legal Action for Women, 2006: 9).

Given this weakness of NGOs in relation to asylum policy, have they been able to advocate or implement any significant advances in terms of gender equality in the asylum determination process? As we argued in Chapter 4, the level of NGO mobilisation around issues of gender equality depends very much on the general discursive opportunity structures for talking about gender equality in any given national context, so that in some states NGOs have been much more active than others in lobbying government to introduce specific policies aimed at taking into account the specific needs of female asylum seekers and introducing more gender equality into the asylum determination process. It seems that perhaps somewhat paradoxically, as asylum policies become more restrictive, so gender issues in the asylum process have gained a higher profile among NGOs in the West. This mobilisation around issues of gender might be explained by the fact that this is seen as one issue where NGOs can still have some influence over government, even if a limited one. The head of Asylum Aid in the United Kingdom, for example, explained that faced with the increasingly restrictive nature of government policies on asylum, his organisation had decided to focus its efforts on smaller battles which it though would be more "winnable" and that gender equality was one of those battles where they estimated they could still have an impact.[8] Having said this, there are still many NGOs which either ignore gender as an issue altogether or else refer to the supposed "vulnerability" of women seeking asylum without seeking to understand the real needs of female asylum seekers. A founder of the All African Women's Group in the United Kingdom points to the fact that her group was founded by women who felt that the major NGOs in the asylum sector had failed to understand their real needs and had failed to listen properly to their stories. The support that the group gives to its members and the fact that they had been unable to find this type of support elsewhere with the NGO sector point to the need for more initiatives which are based on the mobilisation of asylum seekers and refugees themselves. However, obstacles to this type of organising still remain as will be discussed in the following section.

The mobilisation of asylum-seeking and refugee women

What about mobilisations involving asylum-seeking and refugee women themselves? Some members of NGOs and associations have criticised their own organisations for failing to fully take account of the needs and desires of those they are trying to help, in other words women asylum seekers and refugees.[9] Frequently NGO actions for asylum seekers and refugees construct and reinforce power relationships which mirror those of the UNHCR/NGOs and refugees within refugee camp situations. NGOs presume to have superior knowledge and capabilities to act and speak for asylum seekers and refugees, and thus position themselves in a position of power over these people. This presumption of superior knowledge has clearly increased with the growing "technocratisation" of the asylum field, where competence to help asylum seekers is measured more and more by higher degrees of very technical legal knowledge. This "technocratisation" can be seen as a product of the ever more restrictionist asylum systems, within which NGOs try to compete with decision-makers and immigration officials and judges to provide technical legal points which may help their asylum seeker "clients". However, this repositioning of NGOs as more and more technically and legally competent in contrast to the "incompetent" and

"ignorant" asylum seekers has also acted to magnify unequal power relations between the two groups of people. Rather than a mutual exchange
of information between NGO and asylum seeker, more and more often
the situation changes to one in which an asylum seeker is not advised
but told what to do to succeed in their claim. Frequently during the
course of this research, the rejection of an asylum claim was explained
by an NGO employee as the direct result of a failure by an asylum seeker
to listen to the instructions provided to him or her. "I told him/her not
to include that in his/her claim, but he/she just didn't listen to me",
becomes a typical response of an NGO worker to a negative asylum
decision on one of "their" cases.[10]

There is an awareness by some within the NGO sector of this growing
inequality in the power relationships between them and asylum seekers,
and in some cases attempts have been made to overcome, at least partly,
this inequality, by including asylum seekers within NGO organisation or
by sponsoring self-mobilisations of asylum seekers in order to give them
a "voice". In addition, women seeking asylum and women refugees have
spontaneously organised their own campaigns and mobilisations, even
though the conditions of these mobilisations are sometimes difficult.
One of the major barriers to asylum seekers self-organisation and mobilisation is their very precarious legal status which makes it difficult to
plan or carry out any long-term projects. Zetter and Pearl comment of
Refugee Community Organisations (RCOs) in the United Kingdom that:

> With transient membership, limited organisational capacity and
> very constrained access to funding...few RCOs survive to become
> enduring organisations. Reflecting their rather more precarious phys-
> ical and legal status, it has recently been the case that RCOs seem to
> appear and disappear rather rapidly.
>
> (2000: 684)

Similarly, Lesselier points to the way in which various attempts to
create autonomous associations for asylum-seeking and refugee women
in France have led to short-lived mobilisations which have foundered
both because of the precarious legal status of the women involved and
because a lack of recognition for this type of organisation both from
within official government structures and from other NGOs and associations (Lesselier, 2007). In addition, women may find it more difficult
to organise because of the subordinate role that they have been assigned
in many societies. This means that male asylum seekers may not allow
women to take an equal role in associations or political mobilisations.

When it is successful this type of independent mobilisation can be a way of developing a more formal status for those granted some form of protection and a means of integration into the host society. For example, Sales and Gregory refer to the case of Somali women from a local Refugee Organisation who now work with social services in London (Sales and Gregory, 1998). Perhaps even more importantly, these types of associations can provide an arena where women asylum seekers or refugees can express their own political agency and escape from the dominant representations of themselves as merely "victims". As one of the founders of the All African Women's Group in the United Kingdom explained:

> Being together with other women has really helped us to fight. We know that we can help each other, it's very important for women to come together and share our experiences and help each other. We've managed to change our lives.[11]

She described how the group was formed in the wake of protests against the effects of Section 55 of the 2002 Immigration and Asylum Act, which removed the right to welfare support for asylum seekers who failed to make an application "as soon as is reasonably practicable" when arriving in the country (for a fuller discussion of the specific implications of this policy for women see Chapter 6). A group of Eritrean women asylum claimants were refused housing by the Refugee Council under the terms of this Act and organised a public protest outside the Refugee Council offices in London. This group was joined by women from other African countries who shared similar experiences. Semret Fesshaye an Eritrean woman who was one of the group's initial members describes the importance of this self-mobilisation:

> Traditionally, asylum seekers in this country have remained silent for fear of deportation. We have allowed others to speak on our behalf, but because the situation we find ourselves in here is disastrous we are starting to speak up for ourselves.
>
> (Fesshaye, 2003)

This function of providing a voice for asylum seekers and a way for them to speak for themselves is a vital role of grassroots associations and NGOs. In France a group of Algerian women whose asylum claims had been rejected organised a similar mobilisation to protest against their status as "failed" asylum seekers. The group organised support meetings and demonstrations and sent a letter to President Chirac, asking him to consider their cases. Although these actions may have had only limited results in terms of changing their status (a few of the women who were living in France with children managed to eventually get some kind of temporary leave to remain), one of the group members describes the important psychological impact of their ability to organise and to share their own experiences and speak for themselves.[12] Unfortunately, as is the case in international humanitarian actions, these small-scale mobilisations organised by women themselves have little access to funding or official support, and so are likely to remain temporary and sporadic instances, whilst the larger better-funded NGOs will continue in the main to speak for asylum seekers.

Taking account of gender in national and transnational campaigns: moving beyond stereotypes?

In Chapter 4, the variations in the adoption of international norms on gender guidelines in the asylum process into national level policy-making was noted, as was the role of mobilisations by NGOs and other associations in pushing for the appropriation of these international norms. As well as noting a difference in the implementation of norms on the protection of female refugees and asylum seekers, and the recognition of gender-specific forms of persecution between different national contexts, it is also interesting to note that there are differences in terms of the protection offered to women who are victims of different types of persecution. In other words, different forms of persecution have provoked very different levels of mobilisation and varying policy responses. The issue of excision or female genital mutilation, for example, has provoked widespread campaigns in many countries and has often led to the adoption of policies to protect women and girls from this type of violence and to facilitate the access to asylum for women fleeing this type of persecution or trying to protect their daughters. Why have these issues provoked a particular mobilisation and why do they provide favoured access to political asylum? Keck and Sikkink (1998) argue that there are two characteristic types of issues around which transnational advocacy networks have organised most effectively, these being firstly issues involving bodily harm to vulnerable individuals, especially when there is a short and clear causal chain or story about who bears responsibility, and secondly, issues which involve legal equality of opportunity. In the first case, they point out that, "issues involving physical harm to vulnerable or innocent individuals appear more likely to resonate transnationally. Of course, this alone does not ensure the success of the campaign, but is particularly compelling. Nor is it straightforward to determine what constitutes bodily harm, and who is vulnerable or innocent. Both issues of 'harm' and 'innocence' or vulnerability are highly interpretive and contested" (Keck and Sikkink, 1999: 99). The issue of FGM seems to enter clearly into this category of issues which involve physical harm to "innocent" individuals, particularly in cases where the "victims" of this practice are young girls. French associations report that it seems far easier to gain asylum in cases of threatened FGM when the asylum claimant is a mother trying to protect her daughter from this practice, rather than a woman who is fleeing the practice herself.[13] Transnational mobilisation around issues like FGM, as well as having success in creating new international norms and policies regarding these issues, has also been successful in transposing international norms into domestic policy frames. The reasons for this lie not only in the mobilising potential of the cultural toolkit available in this case – the "vulnerable" and "innocent" victims of potential physical harm – but also in the resonance with pre-existing frames in different national contexts. This resonance seems particularly strong where a pre-existing national discourse on the illegality of so-called "traditional" practices exists. In Western societies where a debate has already taken place, or is currently engaged, over the ways in which Muslim cultures might engage in "harmful" practices against women, it is easier for those who wish to mobilise support for women who have been "victims" of this type of practice to place their claims within the existing normative framework and to make strategic alliances with other groups. In France, for example, the issue of whether or not Muslim women should be allowed to wear headscarves in public places had already opened up a more general debate over the ways in which European societies should protect the "rights" of Muslim women (Moller-Okin, 1999; Freedman, 2007a). Similarly, the campaigns to recognise that women fleeing forced marriages should be granted asylum have found an audience within a more general debate over the existence of forced marriages and the need to protect women against them, a debate which has often been brought into public attention through the bias of discourses and policies attempting to limit marriage migration as a source of migrants to the West. However, although there are obvious advantages to the use of such pre-existing frames and debates to increase the success of mobilisations in favour of women's right to asylum by aligning these campaigns within already existing and accepted values and norms, there are also dangers in accepting without question a normative framework which is based principally on Western values and norms. In many cases this pre-existing normative framework is based on a supposedly "universal" set of human rights and women's rights, which are in fact defined according to the experiences and situations of Western women and which ignore the complexities of the situations of many other women. There is not space within this chapter to engage fully in the debates over universal/particular rights. Suffice it to say in this context that the way in which international norms are both defined and then even more importantly transposed into national policies, legislations and norms will have an impact on the effectiveness and impacts of those norms. It is vital that general normative standards are contextualised and embedded in national and local contexts for them to avoid the polarisation of universalism versus culturalism. In other words, as Stivens argues, activists must be aware of the ways in which "claims to rights are embedded in highly specific local contexts and struggles" (2002: 2).

Underlying all the above discussions on the ways that international and national organisations have attempted to "help" refugee and asylum-seeking women is the issue of dominant representations which both portray women refugees as helpless victims and reinforce the difference between "us" and "them", Western women and the racialised "other". This division can be traced back to a primary dichotomy which has been established in international politics between those states which produce refugees and those that accept refugees (Macklin, 1995). Following on from the logic of the Cold War period when the countries of the Western bloc believed that refugees all emanated from the other side of the Iron Curtain, and that political persecution could not happen in their countries, democratic Western States in the post-Cold War era have assumed that they cannot produce refugees as they have laws and policies designed to protect the human rights of their citizens. The refugee-producing countries are others, countries which do not respect human rights in the same way. The problems inherent in this type of distinction are evident from the discussion of gender-related persecution and particularly of domestic violence in Chapter 3. Whilst domestic violence occurs in all countries, the connection is rarely established between violence against women "here" in the West and violence against women over "there" in other countries. As a result the persecutions that take place in those "other" countries are attributed to immutable social and cultural characteristics, and the real dynamics of gender inequality underlying all types of gender-related violence, whether "here" or "there" is not analysed. As Macklin argues:

Recent feminist scholarship from the United States on gender persecution and refugee status evinces a distressing degree of cultural
hyperopia regarding local conditions for women. It seems that when
some North American feminists want to make a pitch for granting
asylum to victims of gender persecution elsewhere, they become
tactically blind to the compelling evidence gathered by other North
American feminists documenting local practices that might constitute gender persecution. At the very moment North American feminists turn to condemn misogyny in the "third world", they lose sight
of the fact that our own culture hardly presents a model of gender
equality.

(1995: 267)

These types of ethnocentric and racialising attitudes may make it
easier for feminists in the West writing about asylum and refugees to
identify some kinds of practices as persecution whilst others are not so
easily recognised. As argued above, female genital mutilation, a practice that is held up as a paradigm of "other" cultures, has been the
subject of many feminist campaigns. Far fewer women have mobilised
to support victims of domestic violence in other countries, or indeed
have suggested that victims of domestic violence in Western states
should themselves be able to seek international protection or asylum
elsewhere. This "othering" of cultural practices and of women seeking
asylum leads to a tendency to disconnect the experiences of Western
women with those of women who seek asylum. As Macklin again
argues:

What this means in the refugee context is that we suppress the
commonality of gender oppression across cultures to ensure that
what is done to Other women looks to utterly different from (or
unspeakably worse than) what is done to women here, that no one
would notice a contradiction in admitting them as refugees. The
logic of the dichotomy of refugee-acceptor/refugee-producer compels
a parallel classification of Western woman/Other woman that serves
to facilitate the admission of at least some women fleeing gender
persecution, but only by adopting a method that is politically and
empirically problematic.

(1995: 272)

How can this problematic dichotomy be overcome in the process
without reverting to a false universalism which ignores divisions among

women produced by race, class or ethnicity? The answer must be to consider the local and international contexts carefully when examining what is persecution against women and what can be done to "help" women seeking asylum or women refugees.

Transnational advocacy campaigns and representations of "refugee women" as "vulnerable victims"

In seeking to understand why there has been in many cases a failure to take into account gender-specific persecutions, it is also necessary to examine critically the global norms that have been created and the frames which are used to represent women refugees and asylum seekers. It might be argued that one of the reasons for the uneven impact of global norms in this area is that they are based on frames which represent women refugees principally as vulnerable victims, thus essentialising a particular set of gendered roles, and failing to take into account the underlying gendered relations of power. Representations of "refugee women" as helpless victims also act to de-politicise these women's experiences and activities (Baines, 2004). Rajaram (2002) points to the way in which humanitarian responses to refugees amount to a generalising and depoliticised depiction of these refugees as helpless victims. Refugees are thus rendered speechless and without agency, and as Malkki argues, they are identified not in terms of their individual humanity but as a group whose boundaries and constituents are removed from their historical context and reduced to norms relevant to a state-centric perspective of international relations (Malkki, 1996). This depoliticisation can be argued to be particularly acute with regard to women refugees and asylum seekers, as women tend to embody as particular kind of "powerlessness" in the Western imagination (Malkki, 1995), and are thus idealised as "victims" without agency.

This use of strategic frames of women as vulnerable victims in need of protection is prevalent amongst practitioners in the international policy community (Carpenter, 2005), and it can be argued that the symbols and signifiers of women as vulnerable victims form a valuable part of the "cultural tool kit" (Swidler, 1986) of these practitioners. Images of women and children in refugee camps have become common in fundraising campaigns by UNHCR and NGOs. In some contexts these images have been shown to be highly effective in raising public awareness of refugee issues and of attracting donor support for particular humanitarian crises or in drawing the attention of political leaders. In Somalia, for example, Loescher comments on the way that "widespread media coverage of starving women and children finally turned policy makers' attention to the disaster" (2001: 303).

However, although such framings might be assumed to be beneficial to women as they are supposed to be used to mobilise support for specific protection measures for women, these frames are in fact essentialising of gender difference and ignore women's agency and voice. Women refugees and asylum seekers are, for example, often symbolised as mothers, and in this framing their primary role is to protect their children. Examples of the use of such a frame can be found in asylum policies in various countries which have sought to protect women whose children are at risk of excision. In this case, protection is offered to women purely in their function as "mothers" protecting their "innocent" children from harm (the mobilising power of ideas of "innocence" and "harm" have been discussed above). A different way to approach this problem of the essentialising nature of the frames used to describe women asylum seekers and refugees and of the framing of particular issues of persecution in terms of pre-existing and essentialising norms is to relate these problems to the question of how gender issues become (or do not become) securitised and the fact that asylum-seeking women themselves are often excluded from the process of "framing" their own claims, because they lack a "voice". In a critique of the Copenhagen School, Hansen uses the example of honour killings in Pakistan to argue that those who are constrained in their ability to speak about their security/insecurity are prevented from becoming "subjects worthy of consideration and protection" (2000: 285). She concludes that "Silence is a powerful political strategy that internalises and individualises threats thereby making resistance and political mobilisation difficult" (Hansen, 2000: 306). This critique might serve as the basis of a wider criticism of the ways in which the "voice" of women asylum seekers and refugees is ignored in the framing of issues relating to gender-specific persecution. The discursive opportunities which exist are not open to these women for reasons of political, social and economic marginalisation and exclusion. The NGOs and associations which make claims for gender-specific policies and legislation do so on behalf of refugee and asylum-seeking women, these women themselves have little or no voice in the process. Speaking for women asylum seekers and refugees leads to representations and framings of them which rely heavily on pre-existing cultural norms as argued above, and which contain these women in their role of "victims". Real understanding of the gendered causes of forced migration would take into account the voices and perspectives of those women who flee and would adapt solutions for protection to specific experiences and to particular national and local contexts. A goal of feminist constructivist analysis must be to give a "voice" to those considered marginal in international politics (Locher and Prügl, 2001). As Steans and Ahmadi conclude:

> Agreements on principles or statements of good intent are of little use if they are not followed up with implementation and enforcement measures or if they are undermined, subsumed or spoken for only by elites. Impediments to women's participation in decision making processes remain, while practices of inclusion and exclusion in relation to NGOs … also silence women's voices.
>
> (2005: 244)

If the interests of women fleeing persecution and seeking protection as refugees are truly to be guaranteed, then the voice of these women needs to be heard. It is important to listen to the voices of women seeking asylum and refugees if the trap of essentialising their experience and treating them as passive victims is to be avoided. Women do need protection and are vulnerable in some circumstances, but this should not be generalised to assume that they are all just "vulnerable victims". Cockburn argues that women should only be treated as "mothers", as "dependents" or as "vulnerable" when they themselves ask for this special treatment. "When, on the contrary, should they be disinterred from 'the family', from 'womenandchildren', and seen as themselves, women – people, even? Ask the women in question. They will know" (2003: 29).

Representations of women asylum seekers

Whilst representations of "refugee women" as vulnerable victims persist in the discourse of humanitarian organisations and in media images of women in refugee camps, other representations exist alongside these, of women using their perceived "vulnerability" to "take advantage" of Western states. These images of female asylum seekers who make "false" claims for protection are also highly gendered and racialised. Women are often represented using their reproductive capacities to make themselves even more vulnerable or to gain extra benefits from an overly generous welfare state. Here we recall again Yuval-Davis and Anthias' arguments about how nationalisms create gendered roles for men and women, within which women are responsible for both the biological and the symbolic reproduction of the national or ethnic group (Yuval-Davis and Anthias, 1989). This type of representation is evident in Lentin's description of the debate over pregnant female asylum seekers in Ireland and the possibility that they might be granted residence permits on the basis that they had children born in Ireland. The media reporting of this issue referred to the managers of maternity hospitals in Dublin who described the ways in which asylum seekers were "stretching maternity hospitals to breaking point" (Lentin, 2003: 314). Further it was claimed that women seeking asylum were becoming pregnant to take advantage of Irish citizenship laws; one report quoted medical personnel as saying, "There are times when you can't get through the front hall because it is so jam-packed with people landing in from the airport ... You don't have to be a genius to see that the system is being exploited" (cited in Lentin, 2003: 314). Here the representations of "womenandchildren" (Enloe, 1993) found in humanitarian discourses on the protection of civilians and refugees are re-contextualised within an exclusionary nationalist discourse where these "womenandchildren" become a threat and a burden for state services, particularly health and welfare services. These representations are closely connected, although these connections are rarely made in the media or in public framing of these issues. As one UNHCR official interviewed for this research commented "we are just not making the connection between the images of the victims over there who we have pity on, and the asylum seekers over here who are resented for 'invading' our country".[14] Chapter 6 will examine ways in which government policies designed to stem this "invasion" have had particular gendered impacts.

6
Asylum Regimes and Their Impacts

This chapter will examine recent changes and developments in asylum law and policy in Western countries, particularly the countries of the EU. It will be argued that these changes have often lead to increasing insecurity and vulnerability for asylum seekers as governments seek to limit the number of asylum seekers who reach their country, and also the number of those asylum seekers who are granted refugee status. Several recent reports have highlighted the impacts of these changes on the human rights of asylum seekers. These issues will be analysed in terms of the differential impacts of new policies and legislation on male and female asylum seekers. It will be argued that whilst the rights of all asylum seekers have been eroded by recent developments, there have been particular causes of vulnerability and insecurity for female asylum seekers in relation to the asylum determination process and also to the provisions for the reception and processing of asylum seekers. The chapter will examine, for example, the debates over the use of reception centres for asylum seekers and the way that the use of such centres can have a particular negative impact on female asylum applicants. It will also examine issues such as housing and welfare, as well as considering the legal and judicial processes for considering asylum claims.

The key issue here is that as has been argued with regard to other aspects of refugee protection programmes and regimes, policies and processes that are in theory gender neutral, in fact have differing impacts on women and men because of existing gendered inequalities and gendered structures of power. These are either ignored or made invisible in many policy decisions, so that the particular effects of policies on women are overlooked. The effects of closing frontiers and making it more difficult for asylum seekers to arrive in Western states will, for example, have differing impacts on women and men trying to reach Europe. We have already argued in Chapter 2 that there are a range of socio-economic, cultural and political factors which make it harder for women to leave their homes and countries of origin and to travel to a Western state to seek asylum. The additional barriers imposed by Western states increase these difficulties and may also mean that women are forced to resort to smugglers or traffickers to help them enter a country, thus exposing them in turn to new risks such as that of forced prostitution. And for those who do succeed in reaching a Western state to make a claim, recent attempts to "discourage" asylum seekers have led to policies designed to restrict their freedom of movement and their rights to welfare, housing and other benefits. Again these policies are in theory gender neutral, but in practice their application is filtered through a system of gendered relations of power and inequalities which may mean that they have differentiated effects on men and women, and on different groups of men and women. All of these different elements need to be explored to determine what the real gendered impacts of asylum policies and processes might be.

European integration – Dublin and beyond

The progress of European integration and enlargement has meant that European Union member states have sought to find common immigration and asylum policies. The difficulties in obtaining unity in this area have been well documented (Geddes, 2000a,b); however, in the key areas of asylum and refugee policy there has been some progress in this respect. The Treaty of Amsterdam of 1997 set out an agenda for harmonisation of asylum policies, and the Tampere European Council called for a common EU policy comprising a Common European Asylum System (CEAS). The emphasis of efforts towards harmonisation have been focused on standardisation of the ways in which asylum claims are treated, and of who exactly should qualify for refugee status, in order to remove existing disparities between national legislation and policies in member states. In effect, EU states have moved towards a harmonisation which aims to keep as many asylum seekers as possible away from European borders, and to reduce the numbers to whom refugee status is granted. It has been claimed that this process has resulted in standards for protection being reduced to a lowest common denominator (UNHCR, 1995a). An Oxfam report on European asylum policies argues that:

While they ought not to require member states to bring their domestic law down to this "minimum" level, the instruments adopted give them the latitude to lower their standards. Member states may fear that if they fail to bring their standards down to the level of their neighbours, their share of asylum seekers will increase...this "domino effect" could mean widespread "harmonising down".

(Oxfam, 2005: 21)

One of the aims of the integrated European asylum policy has been to prevent what has been known as "asylum shopping", in other words, attempts to claim asylum in more than one EU country, so that if a claim is refused in one member state, the asylum seeker can make a new claim in another member state. Under the terms of the Schengen agreement, member countries could and should refuse to grant asylum to any asylum seeker having passed through a safe third country, whilst the Dublin Convention of 1990 signalled that an asylum claim could only be made in one country of the EU – the country that the asylum seeker had arrived in, unless they had relatives in another EU country – and that once a decision was made on this claim that decision should stand for all of the EU countries. The aim of the Dublin Convention was to avoid one person making multiple asylum claims in different countries and asylum seekers being sent, or trying to move from one country to another to find one which would grant them refugee status. Although these restrictions apply to both male and female asylum seekers, they may have a greater impact on women. As discussed in previous chapters, there are differences between EU states in the extent to which any gender guidelines have been adopted with regard to the asylum determination process, and thus it may be beneficial for a woman asylum seeker to have her claim considered in a country which is more receptive to claims based on gender-related forms of persecution. As it is generally hard to have these types of persecutions recognised, then any information that a woman might have about where her claim is most likely to succeed will be welcome and useful to her. Further the particular social and economic conditions which place barriers to women even reaching Europe to make an asylum claim, may also mean that they have greater need of a network of support once they reach Europe, and thus it may be more important for women asylum seekers to get to a particular country where they have some contacts or where they know they will be able to access a community of other women from their own country to claim asylum. The new policies which treat most asylum claims with increasing suspicion, fail to take into account the needs of asylum seekers with respect to choosing a country of asylum, and this can be particularly damaging for women. As Koser argues, the perception that most asylum seekers are "bogus", "fails to take account of data showing that consistently across the European Union over the last decade up to fifty per cent of asylum applicants are granted either refugee status or some kind of temporary protection. It also confuses motivations for leaving with motivations for selecting a country of asylum. It is reasonable to expect that someone fleeing persecution will at the same time try to apply for asylum in a country where he or she has an existing social network, understands the language and has a chance to work" (2001: 88). These concerns about arriving in a country where one has contacts and existing social networks may be even more vital for women for whom making the journey to seek refuge is a choice of last resort.

The attempts to harmonise EU asylum policies have led to several major directives on asylum which should be integrated into each member states' national legislation and policies. The first of these, the qualification directive[1], has been hailed by some women's organisations as an important opportunity to make sure that EU states take gender-related persecution seriously when assessing asylum claims, as the directive specifically recognises that gender-specific persecution should be treated under the terms of the Geneva Convention (see Chapter 4). The directive also recognises that non-state actors may be agents of persecution, which again could benefit the recognition of gender-related persecution by overcoming the distinction between public and private which has undermined attempts to establish recognition of various forms of persecution specific to women, persecutions which largely take place in the domestic sphere and which are undertaken by private or non-state actors. However, despite the apparently promising opportunities offered by this directive for those pressing for greater recognition of gender-related persecution, there are also some possible obstacles such as the directive's reference to the possibility of protection by non-state agents. Thus an asylum claim could be rejected if a member state argued that the claimant could be protected by a non-state agent in their country of origin, where non-state agents would include international organisations or quasi-state entities which control some territory of the state. It has already been remarked that these types of organisations may not be able to offer effective protection to all the population under their control, and this may again be particularly relevant in the case of gender-related forms of persecution. In fact, as has been shown in

Chapter 3, representatives of international organisations such as the UN have in some cases been complicit in continuing exploitation or abuse of women who are supposedly under their protection.

The second major directive aimed at harmonisation of asylum policy, the procedures directive[2], which describes the procedures that should be adopted by member states when deciding asylum claims also contains some elements which have worried human rights organisations and which may have specific repercussions relevant to gender-related persecution. The major point which has worried critics is the idea of creating a common list of "safe" countries for all EU member states. An asylum seeker who has come from or transited through one of these safe third countries on his or her way to Europe could be denied access to any hearing of their asylum claim and sent directly back to the "safe country". The idea of "safe" countries is not new, and many states already have a "white list" of countries that are considered safe. Asylum seekers from these countries may be subjected to a very speedy and limited hearing of their claim before being returned to their country of origin. The presumption is that they have no justification for making an asylum claim and so they have to give very strong evidence of persecution to overcome this presumption. The adoption of these "white lists" by states, and their subsequent expansion as governments try to disqualify a priori as many asylum applicants as possible has come under criticism from human rights groups who argue that to generalise in this way about the safety of particular countries overlooks specific instances of persecution that may still occur within these countries As with many other policies this attempt to define "safe" countries has often ignored gender-related persecutions which may take place in such a country, basing as assessment of safeness on a set of criteria which have no reference to women's rights or the level of protection that women may expect from the state in the case of contravention of these rights. The criteria used to define "safety" are once again based on an underlying assumption of a public–private division which ignore violence and persecution carried out in the private sphere. Moreover, criteria for defining safety require only that a country is safe for the majority of its citizens, so that even where there is clear evidence of gender-based persecution of a substantial minority of the population, this can be ignored. France, for example, has added Mali to its list of safe countries, even though it is well-documented that female genital mutilation (FGM) is a widespread practice in Mali, and despite the large number of Malian women who arrive in France to claim asylum on the basis of fear of FGM (Freedman, 2007a,b).

The case of the United Kingdom's utilisation of a "white list" is also illustrative in this respect. A list of safe countries was established by the United Kingdom in 2003 for use in the processing of asylum claims (and with the specified object of speeding up the treatment of "manifestly unfounded" claims). The criteria used to judge whether a country should be put on this white list included the political stability of the country, the existence of an independent judiciary and democratic institutions. But as Valji argues: "while lip service is paid to the state's role in 'respecting human rights' .... it is doubtful if these criteria were intended to cover rights such as those expounded in the Convention on the Elimination of All Forms of Discrimination Against Women (CEDAW)" (2001: 29). The UK list included the European Union states, the ten (then) EU accession countries and a further seven countries including Albania, Bangladesh, Macedonia and Serbia/Montenegro. The then British Home Secretary David Blunkett argued that asylum seekers from these countries would be deported without appeal on the basis that "It is frankly absurd that people can routinely claim they are in fear of their lives... These are democratic countries which live under the rule of the law" (quoted in *The Guardian*, 24 October 2002). Critics pointed, however, to the inclusion in this list of many countries where human rights abuses regularly took place against some sections of the populations. One concern was with the treatment of Roma people in Central and Eastern European states, and in particular of Romani women. A report published by the Center for Reproductive Rights showed the massive extent of forced sterilisation of Romani women in Slovakia, and also highlighted the physical abuse and discrimination these women faced in accessing maternity and reproductive health care (Center for Reproductive Rights, 2003). Slovakia has now become a member of the EU, and as such is considered a priori a "safe" country from which asylum claims cannot be made in other EU states. It is highly likely, however, that the types of persecutions and infringements of Romani women's rights documented in this report are continuing.

Bangladesh is another country on the United Kingdom's "white list" although violence and persecution of women is widespread in the country. The International Commision of Jurists affirmed their concerns about women's rights in Bangladesh, and about the government's inability or unwillingness to protect these rights in a 2003 report in which they stated that:

Women still frequently face violent attacks, many die as a result of domestic violence and acid attacks on women continue, sparking widespread national and international outrage. NGOs and women's rights defenders complain of a lack of adequate protection and effective legal remedies for the victims of violence. The failure of the Bangladeshi authorities to take prompt legal action against those accused of perpetrating violence fosters a climate of impunity.

(International Commission of Jurists, 2003)

The new procedures directive will go further than the policies introduced in individual member states to identify safe countries, in that the common list established at an EU level will not only serve to expedite claims of asylum seekers who originate in "safe" countries, but will also mean that any asylum seeker who has transited through a "safe" third country can be denied access to the asylum procedure altogether. Asylum seekers will have no opportunity to rebut the presumption that this third country is indeed "safe" and they will have no guarantee that their claim will be considered by this country, which might just return them directly to their country of origin with no assessment of their case for protection. These procedures will thus amplify the dangers already outlined in respect to the designation of "white lists" at national level, and will also act to push the responsibility for dealing with asylum seekers onto countries outside of the EU (for a further discussion of this process of "externalisation", see below). As the Oxfam report concludes: "the very idea that a country can be deemed safe for everyone is problematic. It runs counter to the principle of asylum and the reality that individuals and certain groups may face persecution in seemingly safe places, and that 'safe' places may become rapidly 'unsafe' " (2005: 26).

Safe third country agreements have not only been problematic for the defence of the rights of women asylum seekers in Europe. The United States and Canada signed a safe third country agreement in 2004 which means that any asylum seekers who have transited through the United States will not be accepted into Canada, but must have their claims heard in the United States, and vice versa. Canadian critics of this agreement have pointed to the fact that it has massively reduced the number of asylum seekers who manage to arrive in Canada, especially since the largest national group seeking asylum in Canada in recent years has been Colombians who naturally transit through the United States on their way to seek asylum. In addition, it has been pointed out that this agreement will have gendered impacts because of the differing treatment that gender-related asylum claims receive under Canadian and US procedures for determining asylum claims. Even during the negotiation of the agreement, a Canadian Parliamentary Standing Committee expressed particular concerns about the negative impact it would have on women fleeing domestic violence and suggested that they should be exempted from the terms of the agreement. The Canadian government argued in return that "at a policy level" the United States and Canada have substantively similar approaches to gender-based asylum claims. However, the Canadian Council for Refugees has argued that this is an example where divergences between policy and practice have meant that female asylum seekers who would have received protection in Canada have been "falling through the gaps in the US system" (Canadian Council for Refugees, 2005). The divergences in the two systems stem from the fact that the US gender guidelines are only binding at one level of the asylum determination process, and that female asylum seekers may be forced to enter the system at a level where these guidelines do not apply (see Chapter 4). For example, if a woman is arrested while entering the United States illegally and placed in a removal centre, her case will not be heard by a decision-maker who is bound by the gender guidelines. In addition, other procedural rules, such as the rule that an asylum claim must be made within one year of entering the country, also act against women seeking asylum, as does the failure of US judges to recognise domestic violence as justification for granting refugee status. The Canadian Council for Refugees's (CCR) report on the effects of the Safe Third Country Agreement describes three cases of women fleeing FGM in Guinea and Nigeria whose cases failed because of these procedural rules, and also because in cases of FGM the woman has to prove that she "opposed the practice", in other words that it was done against her will. One woman (named Fatima in the report) had her claim denied on this basis. She had been persecuted by her uncle after the death of her father, and he had instructed her aunts to perform FGM on her. Whilst they were doing it she started to bleed so heavily that the aunts had to take her to hospital to save her life. Her uncle came to see her in the hospital and promised that they would "finish the job" when she was released. With the help of her mother Fatima fled, and filed an asylum case in the United States. Her claim was denied. The CCR report recounts that: "In a response to her appeal the asylum officer admitted that Fatima had proven that she was the victim of female genital mutilation. She had filed within the one-year bar, and the government admitted that Fatima had female genital mutilation performed on her. However, according to the reasons for the denial, Fatima had not proven that the female genital mutilation was done against her will" (Canadian Council for Refugees, 2005). The CRR argues that Fatima, like many other women would have been offered protection as refugees if they had been able to make an asylum claim in Canada. The example of the US–Canada agreement highlights some of the problems with the notions of "safe" third countries evoked above in relation to European policies. Rather than a means of protecting refugees, these type of policies seem to be merely a mechanism for pushing the "burden" of asylum seekers onto other countries, and given the very different interpretations of the Geneva Convention that may exist in national legislations and practices, this "spreading" of the burden can have negative consequences, consequences which may be particularly damaging to some groups of asylum seekers including women.

Securitisation of asylum: The United States and the war on terror

The events of 11 September 2001, and subsequent terrorist attacks in Madrid and London, have provided Western governments with another justification for increasingly repressive policies against asylum seekers, namely the threat that they pose in terms of terrorism. Nowhere has this discourse of asylum as linked to terrorism had such an extreme impact as in the United States, where the Patriot Act of 2001 and the Real ID Act of 2005 have greatly expanded the definitions of terrorist activity, an expansion which has had specific impacts on asylum seekers. The new legislation means that an asylum claim can be denied on the basis that the claimant has provided the "material support" of terrorism. This "material support" is defined extremely widely to include the provision of goods or services to a group of two or more individuals which engages in activities using an explosive, firearm or other weapon. This condition is applied even when the asylum seeker in question has been forced to provide the support to the supposed "terrorists". The perverse effects of this legislation on those who are in fact fleeing terror has been noted by US critics and one of the groups that they point to as having particularly suffered from the impacts of the new laws are Liberian women claiming asylum in the United States. These women who have been kidnapped and raped by militia, and then forced to cook for them, have been labelled "material supporters" of terrorism precisely because of their domestic enslavement and the fact that they have provided food for their captors (Reynolds, 2007). This example demonstrates the ways in which processes of securitisation of asylum policy and "criminalisation" of asylum seekers, can lead to resulting exclusion of these asylum seekers from their rights to demand protection. This type of exclusion is also at work in the European policies of "externalisation" of asylum which will be discussed in the next section.

Europe and the externalisation of asylum

The idea of processing asylum claims far away from state's borders is one that is becoming increasingly popular. As previously discussed, the Australian government has recurrently stopped the boats of asylum seekers from landing in Australian territory, and has moved these people to other locations whilst processing their claims for asylum, in what has become known as the "Pacific Solution". European governments have arrived at a similar solution to their "problems" of asylum, namely the externalisation of European asylum processing to neighbouring states. This idea first appeared in a European Commission communication of 2000[3] although still in very vague terms, and was re-visited by the UNCHR's "Convention Plus" proposals, which the then General Secretary Ruud Lubbers remarked, included ideas concerning the "external dimension of European asylum policy".[4] These ideas were taken up under the Danish presidency of the EU, particularly in discussions between the Dutch and British governments, which led to a series of proposals made public by *The Guardian* on 5 February 2003.[5] The plans revealed by *The Guardian* on the basis of a confidential document leaked to them from the Home Office, indicated that in order to reduce the number of asylum seekers arriving in the United Kingdom, the creation of "regional protection zones" was envisaged. These protection zones would be established outside of the EU and in areas close to the countries from which asylum seekers came, notably Turkey, Iran, Somalia and Morocco, and would be areas to which any asylum seeker who sought to enter the EU could be deported. Other areas of protection were imagined in Zimbabwe or in the Balkans, and a collaboration with the Ukraine and Russia to set up zones for asylum seekers in their countries as well to deal with the potential flows of asylum seekers from Eastern Europe as the EU expanded. The proposals were transmitted to the Greek presidency of the EU in March 2003 for discussion at the forthcoming Thessaloniki summit. In his letter to the Greek Prime Minister, Tony Blair proposed two major ideas: that of regional protection, and of transit processing centres for considering asylum claims before asylum seekers reached the EU. Reaction to these proposals from various human rights groups was critical, arguing that implementation of proposals would infringe asylum seeker's rights and that proper protection could not be assured to forced migrants in regional protection zones or transit processing centres. The Refugee Women's Resources Project reflected specifically on the implications for women, for whom protection might be even more elusive, particularly for those fleeing gender-based persecution:

> The protection of women against gender-based persecution requires the adoption of a gender-based legal framework with specialist knowledge and adequate judicial institutions, which are often lacking in the "protection areas". It is doubtful that there will be political will to incorporate such a framework and guarantee the rights of women to be free from their persecutors and/or be able to prosecute them according to international standards. Further, there is a risk that women who disagree with repressive gender social norms will be deported to regions where such regimes exist.
>
> (Refugee Women's Resources Project, 2003)

Moreover, it was argued that deprived of community support and any form of income, it is also extremely difficult for women to find economic opportunities in countries with already serious needs in terms of food and other socio-economic activities. Many are living in dire conditions common to all refugees and asylum seekers. Shifting further responsibility to these poorest countries by requiring them to accommodate refugees returned from Europe, will only aggravate the welfare and security risks faced by the large number of refugees already in these countries: particularly, women and children.

The British proposals on externalisation of asylum were finally dropped before the Thessaloniki summit because of the opposition of Sweden who threatened to veto the proposals[6]; however, this did not mean the proposals had been abandoned, with a tacit agreement amongst those in favour of the proposals to continue with pilot projects for camps. The following year, the European Commission's Justice and Home Affairs Directorate issued a communication[7] on the same subject which took up Blair's proposals, albeit in a vaguer manner. And in 2004, the Hague Programme called on the Commission to elaborate regional protection programmes in collaboration with third countries and with the UNHCR, using the experience gained from the pilot programmes carried out. The Hague Programme also proposed specific financial incentives to those third countries who were willing to collaborate with the EU in the control of migration.

So what have these processes of "externalisation" meant in practice? And how have they affected the experiences of forced migrants trying to enter the EU? As these processes are in a stage of development it is still hard to predict exactly what shape the attempts to establish regional protection zones might take. So far pilot projects have been agreed with Tanzania, the Ukraine, Byelorussia and Moldavia, but these are still in the planning and early implementation stages, and there is as yet no data about how exactly they will be put in place and what effects they will have. However, it is clear that the momentum for trying to prevent asylum seekers arriving in Europe by keeping them in countries of transit around the EU's borders is increasing. For example, bilateral and multilateral agreements have been signed between EU member states and Morocco and Libya. These two countries have agreed to impose tighter controls on migrants moving through their territory towards the EU and to readmit asylum seekers deported from the member states signatory to the agreements. In 2004 when hundreds of asylum seekers landed on the Italian island of Lampedusa, up to eight hundred and fifty of them were summarily transferred to Libya with no consideration of their asylum claims in Italy (Oxfam, 2005: 38). General concerns about this type of bilateral readmission agreement have been expressed because of the inability of unwillingness of these countries to protect the rights of migrants in transit. In relation to women's rights, particular questions might be raised because of the evidence that high levels of gender inequality already exist in Libya and Morocco, and that these states do little to protect their own female citizens, let alone women who are migrants in transit. A Human Rights Watch report on Libya, for example, described the appalling conditions in which those arrested whilst trying to reach Europe were detained. Whilst both men and women suffered from overcrowding, bad sanitary conditions, lack of food and violence, women were also at risk of sexual violence and rape. The report contains several allegations of this type, and one man described conditions in which the men and women were detained:

> All of the detained men slept outdoors; they were not given bedding. The women and children stayed in a garage-like structure at one end of the courtyard. "The guards would go there at night, and the women would scream," Teclu said. "The men would go see what was going on, but the soldiers would beat them. I can't swear to it, I don't know if any of them were raped. If they were, they wouldn't say so for the shame."
>
> (Human Rights Watch, 2006a,b)

Another woman describes her experiences of the immigration detention centre in which she was held and the women's tactics for self-protection and for resisting threats of sexual violence and rape:

> Anebesa stayed with twelve other women in a small cell that had no showers. They washed with water brought to them in plastic bottles and were allowed only one trip to the toilet per day. They got bread and tea in the morning and one meal of rice during the day. According to Anebesa, the conditions were extremely unsanitary, and many of the women fell sick. She said that one Ethiopian woman died after she went on a hunger strike to protest the conditions, but she could not recall her name. The male guards also threatened the women detainees sexually, Anebesa said. She described the fear in which the women lived: "Whenever we needed to collect the food, we women all went together, all thirteen of us, so that we never left a woman in a room alone. This was successful in preventing attacks. In the same way, at night, the male guards would come with a set of keys and let themselves into our cell. We would always wake each other up when this happened and sit down in a group and start crying and screaming, until they gave up and went out."
>
> (Human Rights Watch, 2006a,b)

Similar worries about the risks to women's rights have been expressed regarding other countries which Europe views as a "buffer zone" between itself and arriving asylum seekers; however, there is as yet little information circulating about what exactly is happening to refugees and asylum seekers in these countries. In December 2006 and January 2007, Moroccan soldiers carried out roundups of sub-Saharan African migrants, removing them from big cities and leaving them near the Western border to fend for themselves. Among these migrants were many women and children. Other reports have criticised the conditions for those asylum seekers stopped at the Eastern borders of the EU and held in the Ukraine. As Europe exerts more and more pressure on its neighbours to stop these asylum seekers before they manage to reach Europe, it is likely that the situation and living conditions will worsen for all of them, and in these situations women's rights will surely be negatively affected. There are also fears that as the development of regional protection plans progresses, more and more countries will be deemed "safe" third countries. Asylum seekers will thus be subject to the same constraints as those from other "safe" countries, with the resulting difficulties for women fleeing gender-related persecutions which are not recognised as detracting from the "safe" status of their country of origin (see above).

The attempts to keep asylum seekers away from Europe's borders have come at a time when some European countries are also looking to attract "skilled" migrants to fill voids in their workforces. The combination of these two policy directions may lead to a "cherry picking" of asylum seekers, so that those who are considered "desirable" in terms of their qualifications, skills or perceived ability to integrate might be chosen to be resettled in one of the EU member states. This type of selection of asylum seekers based not on their need for protection but rather on the needs of the host state for particular forms of labour reinforces a utilitarian rather than a humanitarian framing of asylum and may have important gendered impacts. As discussed in Chapter 5 with reference to humanitarian resettlement programmes, the asylum seekers chosen by European governments will be those with the highest levels of educational qualifications, employment skills or language abilities. But as we have seen, women may well be denied equal access to education or the labour market in their country of origin and will so be less favoured in any such selection process. As Yuval-Davis et al. (2005) comment: "the gendered implications of such a policy are numerous. On what grounds would someone be chosen – a young man compared to a single mother?"

Temporary or subsidiary protection

Attempts to reduce the number of asylum seekers who are granted Convention refugee status (under one of the five grounds enumerated in the Geneva Convention), has also led to the development of forms of temporary protection within Western states. Whilst Conventional refugee status is usually accompanied by the granting of permanent residence, and by access to most or all of the rights and benefits of permanent citizens, temporary or subsidiary forms of protection give access to lesser rights. Temporary protection is not a new measure, the United States used temporary protection schemes for Central American refugees in the 1980s and the 1990s, but what is new is the spread of such measures, and the attempts to harmonise EU policy on subsidiary protection. Temporary or subsidiary protection may also be used in a punitive fashion as in Australia where those deemed to have arrived illegally may be eligible only for temporary protection even if they are recognised as refugees (Gibney and Hansen, 2005). These temporary or subsidiary forms of protection are used to replace refugee status under the Convention when the adjudicators or judges rule that the claimant cannot claim to be persecuted under one of the five Convention grounds, but when they believe that the person in question is still at risk of cruel or inhumane treatment in their country of origin and therefore deserves some form of protection. As argued in Chapter 4, the introduction of subsidiary forms of protection was may be seen as potentially beneficial to women asylum seekers, as this could allow the recognition of forms of persecution which have not been previously recognised as legitimate grounds for asylum claims (such as domestic violence, forced marriage) and could thus widen the range of those who might be offered some form of protection, even though this is less than full refugee status. However, doubts have been expressed about the value of these subsidiary forms of protection which do not offer the same benefits in terms of residence permits and access to welfare as the conventional refugee status. Subsidiary protection may give access only to temporary residence permits which have to be renewed annually; access to the labour market may be limited, as may the right to family reunification. Some NGOs working with women asylum seekers have expressed fears that because gender-related persecution is often not seen as entering under the grounds of the Geneva Convention (see Chapter 4), the granting of temporary protection might be seen as an easy answer to the protection of women, but that this might lead in turn to a further stratification in rights whereby more men are granted conventional refugee status and more women temporary protection.[8]

Gender, trafficking and smuggling

All of these measures to try and restrict the number of asylum seekers arriving in the European Union have led to the development of the market in trafficking and smuggling of human beings. This can be considered as something of a vicious circle, whereby the more restrictive measures the EU states put in place, the greater the demand for the services of smugglers and traffickers becomes (Koser, 2001). The effects of smuggling and trafficking on women may be seen as particularly perverse, for women are more at risk of sexual violence and exploitation whilst being smuggled, and the need to use traffickers can leave them open to the possibility of being forced into prostitution when they arrive in Europe. The definition of "trafficking" is highly complex and has been a matter of concern for policymakers and activists. The EU has placed great emphasis on the fight against trafficking – but these initiatives are firmly placed within the frame of the fight against "illegal migration". Thus although the measures taken are supposedly to protect the "victims" of trafficking, in fact they are often merely a means of excluding more migrants. Although the UNHCR recognises that trafficking may constitute a form of persecution relevant under the Geneva Convention and although in their recommendations regarding the international protection that should be extended to those who have been trafficked it stresses that: "An additional and specific consideration relates to the importance of avoiding any linkage, whether overt or implied, between the evaluation of the merits of a claim to asylum and the willingness of a victim to give evidence in legal proceedings against her or his traffickers" (UNHCR, 2006b), policies and programmes which have been put in place in many Western countries to stop trafficking do not offer refugee status to those women who have been victims of trafficking, but offer them only temporary protection in return for evidence which will help to prosecute the traffickers. Several studies point to the "invisibility" of women who have been trafficked (Thobani, 2001; Jaksic, 2007), and to the way in which the criminalisation of smuggling and trafficking does not in fact protect women, but shifts the focus of policy-making onto the prosecution of traffickers. Thobani argues that recent changes in Canadian legislation on trafficking have been framed as a way of protecting Canadians from the illegality both of traffickers and smugglers, and from the women who have been trafficked, thus pointing to the deportation of these women as the only "solution" to the problem (Thobani, 2001: 24). This kind of approach has been mirrored in other countries, with trafficking being treated from within a security paradigm which leaves little room for the effective protection of "victims" of traffickers.

Increasing internal controls: threatening the welfare of women seeking asylum

At the same time as Western states are attempting to reinforce external and border controls to stop asylum seekers reaching their countries, many are also enforcing internal control measures in order to try and deter asylum seekers from coming to their countries. These internal controls on the rights of asylum seekers are justified by discourses which criminalise asylum seekers, portraying them as "illegal" residents who can thus reasonably be denied the rights of other citizens. Such representations have normalised policies of exclusion of asylum seekers from Western societies, and have allowed the imposition of "deterrents" such as levels of welfare and services well below those of other citizens. The types of internal controls imposed by Western governments have ranged in form from an increased use of detention and imprisonment, to restrictions on where asylum seekers can live, denial of their right to work and limitations on the welfare benefits and health care access available to them. This has led to a continuing stratification of rights within Western states between citizens and other "legal" residents, and asylum seekers and "illegal" immigrants (Morris, 2002). Again, although these restrictions on the rights of asylum seekers are not gender specific, they can be seen to have gender differentiated impacts because of the particular situations of different groups of women and men within the asylum system. Stratification in access to rights and services is thus dependent not only on legal status, but also on a variety of other variables including gender, class, national or ethnic origin, and levels of community networks and support (Sales, 2002). In some countries, women are still treated as dependents of their husbands if they come with them and encouraged to make a joint asylum claim. In this case, the woman will be dependent on her male partner for her status and her access to rights, and in case of marital breakdown or separation she may lose her status. In addition, the right to work or to receive certain benefits may be allocated to the male partner in a couple which will reinforce the woman's dependency. As Bloch and Schuster argue, giving the right to work to the male member of the household cements "the exclusion and isolation of women asylum seekers" (2002: 396). This type of measure causes further stratification in access to rights, as do other policies which distinguish between different types of asylum seeker. In the United Kingdom, for example, the government has made an attempt to separate port applicants (those who make a claim immediately on arrival in the United Kingdom) and in-country applicants (those who make a claim after entry), and to remove benefits from the latter category. Although the removal of benefits from "in-country" applicants has been challenged by the Courts, this type of categorisation further serves to exclude some groups, and may again have particular gendered effects if women have specific reasons for making a later claim, such as a reluctance to talk about sexual violence or rape.

Detention

A phenomenon which has become evident in recent years is the increasing use of detention as a way of controlling asylum seekers and exiles who arrive in Western states. This increased use of detention has in some senses become a "normalised" way of dealing with these people

(Bloch and Schuster, 2005), but has had important implications for the rights of asylum seekers. The expansion of detention has been made possible by the diffusion of a frame of analysis which considers asylum seekers as bogus or fraud, and a threat to the nation, and which leads to a process of criminalisation of those seeking protection. Welch and Schuster describe how a culture of control contributes to punitive social responses towards crime and criminals, and argue that this culture of control is spreading from the United States and the United Kingdom to other European States. A significant feature of the culture of control is the way in which it emphasises the consequences of crime rather than its causes and as a result, "the focus shifts from the crime problem to the criminal problem, paving the way for an emergent criminology of the other in which lawbreakers – and asylum seekers – are characterised as menacing strangers who threaten not only individual safety but also the entire social order" (Welch and Schuster, 2005: 334). Once asylum seekers have been characterised in this way as threats to social order, it becomes easy for governments to detain them with little or no public opposition. The extremes of the utilisation of detention as a means of control of asylum seekers has been reached in Australia where all asylum seekers who arrive to make a claim are placed in mandatory detention until their claim has been decided. However, the United States, the United Kingdom and other European Countries are also increasing their use of detention. In the United States, fear of terrorism fuelled by the events of 11 September 2001 has been used by the government to justify a crackdown on asylum seekers. All asylum seekers are detained on arrival in the United States and although they are eligible for parole if they meet certain conditions, often even those who meet these criteria remain in prison. Asylum seekers who originate from any of the thirty three countries where Al Qaeda has been know to operate are not eligible for parole even if they meet all the criteria required under the system.

In European countries, detention of asylum seekers has usually only been used in order to facilitate their expulsion from the territory, in other words when their claim has failed and they are thus liable to deportation. However, European governments' keenness to get rid of as many failed asylum seekers as possible as quickly as possible, and to show the public that they are doing this, has led to a massive increase in the use of detention. The first asylum detention centres in the United Kingdom were built in the 1990s as the numbers claiming asylum in the United Kingdom increased, and the issue became more and more politicised. The 1999 Immigration and Asylum Act made provision for increasing use of detention and expanded the number of places available in detention centres. By 2004 there was capacity for detention of two thousand two hundred and sixty asylum seekers in the United Kingdom (Welch and Schuster, 2005). There is no legal time limit for which a person may be detained in one of these centres (which have been renamed removal centres by the Home Office, perhaps to make their existence more palatable to the general public). The majority of those detained are eventually released without being removed to their country of origin, either because conditions in that country are too dangerous to allow for deportation, or because they have obtained bail, have been granted leave to remain on compassionate grounds, or because their claim for asylum has eventually been granted after appeal. The use of these detention/removal centres thus seems in many cases to be more of a means of deterrence of punishment of asylum seekers, rather than an efficient tool for their removal from the United Kingdom. Increasingly, asylum seekers are placed in detention on arrival in the United Kingdom as their cases are "fast-tracked". Detention thus acts as a means of expediting the examination of asylum claims with the goal of removing as many "failed" asylum seekers as quickly as possible.

The same point regarding the use of detention as a deterrent has been made by Cimade (2004) in their reports on detention centres in France (Cimade, 2004). As in the United Kingdom, the use of detention in France has a supposedly administrative function, to aid removal from French territory, but in the case of France, detention is limited in time. New legislation passed in 2003 extended the time for which a foreigner may be held in detention to thirty-two days.[9] This new legislation was accompanied by targets issued to police prefectures for the number of foreigners they should try and deport. Cimade argues that this new targeted policy for detention and expulsion has led to the neglect of specific protection needs and rights of individuals, including refusals to register claims for asylum (Cimade, 2004). Asylum seekers have been arrested when they go to the police prefecture to register their claim for asylum, because they do not have legal entry or residence papers, and once in detention, if they are allowed to make an asylum claim it will be treated under "priority" procedures, usually resulting in a refusal within five days (Cimade, 2006a,b).

Other European countries such as Germany and Italy are also increasingly turning to detention as a means of controlling flows of asylum seekers, and are using detention centres to hold not only those whose claims have been rejected but also those asylum seekers who have just arrived in the country (Welch and Schuster, 2005), and these detainees are being held for increasing periods of time – in Germany there are examples of detention for up to eighteen months (Bloch and Schuster, 2005). In Italy, a law passed in 2002 created a new type of detention centre where asylum seekers can be held whilst their nationality and identity is established, and where elements of their asylum claim may be checked (Welch and Schuster, 2005). Various reports have criticised conditions inside Italy's detention centres for foreigners and pointed to the lack of information on and access to asylum procedures (MSF, 2003; Amnesty International, 2005a). The new entrants to the EU are also using detention as a way of dealing with the asylum seekers entering their territory. Amnesty International reports that in Malta, "By the end of 2004, over eight hundred people, including women and children, were held in detention centres run by the police and armed forces. Many were held on grounds beyond those permissible under international norms" (Amnesty International, 2005b: 5).

Detention may entail specific problems for women. These are usually to do with the conditions of the detention which may not be suitable and may expose them to violence and harassment. The "punitive" side of detention of asylum seekers which stems from the processes of criminalisation which have taken place in Western societies is translated where women are concerned into gender-specific forms of humiliation or harassment. Women may be subjected to sexualised and racialised abuse by guards, abuse which relies on cultural and racial stereotypes and constructions of difference between "Western" women and those "other" women who have come to seek protection, but who are treated as criminals. Women may often be kept in unsuitable conditions, with poor food and insufficient provisions for hygiene. Their health needs, particularly in respect to reproductive and sexual health may not be met. Women who have been victims of rape or torture may not be able to access sufficient psychiatric care and support. Particular problems may be posed by mixed gender accommodation (Malloch and Stanley, 2005). One recurring issue is that of the employment of male guards in female areas of detention centres, leading to potentially humiliating or shameful situations for women detainees.

In Australia, since 1999, all those asylum seekers who arrive without valid documents, in other words, without a visa, are subject to mandatory detention for the whole period of time that their asylum claim is being considered. In a study based on interviews with women held in detention in centres on Australian territory between 1999 and 2001,[10] Zurek points to the particular harm suffered by women because of a lack of sensitivity to gendered situations, and to women's specific needs. A basic example of this is the fact that all detainees were kept together, with no separate accommodation for women. In addition to this, there was limited access to showers and toilets and in some cases detainees had to earn the right to have a shower by completing jobs around the centre. However, these jobs were often hard manual jobs which were not suitable for women. There were few female guards in the centres, and male guards were unsympathetic to women's needs, particularly concerning sanitary protection. One woman explains that when a woman needed sanitary products the guards would "be telling everybody. They would be yelling at her and saying this when everybody was in the room" (Zurek, 2004: 37). Many of the women interviewed spoke of how the lack of gender sensitivity compounded the effects of the trauma and torture they had suffered in their country of origin.

A consequence of the rapidly expanding use of detention for asylum seekers in many countries is that there are not enough places in existing detention centres, and so detainees may be housed in very poor conditions. Because of this lack of places, women are often housed in the same spaces as men, with no separate bathroom or toilet facilities. Women in these cases have reported their fears of harassment and abuse. In France it has been reported that: "The massive assignment of women to detention centres has led to serious problems. Instances of prostitution have been noticed, particularly in centres with no effective separation between men and women. Some women have complained of harassment and even of receiving death threats from certain men" (Cimade, 2006a,b: 8).

In the United States and the United Kingdom, NGOs have undertaken specific research into the conditions for women asylum seekers held in detention, which reveal similar concerns about the way that women are treated. A report by the Women's Commission for Refugee Women and Children (WCRWC) states that: "Women asylum seekers are particularly at risk of neglect and abuse. The Women's Commission found that the physical and psycho-social needs of women were not addressed. Inadequate translation assistance results in women being held in prison virtually incommunicado, unable to voice their needs or draw attention to any abuse they experience. Their medical problems are mismanaged or ignored, including critical reproductive health services and gynaecological care. Access to the outdoors is nonexistent in some cases and severely limited in most others. The diet provided to women asylum seekers is often insufficient and almost never culturally appropriate. Most disturbing are reports of abuse at the hands of the officers charged with their care, in some cases eerily reminiscent of the abuses the women fled in their own countries" (WCRWC, 1997: 4). The report also points to the fact that sometimes women are denied services, such as access to interpreters or legal advisors, which are provided for male asylum seekers. Often asylum seekers who are detained in the United States are held in mainstream prisons together with other criminals. This non-separation reinforces the process of "criminalisation" of asylum seekers and has consequences on their living conditions and on the way in which they are treated by guards. Women are more likely to be detained in mixed accommodation with other criminals because the INS argues that the smaller number of female asylum detainees make it impractical to provide separate quarters for them. The WCRWC report points to the resulting indifference of prison guards to asylum seekers, treating them like criminals, and in some cases handing out even harsher treatment than received by other criminal detainees on the basis of racist assumptions and discrimination (WCRWC, 1997). One woman from Guinea was placed isolation for three weeks when she arrived at a prison. She was given a mask to cover her nose and mouth and told she needed to wear it whenever she spoke to anyone, and no prison guards would have any physical contact with her, warning the others to keep away if they did not want to catch the disease. The woman was later released from isolation but was never informed what was supposed to be wrong with her (WRWC, 1997). This type of treatment is clearly motivated by racialised stereotypes of the health dangers posed by Africans, and perhaps in particular the association between Africans and HIV/AIDS.

Most of the attention on women in detention in the United Kingdom has focused on the Yarl's Wood Removal Centre where over thirty African women (principally from Uganda and Zimbabwe) went on a hunger strike to protest against the way that their asylum claims had been treated by the UK authorities. A report by Legal Action for Women on the Yarl's Wood Centre highlighted what it describes as "appalling conditions" within the centre, including "sexual intimidation, racism and brutality from staff" (2006: 16). One of the particular problems highlighted is a lack of privacy for women and forms of sexual intimidation including male officers coming into the women's rooms without warning when they were naked or getting dressed.

Pregnant women are among the categories of those who, according to the UK Home Office regulations, should not be detained. However, there are many known cases where pregnant women have been detained for long periods of time. Jackson reports that one woman was detained for the first five months of her pregnancy whilst still awaiting her appeal hearing (2003: 121). The LAW report on Yarl's Wood also provides evidence of the detention of pregnant women, and points to a lack of adequate healthcare for these women. One three-month pregnant woman complained that she had been bleeding for three weeks, but could not get anyone in the health care unit to take this seriously "even though she was terrified that she would lose the baby" (Legal Action for Women, 2006). Reports from other countries also indicate that the detention of pregnant women has become a regular event. The WCRWC report on the United States describes the experience of a pregnant asylum seeker from Cote d'Ivoire who was denied medical assistance for several weeks, and when she did see a doctor who prescribed nutritional supplements and vitamins for her, these were confiscated by prison staff (WCRWC, 1997). Similar practices of detaining pregnant women and limiting their access to specific healthcare have been noted in France (Cimade, 2004). These particular forms of repression against pregnant asylum seekers might be interpreted in light of what Seu tells us about social narratives and discourses concerning female refugees, and the gendered representations of what she calls "the woman with the baby". In her analysis of these narratives, refugee and asylum seeking women are never referred to as "mothers", but as "women with babies" (Seu, 2003), indicating a questioning of their parental role. In the representations of asylum seeking women as "other", it can be argued that their role as mothers or potential mothers is also that of "otherness", and that their pregnancies are not valued as those of "native" women would be.

These difficulties of motherhood in detention are also evident in respect to the detention of mothers with their children. Although asylum policies in most countries point to children as one "vulnerable" group who should not be detained, in practice the expansion of the practice of detention has affected them as well (Cimade, 2006a,b). The report on Yarl's Wood pointed to the fact that 10 per cent of the women interviewed for the study had their children with them in detention (Legal Action for Women, 2006). Anne Owers, the Chief Inspector of Prisons in the United Kingdom, has condemned the detention of children and argued that the damage done to children who are detained in this way is often overlooked. In evidence to a House of Lords Select Committee she maintained: "The children become invisible, no one looks at what is happening to the child and what damage detention may do".[11]

Asylum and welfare

An idea which has become commonplace in debates over the number of asylum seekers reaching different countries is that the welfare benefits available to these asylum seekers in each country can act like a magnet to attract greater and greater numbers. This idea, together with the perception that asylum seekers place a huge financial burden on national governments, has led to the restriction of many of the welfare rights to which asylum seekers were previously entitled.

In Europe, this process can be seen as a reduction of welfare benefits and support offered to asylum seekers to the level of the lowest common denominator, even though disparities remain in the level of benefits available. In 2003, the EU introduced a Reception Directive[12] which should have been transposed in all member states (with the exception of Ireland and Denmark who opted out of this directive) by February 2005. The Reception Directive is supposed to ensure minimum standards for the reception of asylum seekers in all states which are meant to guarantee them a "dignified standard of living". This "dignified" standard of living seems in many cases not to be a reality though, and often the rights of asylum seekers to housing and other benefits are well below the level of those granted to other citizens. As Düvell and Jordan explain, a process of "benchmarking" has taken place within the EU over the types of accommodation provided for asylum seekers, the level of social benefits and the duration for which an asylum seeker is allowed to claim them. In each case, member states have chosen to adopt models from other countries which are seen as best limiting the number of asylum applicants. Thus the model of dispersal of asylum seekers to accommodation across the country has been copied from Germany and Sweden, and the restriction of benefits from the Netherlands and Denmark. "The overall effect has been a levelling-down of welfare provision and an attempt to speed up decisions in most countries" (Düvell and Jordan, 2002: 505).

Another important aspect of evolution in the provision of welfare and services to asylum seekers and refugees has been the increasing involvement of NGOs and the voluntary sector in this provision as governments have devolved responsibilities on to them. This trend has had a varied impact in different states, depending on the previous structure of the welfare system. In Southern European states, where the welfare regime has not been so developed, the state has never had a major role in providing benefits and services to asylum seekers and refugees and so NGOs have traditionally been the major actors in this sector (Düvell and Jordan, 2002). However under other welfare regimes, NGOs have been brought in to manage the provision of accommodation and services which were previously provided by the state. This might be seen to involve some compromises by NGOs and the voluntary sector and their cooptation by the state, resulting in a lack of independence and an inability to effectively lobby on behalf of asylum seekers and refugees (see Chapter 5). All of these evolutions need to be analysed in specific local contexts to see the impacts they have had on different groups of asylum seekers and refugees.

Accommodation and dispersal

We have pointed above to the specific problems raised by the detention of women seeking asylum, but even for those who are not detained poor on inadequate accommodation can provide a real problem. Policies on housing asylum seekers vary from country to country, but in general a shortage of adequate housing for asylum seekers can be noted. An ECRE report notes that in the United Kingdom, many asylum seekers are housed in "sub-standard private accommodation, which is prejudicial to their health, in a poor state of repair or lacking adequate amenities" (ECRE, 2005: 7). And in France, there are around sixteen thousand places available in reception centres for asylum seekers, whereas the total numbers of asylum seekers arriving in the country in the past decade has been around sixty thousand per year. Although women with children should receive priority in the selection procedures for places in these accommodation centres, in practice these procedures lack transparency, and research has pointed to the fact that the choice of those to whom accommodation will be offered is in fact often based on judgements as to the validity of the asylum seeker's claim and the likelihood of their being successful in gaining refugee status (Valluy, 2007). For those women who do not receive a place in an accommodation centre, the difficulties finding suitable places to live provides an added source of insecurity. One NGO working with women seeking asylum noted that they have found several cases of women exchanging sex in return for a bed in someone's house.[13] A Chechen woman who arrived in France with her two children to claim asylum recounts how she was housed in emergency accommodation in a hotel with no hot water, and only one shower outside. She explains that for her traumatised children "it was very difficult" (Raissa Bataev cited in Cimade, 2006b: 115). This woman was eventually granted refugee status but at the time of her interview with the Cimade was still living in a small hotel room with three children. In other countries, particularly the Southern European states where the welfare states have been significantly less developed, the situation may be even worse. In Greece, there is only one permanent state reception centre for asylum seekers and refugees which can house up to three hundred people. As Greece now receives several thousand asylum applications per year, this means that the majority of asylum seekers in Greece remain in effect homeless and reliant on aid that charities and NGOs provide for the destitute (Sitaropoulos, 2002: 442).

As well as inadequacy of housing, the accommodation offered to asylum seekers is rarely sensitive to the cultural or social needs of particular groups. Examples include housing which does not separate men and women from different families, or which does not meet the specific needs of pregnant women or those with young children. In Germany asylum accommodation centres often house up to five hundred people, and although there may be separate bedrooms for men and women, they are forced to share all other areas including bathrooms and toilets. In some centres women cannot lock their bedrooms (Liedtke, 2002). Ascoly et al. describe the conditions of accommodation for asylum seeking women in the Netherlands whom they portray as waiting for a decision in "cramped, temporary housing, surrounded by strangers, while overwhelmed by loneliness and uncertainty" (2001: 383).

Kennedy and Murphy-Lawless (2003) who undertook at study of asylum-seeking women who were pregnant or had recently given birth in Ireland, point to what they call the "absolutely unacceptable" accommodation conditions for these women. They report that women are housed in hostels or bed and breakfast establishments, often sharing bedrooms with other women and children because of lack of adequate space. Also "it was not uncommon to find women and babies sharing accommodation with unknown men from a family of strangers; where some women had experienced rape, the levels of tension were palpable" (Kennedy and Murphy-Lawless, 2003: 46). Meals were provided on a strict schedule which often did not satisfy their pregnant and postpartum needs. Another report on the conditions of asylum seekers who are pregnant or who have small children in Ireland has reported "experiences of extreme deprivation" including malnutrition (Fanning et al., 2001).

Research carried out in the United Kingdom has pointed to similar problems with accommodation for women asylum seekers. Women, including those who are pregnant, may be housed in mixed accommodation with little concern as to social customs which may require the exclusion of male non-family members (McLeish, 2002; Refugee Action, 2002). Often they have to share toilets and washing facilities with strangers of both sexes. A report for the Maternity Alliance affirms that in these circumstances the women were "very conscious of the embarrassing or even culturally unbearable presence of men" (McLeish,

2002: 20). Other women reported that they were confined to their rooms as they were scared to go out because of fear of harassment or assault by the men with whom they were sharing their accommodation. Whilst the government's asylum support service (NASS) claimed that it was not opposed to considering single sex accommodation it identified difficulties in finding adequate accommodation as an explanation of why it had not yet found such accommodation for women (Clarence, 2003).

In attempts to resolve a perceived "crisis" in which asylum seekers are concentrated in and around certain geographical areas such as major cities or ports, many European governments, including those of Germany, Sweden, the Netherlands and the United Kingdom, have resorted to a policy of forced dispersal of asylum seekers to different locations around the country. This dispersal may be enforced in various ways. In Germany, for example, asylum seekers are not allowed to leave the administrative district in which the accommodation centre to which they have been sent is located, and they are only granted a residence permit for that particular district, thus making their presence in any other part of the country illegal (Liedtke, 2002). In the United Kingdom, those asylum seekers who do not comply with dispersal lose their rights to benefits. These models of forced dispersal often remove asylum seekers from the networks of community support that they may have in the areas from which they are dispersed, as well as disrupting their access to the provision of health and legal services. The dispersal locations may in some cases be remote and difficult to access. In Sweden, for example, one of the most Northern destinations for dispersal is reputed to be highly unpopular because of its coldness and remoteness. An employee in a Stockholm NGO remarked that it is not surprising people are reluctant to go there as "you have to travel two hundred kilometres just to get to a bank."[14] In these types of remote locations, access to special services which asylum seekers may need may be very difficult. Specialised services to care for victims of torture, for example, are often located only in capital cities or other larger cities, and may be unavailable in the locations to which asylum seekers are dispersed. For women who have been victims of rape, access to rape counselling services may equally be inaccessible in the dispersal destination.

The fact that asylum seekers may be forced to remain in accommodation centres for long periods of time produces various material and psychological problems. Ghorashi describes the situation in the Netherlands where asylum seekers are forced to spend an average of four years in such centres, cut off from the rest of Dutch society, feeling trapped and insecure. She argues that in most cases the experiences in these centres overshadow the lives of the refugees even years after they have left the centres (Ghorashi, 2005).

Whilst governments have argued that dispersing asylum seekers should help to relieve racial tensions and discrimination by avoiding large concentrations of asylum seekers in one particular area (Boswell, 2001), in practice asylum seekers may be sent to areas where they are isolated and more vulnerable to racist attacks. Düvell and Jordan argue that: "The model of dispersal and camp-style accommodation has resulted all over Europe in highly visible institutions, exposing asylum applicants to xenophobic attacks, especially where these are situated in peripheral areas with no tradition of ethnic minority settlements" (Düvell and Jordan, 2002: 505).

In the United Kingdom, the 1999 Immigration and Asylum Act set up a National Asylum Support System to coordinate the dispersal of asylum seekers around the country. Under this scheme, whose aims were to shift the burden of housing asylum seekers away from local councils in London and the South of England, people would be sent to accommodation centres or private accommodation across the United Kingdom. If asylum seekers rejected this move or objected to the location they were to be sent to, they lost their right to accommodation and became eligible for subsistence support only (Shaw, 2002; Bloch and Schuster, 2005). The government claimed that when dispersing asylum seekers across the country, account would be taken of the need for community links and for the support of voluntary associations. However, the evidence shows that this has not been the case, and that people have been sent to locations where there are no other asylum seekers from their own community. The result has been isolation and lack of potential community support networks. Highly vulnerable individuals are actually made more vulnerable by the uncertainty and insecurity which accompanies the dispersal process (Clarence, 2003).

The system of dispersal and accommodation centres pursued by the UK government has also had particular gendered impacts. Sales points to the fact that single men were more able to opt out of the dispersal system and move back to London to rely on family and community support. This was much harder for women, and especially those with children, who could not afford to lose the accommodation and benefits that were provided within the national dispersal system (Sales, 2002). In its report on the dispersal system the Audit Commission highlighted the lack of adequate support for claimants who were dispersed. Outside of London interpreting services were found to be "ad hoc" and limited (Audit

Commission, 2002). Moreover, for those women who had been raped or suffered sexual violence, problems arose through disruption in medical and psychological care and counselling. Many of the specialist services that are required by these women were not available in the locations to which they were dispersed (Refugee Action, 2002). As Clarence argues: "Continuity of care and the provision of services which understand the complex problems women asylum claimants who have experienced sexual violence present with, are crucial if the physical and mental health needs of such women are to be addressed. Dispersal clearly does not consider such needs" (2003: 27).

Dispersal was implemented even when women were heavily pregnant and near to giving birth, or when they had just given birth and were looking after very young babies. A report by the Maternity Alliance and Bail for Immigration Detainees highlighted the way that this dispersal could compound what was already a difficult situation for these women, both removing them from friends and family who might support them, and forcing them to abruptly change their medical carers. Further, the report found that it was not uncommon for women with young babies to be moved around frequently from one accommodation centre to another with all the disruption that this entailed (Maternity Alliance/Bail for Immigration Detainees, 2002). For those women who were placed in full board accommodation, other problems emerged. They would sometimes miss their medical appointments if transport was not available and the provision of meals also created difficulties. There was often a lack of flexibility surrounding meal times and thus women missed meals completely if they were attending hospital appointments. For those with young babies, neither baby milk formula nor jars of baby food were available, and women were required to purchase these themselves (Maternity Alliance/Bail for Immigration Detainees, 2002).

Welfare payments: towards a minimal standard

Part of the drive to reduce the attractiveness of countries for asylum seekers has been a reduction in the welfare payments to which they are entitled. In many Western states, asylum seekers no longer have the right to work, which has both material and psychological effects on their well-being (see Chapter 7). The move to take away asylum seekers' access to the labour market has been accompanied by a reduction in their access to welfare payments, or the replacement of cash payments by payment in kind and voucher systems. These types of restriction both place the living standards of asylum seekers well below those of other categories of citizens relying on benefit, and act to stigmatise them and "abnormalise" their daily life (Liedtke, 2002). The lack of legal access to the labour market often means that asylum seekers are forced to work illegally and therefore without any form of protection from their employers. For women, this type of employment is often in the form of domestic work or cleaning (Jaubany-Baucells, 2002). Female asylum seekers have pointed to the material hardship they have encountered as a result of the limited welfare payments to which they have been entitled. In France, for example, where the allowance to which asylum seekers are entitled works out at less than ten euros per day (Bousquet, 2006), women complained that they did not even have enough money to buy nappies for babies and young children.[15]

In Australia, those asylum seekers who are living outside of detention on a "bridging visa" (this group includes mainly those who arrived in Australia with a valid visa and then lodged an asylum claim whilst in the country), may often live without any rights to housing, welfare payments or medical care. A report by the Hotham Mission describes the condition of destitution that faces many of these asylum seekers, and their reliance on charities for support. They describe the particular difficulties faced by women supporting children, many of whom have had difficulty providing food and medical care for these children. One mother who had arrived from South Asia with her three children had no form of income and thus "she could not afford to pay for food or rent forcing her and her three children into homelessness and severe poverty" (Hotham Mission, 2003).

An analysis by the Cimade argues that the restrictions on the right to work and on welfare benefits for asylum seekers in France have forced them into a "parallel economy". In the case of women, especially those on their own or with young children, "the absence of effective protection, accommodation or welfare payments can compel them to enter into forms of domestic slavery or prostitution" (Cimade, 2006b). One of the interviews included in their study is with a young Congolese woman who arrived in France to claim asylum after having been raped by police in Congo. With nowhere to live and no means of supporting herself she was forced to enter prostitution to survive. She recounts her story thus:

> Today I have no one. I sleep in emergency shelters. I've got into prostitution, I don't have any choice. It's France which has forced me into prostitution... when we come to France we're treated like dogs, we're nothing.
>
> (Rosalie Masimba, cited in Cimade, 2006b: 66)

Systems which provide payment in kind or vouchers may also have deeply exclusionary and gendered impacts on asylum seekers. One example is the voucher scheme which was introduced in the United Kingdom following the 1999 Immigration and Asylum Act. Under this system, rather than receiving cash benefits, asylum seekers would be entitled to vouchers which could be redeemed for goods in certain shops and supermarkets (Geddes, 2000a; Shaw, 2002). The vouchers were worth only 70 per cent of the benefits provided to other welfare claimants, and provided for only a basic subsistence level of support. A report for Oxfam and the Refugee Council (2002) claimed that the level of support provided by the vouchers was below the minimum necessary for an "acceptable standard of living". The impact of the voucher system was in fact to reduce the living standards of asylum seekers drastically, leading to hunger and an inability to purchase basic necessities. One survey reported that 85 per cent of the asylum claimants interviewed had experienced hunger as a result of the voucher system (Oxfam and Refugee Council, 2002). Again the effects of this seem to have been worse for women, as many organisations noted that women would go hungry in order to be able to feed their children and ensure that they had sufficient clothing (Maternity Alliance/Bail for Immigration Detainees, 2002).

Not only did the vouchers provide inadequate support but using them was found to be a humiliating experience as they very clearly and publicly labelled people as "asylum seekers". For women, there were added problems associated with the use of the vouchers. The first of these stemmed from the fact that many women had had their claim registered as dependents of their male partners or husbands. As the vouchers were printed with the name of the principal applicant (the man) on them, women encountered difficulties when shopkeepers refused to take their vouchers as they were not in their name. Home Office research accepted that women had been prevented from using the vouchers because they had the name of the principal (male) applicant and shops had refused to accept them (Eagle et al., 2002: 20). Public refusal, in what was already considered to be a difficult and potentially demeaning situation, contributed to women feeling isolated and marginalised. It also lessened the control and influence women could have over the way in which vouchers were spent (Clarence, 2003: 23).

The voucher system was, on the whole, insensitive to the needs of women who were pregnant or had young children. Even the maternity grant of three hundred pounds (payable in vouchers) was implemented in such a way that women had difficulties in accessing it. The grant was available, on application, within four weeks of the birth or two weeks after it. No extra support was available earlier in the pregnancy to buy maternity clothing or any other items which pregnant women may require; those extra needs had to be met out of the standard voucher and cash payments. In an Oxfam and Refugee Council survey, 65 per cent of organisations reported that the maternity grant was an inadequate amount to meet the needs of women in the period immediately before and after birth (2002: 12–13). Organisations reported that women had entered hospital for the birth of their child without such basics as nappies because vouchers had not arrived in time. The six-week application "window" ignored the potential difficulties which impacted upon the ability of a woman to meet the deadlines. Women who had not applied before the birth and remained in hospital for more than two weeks found themselves without the grant because they had missed the deadline (Oxfam and Refugee Council, 2002: 12–13). Compounding all of these difficulties was the requirement to spend maternity grant vouchers only in specific stores – the option of buying (cheaper) second hand baby goods was not one therefore available to women claimants.

The low weekly allowance that women received also meant that those with young babies were not able to purchase milk formula. A public debate arose over this issue because of the (potentially fatal) harm that this posed to women who were HIV positive and who were recommended not to breastfeed their babies. The government claimed in a joint Department of Health/Home Office statement that "Selective provision of formula milk (through milk tokens) to HIV-infected asylum seeking mothers could result in deductive disclosure of the women's HIV status" (Community Care, 2002). It went on to claim that if all asylum claimants were given milk tokens, it would have a negative impact on breast-feeding promotions, although this ignored another government campaign to reduce mother to baby transmissions of HIV of which the provision of milk formula is a key component. The statement pointed to the vouchers provided by NASS and the additional maternity allowance as evidence of the government's financial assistance to asylum claimants and stated that "Asylum seekers may be able to access formula milk free or at reduced prices through local schemes operated by community clinics or hospital services" (Community Care, 2002). This failed to acknowledge that the National Health Service did not accept vouchers and thus women were unable to purchase the reduced cost milk formula on sale within hospitals unless they used their small cash allowance, which was also required to fund their travel and communication needs (Clarence, 2003).

After much protest, the government finally agreed to phase out the voucher system and to pay asylum seekers in cash. However, the low level of benefit has remained. Successive legislation also introduced more exclusionary measures with regard to welfare payments. Section 55 of the 2002 Nationality Immigration and Asylum Act stipulated that asylum seekers would not be eligible for welfare support if they did not make a claim immediately on arrival in the United Kingdom or "as soon as is reasonably practicable". We have already referred to the social and psychological difficulties that some women face in making an asylum claim, especially when this involves rape or sexual assault, but the new legislation does not accept this as a valid excuse for making a late claim. Women who had been registered as dependents to their husband's asylum claim, and who then chose to make an independent claim would also be considered as late applicants and denied support. Asylum seekers and their supporters have mobilised to protest against the hardship and destitution that is caused by this policy, and six asylum seekers brought a successful case against the government in which the Court of Appeal ruled that the implementation of section 55 was inhumane and could lead to a real risk of destitution. The government's response to this defeat, however, was not to repeal this section of the legislation, but merely to argue that whilst the asylum seekers in this particular case had been treated unfairly this did not mean that section 55 should not be applied in the future if certain amendments were put into practice, such as making greater efforts to understand the reasons for late applications (Schuster and Solomos, 2004).

These examples from the United Kingdom are illustrative of what is happening all over Europe and in Canada, the United States and Australia, as governments seek to make their country less attractive to asylum seekers. There is no evidence that these restrictions and exclusionary measures actually do discourage asylum claims, but there is very compelling evidence that they have a highly negative effect on the welfare and rights of asylum seekers.

7
Women Asylum Seekers and Refugees: Experiences from France

The previous chapters in this book have described the ways in which gendered inequalities underpin the neutrality of refugee and asylum laws, conventions and practices, and how this has a particular impact on the experiences of women refugees and asylum seekers. In this final chapter, we will examine the particular experiences of female asylum seekers in France, using data from qualitative interviews carried out with asylum seekers and refugees, with members of NGOs and associations supporting these women and also with lawyers, policy makers and officials involved in the determination of asylum claims.[1] France has been chosen as a case study as in recent years it has been constantly among the top destination countries for asylum seekers. In 2005 and 2006, France received more asylum applications than any other industrialised country. The material presented in this chapter should provide a direct insight into the experience of women who arrive in a European Union country to claim asylum and will follow their progress through the asylum application process, examining the ways in which both the official procedures and the more "informal" contacts with NGOs and civil society have particular impacts on men and women. We will also examine the ways in which material problems such as poor housing and lack of income have specific impacts on the women who seek refugee status.

The experiences of women seeking asylum in France tend to reflect the tendencies described in previous chapters, in that their situations have been made increasingly insecure by government attempts to reduce the numbers of asylum seekers and refugees and by the gendered impacts of asylum policies and legislation. Despite what some officials and members of civil society have pointed to as "favourable" advances in jurisprudence – the acceptance, for example, that some categories of women might be considered as part of a "particular social group" under the terms of the Geneva Convention, the way in which women and men are constructed in the asylum determination process and the way in which gender-related persecution is framed mean that the asylum process is still highly gendered. Further, recent changes in asylum policies relating to welfare and housing have impacted differently on male and female asylum seekers, leading to gendered outcomes in the situations and experiences of these asylum seekers.

The methodologies employed for this research sought to allow female asylum seekers to document their own particular experiences of the asylum reception and determination processes, thus revealing experiences which have previously been ignored or have been categorised and represented in ways that have denied these women their own identities and agency. The use of interviews with these women asylum seekers is intended to some extent to overcome the problem of the absence of their voices from academic research and policy-making on asylum. As Tickner argues: "This re-writing of (in)security using the voices of marginalised lives constitutes a political act that can challenge dominant and oppressive ways of documenting these lives" (2005: 9). We will begin the chapter though with a brief overview of recent developments in the French asylum system to set the context for a discussion of the experiences of asylum seekers.

Developments in asylum policy – the French context

The French experience is similar to that of other European states in terms of policy responses to asylum seekers, with an increasingly restrictive regime being put in place in order to discourage asylum seekers from coming to France and to limit the numbers to whom refugee status is granted. As with other European states, policy making on asylum does not take place on a purely national level, as attempts to construct a unified European asylum policy impact on the policies of national governments, creating a complex multi-level policy field. Thus policy-making on asylum in France is constrained both by international conventions and the actions of international organisations (principally the UNHCR) and by European institutions and policy-making bodies.

The institution responsible for adjudicating on the granting of refugee status in France is the Office Français de Protection de Réfugiés et Apatrides (Ofpra), set up in 1952 for this purpose. The Ofpra is responsible for assessing the dossiers of asylum seekers in which they set out their claim for asylum, in most cases they then interview the asylum seeker and come to a judgement on whether or not they should be granted refugee status. Although an interview should take place with every asylum seeker, interviewees for this study remarked that the pressures on officers working at the Ofpra to speed up the asylum process and to deal with as many cases as possible in a short space of time had led to an increase in the number of dossiers which were considered as "manifestly unfounded" and therefore rejected without any interview taking place. If the asylum claimant receives a negative decision from the Ofpra, they may then take an appeal to the Commission de recours des réfugiés (CRR) where a rapporteur (or assessor) will review their case, and then the claimant will be called to a tribunal with three judges who make a final decision. The judges who sit in the CRR are not permanent judges trained in immigration law, but are drawn from differing sources. Each sitting of a CRR tribunal has one "president" who is drawn from the administrative elite, normally the Conseil d'Etat, a second judge represents one of the Ministries to which the Ofpra is responsible (the Ministry of the Interior or the Ministry for Foreign Affairs) and the third judge is appointed by the UNHCR's bureau in France.[2] The CRR's decisions can be annulled by the Conseil d'Etat (the highest administrative court), but this is rare.

In the first twenty years of Ofpra's existence the number of asylum claims it dealt with was relatively small and the rate of refusal of asylum claims was negligible (Legoux, 1995, 1996). The number of claims began to increase after the suspension of immigration in 1974, with France becoming one of the leading European countries in terms of the numbers of asylum claims it receives. Figures for 2004 show that France was the first asylum destination in Europe, with sixty-one thousand six hundred first time applications, and this status as the leading destination for asylum seekers has been maintained in 2005 and 2006.[3] And as the number of claims has increased, the criteria for granting refugee status have become stricter and the proportion of asylum claims rejected has grown.

Government policies to reduce the number of asylum seekers have taken a two-pronged approach, with one set of policies designed to reduce the attractiveness of France as a destination for asylum seekers, and another set designed to reduce the numbers to whom refugee status is granted and to expedite the deportation of failed asylum seekers. Internal controls aimed at deterring asylum seekers have included restrictions on their rights in terms of welfare, housing and education. In 1989, housing grants to asylum seekers were suspended, meaning that they had to turn to specialised housing provided either by the government in reception centres or by charitable associations, or else rely on help in finding lodging from community support networks already in place. Family allowances for asylum seekers were also suspended. Then in 1991 asylum seekers' right to work was revoked creating an almost impossible financial situation for many. The government provided an extra two thousand five hundred places in reception centres, but this was not sufficient for the needs of all those arriving to seek asylum in France. The result of these reforms was to create an impossible financial and social situation for many asylum seekers. As Brachet comments: "From the start of 1992, the new arrivals who did not find a place in a reception centre, were objectively incapable of surviving on their legal allowances. The meagre minimum allowance (about 1300 francs at the time) that was granted to adults for twelve months only, irrespective of the number of children dependent on them, was evidently not sufficient to live on" (2002: 55). Many asylum seekers were thus forced to work illegally, leaving them vulnerable to exploitation in the labour market, and also allowing governments to confound the issue of asylum seekers with that of illegal employment and to label many asylum seekers as mere "economic migrants" who were taking advantage of the French system.

A second part of the strategy for controlling asylum flows has been to apply stricter criteria to those asylum applications which are received, so that fewer of these are successful. The total number of persons granted refugee status in France has fallen continually in the last decade, in real terms and as a percentage of asylum claims received. In 1985, only 57 per cent of asylum claims were rejected, but by 1995 that figure had risen to 84 per cent, and by 2003, 90.2 per cent of asylum claims were rejected by Ofpra (UNHCR, 2005). Politicians have used the growing number of refusals of asylum claims to support their argument that most asylum claimants are in fact "false" refugees. However, others have argued that the figures for rejections of asylum claims demonstrate not that most of these claims are "false", but that governments are increasingly rejecting the notion of asylum itself (Valluy, 2005). The most recent legislation on asylum in France, in 2003, went further down this route, with measures designed to expedite the asylum process and to ensure the quick removal of failed claimants from French territory. The legislation reduced the time allowed for an asylum claimant whose first claim had failed to lodge an appeal, and prolonged the period for which failed asylum claimants could be detained in order to ensure that the maximum number of failed claimants are returned to their countries of origin. The number of available places in detention centres has been increased, and the government has announced that it intends to use more and more "charter flights" to deport failed asylum seekers en masse. All of these measures indicate a strong desire to reduce again the number of those who are granted refugee status by the French state, and to remove from France as quickly as possible anyone whose demand is judged "unfounded". Critics have argued that these new laws could signal a real crisis for the right to asylum in France (Wihtol de Wenden, 2002).

Experiences of migration

The histories of exile of the women interviewed reflect a diversity of experience which illustrated the danger of generalising about the motives and trajectories of women asylum seekers and refugees. Their explanations about their motives for leaving their countries of origin, and about the journeys they had undertaken to arrive in Europe demonstrate the impossibility of categorisation, and of defining "real" and "false" refugees, with a mixture of motives and constraints present in many of their narratives. Some of the women interviewed had suffered from persecutions specifically related to their status as women such as the threat of forced marriage or forced genital mutilation; others had been persecuted for more traditionally "political"[4] activities such as being militants in opposition parties. One of the women interviewed had fled because her sexual orientation made her the target of violence and persecution. They may have been persecuted because of activities that they had undertaken themselves, or because of activities undertaken by their husbands or other relatives. One woman from the Democratic Republic of Congo explained, for example, that she had been targeted because of her father's political affiliation. Her father and mother had been murdered in front of her and she had then been the victim of rape and torture. For others, the motives for persecution were mixed, for example, women who had been persecuted because of their belonging to one political party or opposition group, but whose persecution had taken the specific form of rape or sexual violence because they were female. All expressed the difficulties, both psychological and material, that they had experienced in leaving their countries, the choice of exile being one of "last resort" when they felt that they had no means of guaranteeing their security, or that of their children. Some had in fact fled in such desperate circumstances that they had been forced to leave their children behind in their country of origin, a situation which made their exile even more difficult to bear.

The experiences of one woman from Guinea illustrate the emotional, physical and economic obstacles involved in leaving one's country of origin. Her father had threatened to marry her to an "uncle" who was fifty years older than her. When she refused this marriage, she was locked in a room and severely beaten by her father and her brothers. She eventually managed to flee her home with the help of one of her sisters, and escape to Conakry where she hoped to work, but she was pursued by her father and brothers who attempted to recapture her and bring her back to her village. She explains that:

> I only wanted to stay in Guinea, to stay in my village. I didn't want to leave. But I thought that if my father found me he would kill me and I couldn't marry that man, that old man. I didn't know what to do, I thought I would die, that my family would kill me. So my friend lent me some money to take a bus and leave. I didn't want to go, but I thought I must leave otherwise I would die.

None of the women interviewed expressed any explicitly "economic" motive for coming to France, and indeed many commented that becoming an asylum seeker in France had worsened their economic situation and lowered their standard of living. Some of them did, however, explain that part of their motivations for flight was the fact that the material conditions under which they were living had become untenable – one woman, for example, had lost her job because of the political opinions she expressed, and this, together with other forms of harassment, such as police following her and her family, had made her situation unbearable. This accords with the findings of other studies on the causes of asylum flows into Europe which show that poverty is not in itself a major push factor in asylum migration, and that asylum seekers who succeed in reaching Europe tend to come from intermediate groups who possess the cultural and material resources necessary for mobility (Castles et al., 2003). As argued in previous chapters, however, economic motives cannot be completely separated from other motives for seeking asylum, and so any attempts to neatly categorise asylum seekers separately from "economic migrants" will result in a false dichotomy.

Whilst some of the women interviewed had travelled directly to France entering the country either on a tourist visa or with a false passport bought often at great expense in their country of origin, or travelling without papers, others had long journeys involving travelling through many countries with many means of transport. One woman from Sierra Leone, for example, recounted how her journey to France had taken eighteen months in total and involved walking, hiding in lorries, and travelling on a small "African" boat from Morocco to Spain before finally managing to take a train to Paris. She had few financial resources to pay for her voyage, and thus spent two months working as a domestic worker in Senegal, a job which also helped her to get in touch with the "passeurs" ("smugglers") who helped her eventually to reach Europe. Other women also talked about their use of "smugglers", but these were all informal types of arrangements made through a network of acquaintances, sometimes involving domestic work in return for help with their passage. None of the women mentioned any contact with one of the very organised criminal "gangs" of smugglers, so much talked about in the European media. In fact, those who helped to smuggle some of the women were not viewed by them as "criminals" or exploitative, but more usually as people who would sell them a service in return for cash or payment in kind. Networks of acquaintances or family members were also cited as the main reasons chosen for coming to France to seek asylum, although a few women said that they had not had any preference for which European country they came to, and had somehow arrived in France by chance. Again the idea that the circulation of information about different asylum regimes and their relative benefits may act as a "magnet" for asylum seekers who will choose to go to the country with the most lax policies on asylum and the greatest welfare benefits seems to be totally unfounded in the data collected in the interviews. None of those interviewed had chosen to come to France because they believed their asylum claim would be more successful here than in another country, and none had any real idea about the kind of rights or benefits they would be entitled to in France in comparison with those of different European states. By contrast, several had come to France because they already spoke French, coming from a country with previous colonial links, and several said they had come here because they knew of friends or other family members who had already made the same journey.

Isolation and rejection: how asylum seekers understand their reception in France

> I have the feeling that I am dead. I cannot dream. I have no projects for the future

These were the sentiments expressed by one Guinean woman interviewed for this research, feelings which were echoed by other women who felt desperate and isolated during the process of claiming asylum, a process which for many was far harder than they had imagined when they had decided to leave their country of origin. Another woman remarked on the fact that she felt defined by her status as an asylum seeker and had lost her own identity during the time that she had spent in France. These types of remarks were fairly frequent and expressed regret that for many their traumatic personal stories and narratives were ignored or dismissed by the French authorities, and that they had little chance to integrate into French society, but were kept at a distance both through material circumstances and through attitudes which were perceived as hostile. One woman commented that as soon as she arrived at the police prefecture to register her claim for asylum she could feel the contempt of the French officials and that these attitudes of scorn and disbelief accompanied her through the whole asylum process. She pointed to the way that simple issues like making asylum seekers queue for hours to register their claim and the prefecture, and then suddenly closing the counters when there were still many waiting to be seen could make these asylum seekers feel that they were "rejected" even before their claim had been assessed. Another woman recounted that when she arrived at the prefecture, asylum seekers were given different coloured tickets on the whim of the officer at the reception, and that those with one particular "unfavourable" colour could be kept waiting hours and hours, whilst those who the reception officer like the look of would be given a ticket that gave them much quicker access to the front of the queue. These remarks about the way in which officials within the police prefecture treat asylum seekers are confirmed by research carried out by Spire who describes the prefecture as a site of denial of the right to asylum, where the asylum seeker is constructed a priori as someone who will become an illegal resident to be deported from France, and where the suspicion that each asylum seeker is "fraudulent" shapes the way in which he or she is treated. Within this system, however, some nationalities are supposed to be more "genuine" than others, and this will affect the way in which they are treated in relation to other asylum seekers from less "favoured" nationalities (Spire, 2006). Constructions of asylum seekers from particular countries of origin as more "genuine" than others, and of some as clearly "fraudulent" were also evident in qualitative research carried out with officers from the Ofpra and from the CRR as explained below.

Despite the various persecutions they had suffered and the difficulties that they had experienced in reaching Europe, women asylum seekers and refugees interviewed for this study expressed the feeling that the French state failed to recognise their persecution as valid, and that they felt rejected and stigmatised as a result of this. Some of the women interviewed had eventually been recognised as refugees, but none of these had been granted refugee status by the Ofpra in the first instance, and thus all had had to resort to an appeal before the CRR, or even had their claim re-opened and re-examined before their refugee status was accorded. The discrepancies between judgements in the first and second instances of decision-making (Ofpra and CRR) are statistically well documented, and correspond with similar differences between first and second instance decision making in other states. In 2005, only 30 per cent of those eventually granted refugee status received a positive decision from the Ofpra and the rest had to make an appeal to the CRR to receive a positive decision (Ofpra, 2006). This variation in decision-making can be seen as a reflection of the structure and operation of the two instances and also of some degree of "competition" between them (see below), but its impacts are particularly felt by those asylum seekers who have experienced very traumatic events and who are forced to repeat their stories over and over again to various different officials before eventually receiving a decision.

A Congolese woman recounted her experience of having to tell her story of rape and sexual violence again and again before numerous officials and judges:

> It was horrible because I didn't want to keep telling my story to everyone. It really wasn't easy to talk about my life, because I'm a person who has my dignity. I felt really bad because I saw all my past again...that's it...in order to get out of my situation...first at the Ofpra and then at the Commission...I saw my film again, and I became really cold...the friend who was supporting me took my hand and said I was completely cold, I wasn't in my body anymore...it was no longer me...I was cold.... The French state forces you to go through that and to tell your story again and again in order to have your papers.

This account of being "cold" and not "in my body" evokes the symptoms of panic which may well be evoked in a court setting by those who have suffered trauma or torture (Rousseau, 2000). Many of the women used similar language to evoke the painful procedure of recounting stories of trauma and violence again and again, and some described this experience as one of re-living the violence they had suffered. A volunteer in an NGO who helped women to prepare their dossiers and accompanied them to the CRR hearings also judged that she had a role in perpetuating violence by forcing the women to speak about their experiences again and again in minute detail.

Another demand which caused added trauma for some women was that of providing sufficient evidence to support their claims. In some cases, this involved several medical examinations which could be perceived as humiliating or demeaning. This was particularly noted in cases where women were claiming asylum on the grounds that they wished to protect their daughters from female genital mutilation (FGM). In these cases, the Ofpra demanded not only a medical certificate to confirm that the daughter had not yet undergone FGM, but also a certificate to prove that the mother had herself been a victim of this practice.

Women felt strongly that during their interviews at the Ofpra and (to a somewhat lesser extent) during their hearings at the CRR, the officials with whom they came into contact had generally not believed their stories and had tried to "catch them out" by asking very detailed questions about the exact circumstances of their migration and exile, questions which the asylum seekers did not always see as relevant to their claim. These questions often related to precise dates or place names, all of which may be confused or forgotten during the trauma of flight. As one woman put it:

> I was just trying to get away, I can't remember exactly the date I left…it's all a bit confused for me.

This type of confusion and forgetfulness although clearly symptoms of trauma and of the precipitate conditions of an applicant's exile, were in some cases construed by officials as signs of the fact that they were telling a false story.

The culture of disbelief surrounding asylum seekers' stories, and the propagation of negative attitudes towards them through government and media discourse, led to some of those interviewed admitting feelings of shame, and of wanting to hide the fact that they were an asylum seeker. Several women told me that they kept away from the other parents at their children's schools because they did not want anyone to find out about their status as an asylum seeker. They thought that this discovery would bring shame both on them and on their children who might be teased or ostracised by their classmates as a result. Others, however, had been surprised by the positive reactions that they had encountered from "ordinary" French citizens. One woman who had been reluctant to let anyone find out that she was an asylum seeker expressed her delight and surprise when parents and teachers at her son's school organised a campaign to support her following the rejection of her claim for asylum. This type of experience which was confirmed by that of other women demonstrates the need to have a more subtle understanding of public attitudes towards asylum than that which attributes merely xenophobic and anti-asylum sentiments to public opinion.[5] The fact that racism or rejection is by no means a uniform reaction of French citizens when faced with asylum seekers reinforces the arguments that rather than being pushed by hostile public opinion into restrictive policy-making, the restrictions on asylum come from the "top down" (Statham, 2003). It is also interesting to contrast the ways in which women seeking asylum experienced their contacts with bureaucrats and immigration officials, to the way in which they perceive their contacts with ordinary citizens. The former were invariably described as "rude", "dismissive" or "unsympathetic", whilst the opinions of the latter were mixed, with some individuals showing what were construed as "racist" opinions or actions whilst others were perceived as "supportive" or "sympathetic". This tends to reinforce the idea that rejection of asylum seekers may be more a product of bureaucratic implementation of repressive policies, than of public racism.

Poverty and the struggle to survive

A major issue for many women was that of poverty and lack of means to buy even the most essential items. Asylum seekers who are not living in accommodation centres are entitled to an allowance of three hundred euros per month in France. Up until now this support has been limited to the first year of their claim, although the time limit has recently been removed to bring France into line with European directives on the reception conditions for asylum seekers. However, even though asylum seekers are now entitled to receive an allowance throughout the period that their claim is being processed, many found that this allowance was not nearly enough to support them, and this was particularly the case for women with dependent children, who had to pay for their accommodation, food and clothes all from this small sum of money.

The women interviewed also talked about their struggle to survive financially, and about the hardship imposed by the fact that they did not have the right to work. An Ivorian woman with two young children aged two and a half and seven months, respectively, explained that she had to leave her young baby in the same nappy all day, as she could not afford to buy enough nappies to change her regularly. Others said that they relied on charities to provide clothing and food for them and their children as they simply could not afford to do so themselves. One woman remarked that:

> Our daily life as an asylum seeker is a race for survival. We spend our whole day running around trying to find enough food, somewhere to sleep, clothes for our children, never mind trying to find a lawyer to help us with our claims.

This poverty and lack of necessities was attributed both to the low level of state support and to the fact that they were not, as asylum seekers, allowed to work. Many women talked about the fact that they would like to work and remarked that they felt being deprived of the right to work, as well as causing financial hardship, undermined them psychologically and constituted an attack on their personal dignity. One woman remarked that the "hardest thing for me is not being allowed to work". Some reported feeling "humiliated" because they did not have the right to work and had to ask for financial help from charities. Another woman who had been a radio journalist for the national radio station in Guinea, a well-respected and well-paid job, told me that she felt she had become a "nobody" in France because she could not work and support herself. She described the way in which her life had been transformed from that of an independent woman, working and supporting three children, to that of a dependent, excluded from society. She felt anguished about the fact that she could not afford to buy her children clothes or books, and about the fact that she was forced to travel on the metro without a ticket as she could not afford one. This type of hardship would never have occurred in her previous existence.

Several women had started to do voluntary work to overcome this feeling of lack of personal dignity and confidence, caused by lack of access to the labour market. Others had become involved in support groups or associations. All said that they would rather have paid employment, but that becoming involved in some kind of voluntary work had helped them to escape from the isolation they had experienced and to give some kind of purpose to their lives, thus aiding them in the wait for a decision on their asylum claim.

The lack of a work permit means that some of the women asylum seekers I interviewed were working illegally. Although for some this was a situation which worked out reasonably well for them, allowing them a degree of financial independence and providing them with a means of interacting with the host society, for others, the situation was difficult either because they lived in constant fear of discovery, or because illegal work had led to some form of exploitation or abuse. A Congolese woman explained how she had become a live-in nanny and housekeeper for a single man and his daughter, but that despite her working long hours to take care of the child and do the cleaning and cooking, her employer told her she was not working hard enough and refused to pay her. When she protested, he simply threw her out of the house. Another Algerian woman explained that her employer had insisted on paying her by cheque although he knew quite well that she did not have a bank account and had no means to cash the cheque. She was forced to ask an intermediate to cash the cheque for her, but was then cheated out of the full amount of money.

The EU Reception Directive (see Chapter 6) states that all EU member states should determine a fixed period of time during which an asylum seeker may not have access to the labour market, and that after this fixed period they should have a right to work. Whilst this measure can be seen to be a move towards a "lowest common denominator" in that it allows member states the right to block access to the labour market for a period of time, it could be interpreted as implicitly stipulating that asylum seekers do have a right to work. France is one of only three EU countries which still removes asylum seekers' right to work indefinitely (ECRE, 2005), and from the evidence gained from interviews, this is one of the restrictions on their rights that asylum seekers feel most strongly both in terms of the poverty or exploitation to which it exposes them, and in terms of the psychological effects of unemployment.

Housing: a divide between those within accommodation centres and those outside

Linked to the problem of poverty is that of finding somewhere to live. France provides about sixteen thousand places in accommodation centres for asylum seekers (CADA), which is obviously insufficient for all of those who come to seek asylum, and so many are left to fend for themselves in terms of finding somewhere to live. These CADA are managed by NGOs under contract with the state which pays a daily per capita rate for each asylum seeker housed. The selection process for admission to a CADA is supposedly carried out according to criteria relating to the need or vulnerability of each asylum seeker, and so women who are alone with children should receive a high priority in the choice of those who will get a place. Thus judgements based on the relative "vulnerability" of women may act to their advantage in this case. Some research, however, has pointed to a more opaque selection system whereby the NGOs and associations managing the CADA try to select those asylum seekers whose claims they think will succeed in order to maintain a high rate of "success" for claimants within their centre (Franguiadakis et al., 2004; Valluy, 2007). In this case, the types of judgement which are made by other officials in the system will be generalised and reproduced in the selection of those who will receive places. Valluy describes a process whereby NGO staff working in CADAs and sitting on the selection committee for entry to the centres act in the same way as officers of the Ofpra or judges at the CRR, making judgements about who is a genuine asylum seeker and what motives are "real" motives for seeking asylum, which act to exclude those who are judged "false" or "bad" asylum seekers. This may affect women whose claims are based on motives which are still not generally admitted as "serious" motives for claiming asylum.

Women housed within accommodation centres in general expressed a feeling of relative security with respect to everyday living conditions, and realised that they were not faced with the same difficulties in finding accommodation as others. Several expressed satisfaction with the overall quality of accommodation and with the help that they received with their asylum claim by staff at the centre. Some women did, however, feel that they had lost a lot of their independence, and that their behaviour was constantly monitored and judged by those working in the CADA. As one woman explained:

> The people who work here judge us all the time. If we don't go and join in with the activities and outings they organise for us they aren't happy with us.

This experience of being "judged" by those working in the CADA is confirmed by research carried out by Kobelinsky who argues that social workers and others employed within the centres classify asylum seekers according to their own definitions of the genuine refugee or "hero" and the "impostor" (Kobelinsky, 2006).

Despite these inconveniences, however, the fate of women who had secured a place in an accommodation centre was far easier than of those who had to seek their own accommodation and frequently spent their days looking for somewhere to sleep that night. Some of these women are accommodated in emergency hotel or hostel accommodation, but although this guarantees them a roof over their heads, the living condi-tions can be very poor. One Algerian woman interviewed was living with her husband and two-year old daughter in a tiny hotel room where there was no room for a cot or separate bed for the child, and only one small gas ring and fridge to cook on. She shared her bathroom and toilet facilities with about fifty other people and told me there were often queues and that the facilities were usually dirty. Women also recounted stories of fights and attacks within this type of emergency accommod-ation, and expressed anxiety about the fact of sharing accommodation with men who were not from their families. A woman living in an emer-gency hostel in Montelimar told me that she was scared to leave her room because she had encountered sexual harassment from some of the men living there.

For those who are housed neither within a CADA nor in an emer-gency hostel or hotel, the task is to find a place to stay either with friends or acquaintances or through some kind of exchange of services for accommodation. Some asylum seekers have friends or family already in France when they arrive and are thus spared most of the difficulties of finding accommodation (provided of course that these friends or family member have themselves found adequate accommodation). Others try and mobilise help or support from within a community of asylum seekers from the same country of origin in order to find a place to live. As the quote from one interview cited above shows, for many asylum seekers the search for a place to sleep is a daily task which takes up a lot of their time. For women with small children, ensuring that they have a decent place to sleep can be particularly problematic. Another issue which arises is the fact that women may be forced to exchange sex for a place to stay, thus engaging in a form of prostitution in order to live. Representatives of one NGO's women's committee pointed to the fact that several of the women asylum seekers they were helping with their claim had been forced into sexually exploitative relationships in order to find somewhere to live.

Changing relations within the family

Although many of the women interviewed had come to France alone, or with their children, others had come accompanied by a husband or male partner, and in this case their narratives often reveal the complex-ities of gender relations within a family when seeking asylum. Problems that occurred within couples were exacerbated by the difficult material conditions experienced by asylum seekers, and in conjunction with the psychological stresses that are involved in the asylum process this often led to conflict or violence. Women were often expected to perform the same roles and to behave according to the same "feminine" norms that they had conformed to in their country of origin, but this was complicated by the material and emotional conditions of asylum. One woman explained, for example, the difficulties she had in cooking adequate meals for her husband in their small hotel room with only one gas ring. She explained that her husband had complained that she was not cooking for him in the same way as she had done in Algeria, and these complaints had led to conflict and violence. Another woman explained that the only way in which her and her husband could find accommodation was for her to find a job as a housekeeper for another man. The fact that this man was older and single was particularly annoying to her husband who felt that she should not be alone in his company.

As other studies have revealed (see Chapter 2 for more details), the question of employment is one that is particularly problematic in terms of changing relationships between men and women seeking asylum. Although officially asylum seekers do not have the right to work in France, many work "illegally", often engaged in low-paid jobs and frequently in domestic jobs such as cleaning or childcare (some also work in prostitution). Whilst men can find work in these areas, or may be employed in more traditionally "male" jobs such as building work, it seems from the interviews carried out that women could often find work more easily than their husbands, and this might lead to tensions. Several women were undertaking housekeeping or cleaning work like the woman mentioned above, and one of these in particular spoke of the anger her husband felt at being "left alone" whilst she went out and earned money. These feelings of anger stemmed both from the loss of men's traditional roles and the thought that their wives might be behaving "inappropriately" during their time at work. This fear of "inappropriate" behaviour which transgressed the gender norms of their countries of origin was also evident in male wariness about their female partners engaging in any kind of associational or voluntary work. Another Algerian woman, who was part of an informal association of women asylum seekers organised by the Red Cross, found that her husband resented her going out to meetings of this group, especially when the meetings were held in the evening. She explained:

He thinks I should stay at home in the evenings, so if I go to a meeting of our group I have to make sure I am back in time, or else he will think I have been doing something wrong. He thinks it is not normal for women to be out alone, and that I should stay at home with him.

This type of reaction was fairly typical of those interviewed, and it seemed that there was a strong tendency for the possibilities of change in the gender relations within a couple to be constrained by conflict or violence over the new roles which women might adopt. One extreme example was provided by a woman who admitted that her husband had become very violent towards her in their new situation in France, and that she would like to leave him but was scared to do so. Other women, however, estimated that their relationship with their male part-ners had survived well in the process of claiming asylum and that their partners were ready to make compromises and to come to an understanding regarding new forms of gender relations. The diversity of experiences did not depend on the country of origin from which these families came, although it can be seen that where conflict did occur within relationships between men and women, it was often based on a reappropriation and reinforcement of unequal gender relations that had previously existed in this country of origin. The reproduction of gender roles that had existed in the country of origin was not just a question of men trying to impose particular role and modes of behaviour on their female partners (although this did occur) but also of women interiorising and reproducing norms of behaviour to which they had conformed in this country of origin. These norms were often felt strongly in relation to their domestic roles – they felt it was they who should be responsible for feeding the family and so on – and also in relations with other men outside of their family, where norms of "modesty", for example, were still important.

Support for women seeking asylum: the NGO sector

Earlier in this book (Chapter 5), we discussed the sometimes ambiguous position of NGOs and other associations which set out to assist asylum seekers and refugees, in particular with relation to their cooperation with (or cooptation by) the state. This ambiguity is clear in the positions of some of the NGOs in the asylum sector in France, a sector which seems particularly weak, largely due to fragmentation and disagree-ment between some of the major NGOs in the field. The Coordination Française pour le Droit d'Asile (CFDA) is a group which supposedly feder-ates most of the NGOs and associations working in the sector, although its meetings often show evidence of far more disagreement than agreement between the different representatives. These meetings were even described as "civil wars" by one interviewee.

A clear tendency that emerged was that of employees within NGOs to reproduce the categorisation of "false" and "genuine" asylum seekers that have been established in official and political discourse. Thus in one discussion between two people working for different NGOs, the question arose of what to do if an asylum seeker approached the organisation for help with their claim, but their story was not believable. The consensus in this case seems to be expressed by the view of one employee who says that:

> If I don't really believe what an asylum seeker is telling me, and if I think that they are not really genuine, then I will help them with their dossier, but I won't really invest a lot of time in it. I'll help them, but just a bit, not with a lot of effort.

This point of view was expressed by others, who whilst criticising the government's increasingly restrictive policies on asylum, also complained about their huge workload and the fact that they were swamped by requests for help from asylum seekers, some of whom they believed were just trying to "take advantage of the system". With regards to gender-related persecution, dominant political constructions also seemed to be fairly widely reproduced. One (female) NGO employee, for example, expressed the opinion that she was pleased that rape was now sometimes recognised as grounds for granting refugee status, but that she now thought that "all women asylum seekers say they've been raped as they think it's an easy way to get their claims accepted". This comment was an extreme version of a general sentiment expressed frequently, in other words that women would "use" their supposed vulnerability to rape, sexual violence and FGM, to try and "cheat" the system.

These sentiments are not representative of all of those who were interviewed, some of whom expressed much more sympathetic and gender-sensitive approaches to women seeking asylum. Some NGOs have also set up specific women only consultation sessions to respond to a perceived need to listen to women's stories in a non-mixed setting where it would be easier to build a relationship of confidence with these female asylum seekers. There are also a couple of smaller associations which are run by women and targeted exclusively at women migrants, these groups are very marginalised within the wider NGO sector, however. Moreover, within larger NGOs where there is a specific women only initiative it has often been created at the instigation of one particularly "gender-aware" figure within the organisation, and if this person leaves, the whole initiative may disappear.

The relative marginalisation of gender-specific initiatives within the NGO sector can be linked both to the political and economic circumstances within which NGOs in France operate – a heavy dependence of the larger NGOs on state funding and cooperation with government in running CADA (Dufour, 2006; Valluy, 2007) – which lead to them reproducing dominant categorisations, and to the fact that feminist analyses or understandings have made few inroads into this sector. A feature which emerged strongly from the NGO sector in France was its general resistance to the idea of any kind of separate action for women asylum seekers or any kind of gender-sensitivity within analyses of asylum policies. One of the managers of the largest NGO in this area, France Terre D'Asile, told me that his organisation (which has over four hundred and fifty employees) did not have any employee who dealt specifically with women or with gender issues, and that they had no policies targeted either at women asylum seekers or refugees or at gender equality. He did not seem to find this absence surprising and explained that in the view of his organisation, women and men had "equal access to the law", so there was no point in making any distinction between them.

This belief in a "universalism" which does not necessitate any kind of separate treatment for different categories of asylum seeker can help to explain why there has been very little substantial activism or mobilisation on the issue of asylum and gender-specific persecution in France, and why what mobilisation there has been has had little or no impact on policies or legislation. On several occasions the issue of women asylum seekers and gender-related forms of persecution has been discussed both by feminist groups and amongst associations and NGOs working with asylum seekers and refugees, but this discussion has never led to any real agreement on the goals of a mobilisation, or to a widened participation in the mobilisation beyond a few activists. The "major" associations and NGOs dealing with asylum have neglected this issue, or dismissed it as unimportant or even "divisive". Sporadic and fragmentary organisation and mobilisation around this issue can be traced back to the start of the 1990s when the FASTI[6] organised a forum on the subject of "Droit d'asile pour les femmes" (the right to asylum for women), which assembled various other organisations[7] to denounce the non-recognition of gender-specific persecutions such as excision and forced marriage in French asylum law, and to call for a recognition of the difficulties faced particularly by women in pursuing an asylum claim in France, and action to overcome these difficulties (for example, the right for women making an asylum claim to be interviewed by a female official at the Ofpra). This meeting held in December 1993 had no real follow up however, and mobilisation around these issues remained highly fragmentary and limited, until in June 2004, when a public meeting was organised at the Bourse du Travail in Paris on the subject of women and the right to asylum. This meeting led to the formation of a working group drawn from various associations active in the field of asylum and refugee support, the Groupe Asile Femmes (GRAF) which has undertaken various information and mobilisation activities, including meetings with the heads of the institutions which process and judge asylum claims, publication of newsletters and petitions and the organisation of public meetings. However, the group has remained small and its activities have had little impact beyond a very restricted number of activists. Moreover, despite the small size of the group it has shown signs of the fragmentations and divisions which are generally very visible in this NGO sector. One of the members of the group thus confided that she and some others were "suspicious" of the representative from Amnesty International who did not seem to share their values or goals. Although the GRAF has lobbied decision makers, there is no evidence that their own guidelines concerning the treatment of female asylum seekers will be integrated into national policies as has been the case in other countries.

One of the major reasons for the failure of the GRAF, or of similar initiatives, to have an impact in France can be seen in the lack of discursive opportunity structures for framing asylum and refugee issues in terms of gender. Within the wider network of associations dealing with the right to asylum, the fact of considering women asylum seekers and refugees as a separate category has met with opposition or incomprehension from many militants. At a meeting of the CFDA, a representative of one large association working for the rights to refugees and asylum seekers argued that to treat women asylum seekers as a separate category would be to disadvantage male asylum seekers.[8] A member of the GRAF explains that this type of reaction was fairly typical of those working within the associative field in this domain, many of whom believed that any measures to provide specific procedures or support for female asylum seekers would inevitably deprive male asylum seekers of some of their rights and support. This type of argument against gender-specific policies or procedures is often framed in terms of the necessity of maintaining "universalism" which is strongly anchored in the French tradition. However, as one woman activist remarked, behind this pretence to universalism, is often a hidden anti-feminism: "As soon as someone in one of the associations thinks that you are acting on behalf of women, they call you a feminist, which is a kind of insult here".[9] Another woman activist pointed out that, "French associations just don't understand the need for specific actions for women. When anyone suggests such a thing, they are greeted with incomprehension".[10] Thus it can be argued that a key element in the failure of France to adopt at national level any of the international norms on gender-specific persecution, has been a discursive opportunity structure within which gender is either absent, or else has negative connotations. Within this context, the few mobilisations that have taken place around this issue have been led only by women, and have not received support or legitimacy from the rest of the associational network in this area.

The Ofpra and CRR: deciding on asylum claims

The research carried out in France also included interviews with officials working at the Ofpra and the CRR, and observation of sittings of the CRR.[11] These interviews confirmed much of what had been revealed by interviews with asylum seekers and with NGOs, namely an experience of the exercise of discretionary and often arbitrary power by officials and judges who based their decisions on their impressions of whether or not an applicant was "credible". These impressions and judgements are in general formed on the basis of a short written dossier, an interview by an immigration official at the Ofpra (although not all asylum seekers are granted an interview if their dossier is judged, for example, to be "manifestly unfounded"), and then an appeal hearing at the CRR which lasts on average for half an hour, during which the asylum seeker will be able to put forward their case for roughly ten minutes. The limited amount of time given to asylum seekers to explain their stories was a point highlighted by many of those interviewed for this study, and is clearly problematic in terms of the ability of any person to recount their life story accurately under such limited time constraints. However, the pressures put on the system to "process" the maximum number of asylum claims possible in a short time span means that this rapidity in assessing applicants' stories is inevitable.

Interviews with officials working at the Ofpra or the CRR revealed an institutional culture within which judgements were often made on the basis of assumptions or stereotypes regarding certain nationalities or ethnic groups, or on ideas about correct behaviour in certain circumstances. One rapporteur at the CRR explained, for example, that she was fed up of all the applications received from Chinese asylum seekers who she believed just "cut and pasted" their dossiers from one another, and all told the same, fabricated story. She continued to justify her antagonism towards these asylum seekers from China by arguing that

> None of them are real asylum seekers anyway, they just want to come and work in France, and if they make an asylum claim they think they can stay longer. They're just using the system to stay here and make money.

These judgements on the basic "fraudulent" nature of Chinese asylum claims were repeated by several other interviewees, leading to a supposition that it may be much harder for a Chinese applicant to make a case for protection than someone from a country of origin whose claimants are believed by officials to be generally more credible. A judge at the CRR expressed similar feelings of exasperation with Sri Lankan asylum claimants, whom he also believed always told the same story. He expressed the opinion that their claims all involved personal or familial feuds, or as he put it "fights over money and business", and were not in the least politically motivated. This type of construction of difference between asylum seekers of different origins, with some nationalities being judged as a priori more "genuine" than others seems to provide evidence against the belief that decisions on asylum claims are made on an "objective" basis, and reinforces Spire's observations in the police prefecture discussed above (Spire, 2006).

Evidence from the interviews as well as from observations carried out at the CRR supports the view that decision-making on asylum claims is a highly arbitrary process. Several rapporteurs at the CRR expressed the opinion that the outcome of a claim would be highly dependent on the personality of the judge who was president of the sitting. Some presidents were reputed within the organisation to be overly harsh to asylum seekers, whilst others had the reputation of being kinder and fairer. The rapporteurs also criticised the fact that the judges had no specific training in asylum law, and that they did not come and consult the relevant dossiers before a hearing, so that in many cases their decisions seemed to be based solely on their first impressions of the claimant. This type of criticism of judges by rapporteurs is revealing of a deeper split between the rapporteurs who are employed by the CRR and who judge themselves to be "experts" on asylum, and the judges who are drafted in on a part-time basis from other organisations and frequently have less "technical" knowledge of asylum, but more power in that they are charged with making the final decision on the asylum claim. Many of the female rapporteurs interviewed expressed the opinion that it was they who were responsible for pushing forward the positive jurisprudence with regard to gender-related persecution because they had persuaded the judges to follow their advice in several key cases. Hostility or suspicion was also expressed by employees of the Ofpra and the CRR with regard to the role of the other institution in the asylum determination process, revealing a kind of rivalry between the two instances of decision. Some Ofpra employees saw the CRR as trying to "undermine" their decision, whilst several rapporteurs at the CRR explained that they found the protection officers at the Ofpra too narrowly focused on their own geographical region and unable to take into account the wider issues of persecution in the asylum determination process.

A university lecturer who had served as one of the UNHCR's appointed judges explained how even as someone hoping to "subvert" the government's repressive asylum policies, he had become sucked into the system and "institutionalised". He realised that refugee status would only be granted to a small proportion of asylum claimants and thus entered into a logic of trying to pick out a few cases that were "worth fighting about". "I thought that if I had 'saved' one person each sitting then I was doing a good job". This type of attitude shows that even those judges "favourable" to asylum seekers are drawn into the logic of selecting and categorising the "good" from the "bad" claimants.

The process of "institutionalisation" of those working within the Ofpra and the CRR can also be seen in an effect of becoming "immune" to the suffering recounted by asylum claimants. Rousseau et al. describe the way in which constant exposure to traumatic stories can trigger "defensive reactions that lead to trivialisation of horror, cynicism and lack of empathy" (2002: 49). Several of those interviewed described a process whereby, as one interviewee at Ofpra explained: "you arrive thinking you can change things and then when you've heard all these terrible stories again and again, you just start not to believe them, or to not really care so much". These processes of "vicarious traumatization" (Rousseau et al., 2002) are also present in the responses of NGO employees working with asylum seekers. One interviewee explained that "you have to stay detached from their stories, otherwise you can't go home at night and relax and lead a normal life". Psychological processes such as these interact with the more structural institutional pressures and the dominant social representations of asylum seekers to create a general tendency towards suspicion and disbelief on the part of those working within state institutions dealing with asylum.

Gendered constructions of asylum seekers and refugees

In France, as in other Western countries, there has been some progress towards the recognition of gender-related asylum claims. Interviewees (and particularly those from within the Ofpra and CRR) pointed to what they saw as "landmark" judgements which advanced French decision-making in the area of gender-related claims. However, these decisions seem to reveal not an overall change in the way that gender-related claims are constructed and understood but rather arbitrary outcomes of a decision-making process which is operated through the discretionary power of different officials, and within which the dominant representation of an asylum seeker is that of a "fraud". Within this system gender relations still represent women seeking asylum largely as apolitical beings whose place is in the family. When their claims are recognised, it is largely because of persecutions understood as the product of "oppressive" Third World cultures. The barriers to women making effective asylum claims are still in existence. Moreover, as well as continuing barriers to having their asylum claims recognised, women are facing increasingly exclusionary pressures through the restriction of the right to work and to accommodation and welfare benefits. This can lead to huge material and financial difficulties which can be interpreted as an attack on their dignity and an infringement of their rights. It would be wrong, however, to portray these women as merely "victims" of persecution and of the French asylum system. None of them had been passive subjects in the face of the persecutions and difficulties they had faced, but all had shown a huge willingness to fight to establish their rights to be recognised as a refugee and to have a decent standard of living for themselves and their children. As Kelly (2000) points out, women's agency may be demonstrated just in their survival and the ways that they continue to provide for themselves and their families in the face of major obstacles. The courage of these women and their willingness to continue to struggle to obtain their rights is impressive.

Sadly it seems that for these women, as for all those displaced by conflict and persecution, the hope of protection may remain elusive. Conflicts that produce displacement are not going away, but the policies of containment pursued by governments in the West are likely to keep more and more refugees away from their state borders. Moreover, those asylum seekers who do manage to reach Europe, North America or

Australia will continue to be treated as unwelcome intruders, and the decisions taken on asylum claims are influenced by this framing of asylum claimants as "fraudulent". The asylum seekers remain at the mercy of discretionary power and arbitrary decision making which is cloaked in a discourse of objectivity.

Conclusion

The attempt to consider gender issues in the politics of asylum and refugees reveals a complex and varied set of relations and represent-ations. Within dominant political discourses, this complexity is often hidden beneath dichotomous and opposing constructions: the refugee as a victim and an object of pity versus the asylum seeker as a menace and an object of dislike; the "refugee woman" alone with her chil-dren as a vulnerable victim in need of special protection versus the asylum-seeking single mother as a "sponger" using her maternity to gain benefits from the welfare state. Within these broad categories of oppositions, more distinctions and oppositions emerge created around stereotypes relating to national or ethnic categories or to causes of flight: asylum seekers from the ex-Yugoslavia may be more easily accepted in the West than those from Africa, being seen as ultimately more easy to "integrate" and somehow more "deserving"; those who have been perse-cuted for leading a political opposition party more worthy of protection than those who are "merely" fleeing a forced marriage or domestic violence. All of these dichotomies and divisions and the many others that exist are shaped by national and international pressures which define and re-define who exactly is a refugee or an asylum seeker. As we argued in the introduction to this volume, the nature of contem-porary migratory movements in fact makes it almost impossible to set up clear definitions and categories, and to distinguish between volun-tary and forced migration, an asylum seeker or an economic migrant. The causes of migration and its routes and consequences are so complex that all of these categorisations and distinctions become irrelevant. And yet international organisations and political leaders continue to make policies based on these categorisations and divisions. Exclusionary asylum policies in the West are, we are told, designed to keep out the economic migrants who are trying to cheat the system so that the "genuine" asylum seekers and refugees can benefit from protection.

A first step in trying to understand more clearly what lies beneath these constructions and representations which establish binary categor-isations and divisions is to reveal the fact that they are just that: political constructions which correspond not to "reality" but to a particular representation of that reality. The international conventions on the protection of refugees in theory set up a challenge to the sovereignty of a nation state and its ability to control its borders: states should in theory open their borders to all who are in need of protection, and they have a duty to "non-refoulement" of those who ask for this protection. In practice, however, the application and implementation of these conventions has been subverted in the interests of the defence of the nation state and its sovereignty. The right to choose who is a "good" and who is a "bad" migrant rests firmly with the state and its officials.

What about the women? This book has tried to provide some understandings of the varied situations and experiences of women through the forced migration process: the causes of migration, the experiences of displacement and exile, lives in a refugee camp, as an asylum seeker in the West, or once recognised as a refugee by a Western state. One of the major questions to be asked in writing about these women's lives is whether it is possible or useful to search for any commonalities of experience? Or are differences of location and of class, ethnicity, race, sexual orientation and age – to mention just a few of the things that separate women – too great for it make any sense to talk about women asylum seekers and refugees in any sense more meaningful than a description of women who are at some point of forced migration? The research carried out for this book seems to show that despite the multiple differences that exist, there is some point in trying to talk about women and about gender in the forced migration process. It can be argued that the same processes of construction of dichotomised representations of "good" and "bad" refugees are both reinforced by and in turn inform and reinforce gendered relations and structures of power. The representations of women in refugee camps as "vulnerable victims" are thus part of a framing of international humanitarian politics which is at the same time a politics of containment of refugees within these camps. The use of images of "women as victims" (or "womenanchildren"), together with a discourse of aid to these victims, reinforces the idea that international institutions such as UNHCR and national governments in the West are doing their best to support the vulnerable. Both those aiming to gain financial support from donors and those aiming to garner public support for a military/humanitarian intervention may utilise such images within their discourse. These images rely on gendered assumptions about the greater vulnerability of women and on the contrary the invulnerability of men. And at the same time these constructions of women as vulnerable victims both reinforce pre-existing gendered inequalities and create new ones by framing women as passive and without agency, requiring others to speak for and to "save" them. Constructions of women within the asylum policies and legislation of Western states also takes place within this dichotomising framework, framing asylum seekers as "bogus" or "frauds", a threat to the nation. These framings mean that those who work to assist or accompany women asylum claimants are thus reduced to battling for small victories, such as the acceptance that in a certain case a woman from a particular area of a specific country may be considered as part of a particular social group if she has suffered from domestic violence. To gain the protection of a Western state as a refugee, a woman must demonstrate that she fits into the categories of "refugeeness" established by that state, categories which are informed by the dominant framings of asylum seekers as "false" and by gendered constructions of the division between public and private, and of the proper way for a woman to behave. Behind all of the debates on whether or not certain women should be accepted as part of a social group or whether a certain form of violence should be classed as "persecution", we can see an underlying construction of the asylum seeker as a "threat", the threat that if one woman is admitted to refugee status because of a fear of FGM, domestic violence or rape, then millions more, or "half of humanity" will follow. These framings also reinforce gendered constructions of women's apolitical role (their persecution never appears as political), and of the naturalness of some of the violence that they suffer.

Gender inequalities are widespread and far-reaching. They inform all aspects of forced migration. But at the same time the way these inequalities are constructed and the way that they are experienced will vary widely from one context to the next and from one woman or man to the next. How then should any action to address these inequalities best be addressed? Whilst stressing the commonalities that thread through women's experience, it is also important not to overlook differences, and to make sure that different situations and experiences are analysed in context. The best people to know how to move beyond stereotyped representations are the women refugees and asylum seekers themselves. To understand how gender operates as a relationship of power in conflict, in forced migration or in exile, we need to ask those involved how they experience these relationships, and how best to modify them. To give asylum seeking and refugee women back their voice.

Notes

1 A gendered approach to refugee and asylum studies

1 For a fuller discussion and critique of the refugee-aid worker relationship and its "victimisation" of refugees see Chapter 5.

2 Boltanski describes the way in which a politics of pity is based on the notion of suffering at a distance (Boltanski, 1993).

3 For an analysis of the relationship between humanitarian and military interventions see, for example, Agier (2003).

4 These figures provided by the UNHCR are disputed by other agencies and researchers whose estimates range widely. Harris, for example, argued in 1996 that there were seventy million refugees and seventy million internally displaced persons in the world (Harris, 1995). Although these figures are clearly at the top end of the scale, it is agreed by many that the UNHCR figures are an underestimate.

5 For a more detailed discussion of the 1951 Convention and particularly its gendered impacts, see Chapter 4.

6 This figure includes only those Afghan refugees living in official UNHCR camps, at least as many are probably living in Pakistan outside of these official structures.

7 Office français de protection de réfugiés et apatrides, the official body which processes and decides on initial claims for asylum.

8 *Journal Officiel* 6 June 2002.

9 This is the point of view expressed by many NGOs working with asylum seekers, and by asylum seekers themselves, expressed in interviews with the author during 2005 and 2006. The same judgement on the arbitrary nature of decision-making on asylum seekers was also put forward by former judges at the French Commission de Recours de Refugiés (Refugee Appeals Commission) in interviews with the author.

10 This figure is seen as a conservative estimate by many as it does not include the many undocumented migrants. Others have suggested that if all undocumented migrants were accounted for, the figure would rise to about 7 per cent.

2 Who are the "refugee women"?

1 Email correspondence with author, 2006.

2 Email correspondence with author, 2006.

3 Interview with author, December 2006.

4 Email response to questions, January 2006.

5 The Ofpra which is the official body that judges initial asylum claims was given the powers to grant subsidiary protection as well as convention refugee status under a new immigration and asylum law of 2003, the "loi Sarkozy".

6   Interviews with author, 2005 and 2006.
7   Figures provided by the CGRA, personal communication.
8   Kreitzer points, for example, to the fact that there is no facility for childcare to enable women to participate in planning meetings within the camp (Kreitzer, 2002).

3   Gender related persecutions: why do women flee?

1   For a discussion of why women are under-represented amongst those seeking asylum in industrialised countries, see Chapter 2.
2   CEDAW, General Recommendation 19, Violence against Women (Eleventh session, 1992), Compilation of General Comments and General Recommendations Adopted by Human Rights Treaty Bodies, UN Doc. HRI\GEN\1\Rev.1 at 84 (1994).
3   A report for the European Parliament suggests that up to sixty thousand women have been victims of FGM in Europe, the United States, Canada, Australia and New Zealand, and that another twenty thousand women are at risk of this practice (European Parliament (2001), Report on female genital mutilation, 2001/2035 (INI)).
4   Although this does not mean that male circumcision may not also be criticised as a harmful practice as it is for example by Carpenter (2004).
5   Although the Department of Homeland Security did finally grant her leave to remain in the United States.
6   This was notably the case during the conflict in Algeria during the 1990s when women, and particularly single women or women labelled as lesbians were targeted by Islamic groups. France created a specific form of "territorial asylum" to deal with these cases of civilians escaping from persecution by Islamic groups in Algeria, and although almost all claims for this form of asylum were rejected, three Algerian lesbians did benefit from this status.
7   For a discussion of the issues involved in the definition of a "particular social group" under the terms of the Geneva Convention, see Chapter 4.
8   New York Times, 22 June 2005.
9   "Sex and death in the heart of Africa", *The Independent*, 25 May 2004.
10 "Sex and the UN: when peacemakers become predators", *The Independent*, 11 January 2005.

4   Gender and asylum in international law – the geneva convention revisited

1   The *OAU Convention on the Specific Aspects of Refugee Problems in Africa* (Addis Ababa, September 1969) and the *Cartagena Declaration on Refugees* (Cartagena, 1984) provide some elements of regional refugee definition which are applicable to situations in Africa and South America respectively.
2   Interview with author September 2005.
3   Interviews, 2005 and 2006.
4   Interview, March 2006.

5 Resolution on the Application of the Geneva Convention Relating to the Status of Refugees, 1984, OJ (C127)137.
6 UNHCR Executive Committee, 1985, Refugee Women and International Protection Report, 36th Session, UN A/A96/673.
7 See http://www.womenlobby.org/asylumcampaign/EN/PRE/lau.html.
8 United States Immigration ad Nationality Service, *Memorandum: Considerations for Asylum Officers Adjudicating Asylum Claims from Women*, 1995.
9 www.ind.homeoffice.gov.uk/ind/en/home/law_policy/policy_instructions/gender_issues_in_the.html
10 *Convention on the Elimination of All Forms of Discrimination Against Women*, adopted by the General Assembly of the United Nations in 1979.
11 Decision no. M91-04822 (1991).
12 Interview with author, January 2007.
13 The RWRP was established by Asylum Aid in 2000 and is now one of the NGO's major foci of action.
14 Interview with author, January 2007.
15 Swedish Aliens Act (Code of Statutes no. 1996: 379), chapter 3, section 3.
16 Swedish Aliens Act (Code of Statues no. 2005: 716), chapter 4, section 1.
17 Interview with author, December 2006.
18 Interview with author, November 2006.
19 It is apparently common knowledge that the French-speaking section of the CGRA is much more likely to make positive judgements in asylum cases than their Flemish-speaking counterparts, leading to very similar cases receiving different judgements from the two different sections. This knowledge apparently leads asylum claimants "in the know" to swap tickets in the waiting room in order to ensure their case is taken by an officer from the French-speaking section.
20 Interview with author, December 2006.

5 Supporting women refugees and asylum seekers

1 The ten largest donors are in order the United States, the European Commission, Japan, Sweden, the United Kingdom, the Netherlands, Germany, Norway, Denmark and Canada.
2 See for example Agier and Valluy's critiques of the UNHCR's role in European policies for the "externalisation" of asylum (Agier and Valluy, 2007).
3 For a more detailed discussion of the "externalisation" of asylum and its consequences see Chapter 6.
4 By the mid-1990s UNHCR employed over five thousand staff worldwide.
5 Interviews with the author at UNHCR headquarters and in national bureaus in Europe, 2005, 2006 and 2007.
6 Interviews, 2005, 2006 and 2007.
7 This view was expressed relatively frequently in interviews with NGO employees in France and the United Kingdom.
8 Interview, January 2007.
9 Interviews with author, 2005 and 2006.
10 Evidence gained from interviews with NGOs and observation of meetings between NGOs and asylum seekers, 2005 and 2006.

11   Interview, January 2007.
12   Interview, December 2006.
13   Interviews with FASTI, CIMADE, September and October 2005.
14   Interview, December 2006.

6   Asylum regimes and their impacts

1   Council of the European Union, "Council Directive on Minimum Standards for the Qualification and Status of Third Country Nationals or State-
less Persons as Refugees or as Persons who Otherwise Need International
Protection and the Content of the Protection Granted".
2   Council of the European Union, "Amended Proposal for a Council Directive
on Minimum Standards on Procedures in Member States for Granting and
Withdrawing Refugee Status".
3   Communication from the Commission to the Council and the European
Parliament, "Towards a Common Asylum Procedure and a Uniform Status,
Valid Throughout the Union, for Persons Granted Asylum", COM (2000: 755).
4   Statement by Mr Ruud Lubbers, United Nations High Commissioner for
Refugees at an informal meeting of the European Justice and Home Affairs
Council, Copenhagen, 13 September 2002.
5   "Shifting a Problem Back to its Source: Would-be Refugees May be Sent to
Protected Zones near Homeland" and "Safe Havens Plan to Slash Asylum
Numbers" (*The Guardian*, 5 February 2003).
6   There was also some opposition from Germany but the German government
was in fact divided on the issue.
7   Communication from the Commission to the Council and the European
Parliament, "The Managed Entry in the EU of Persons in Need of International Protection and the Enhancement of the Protection Capacity of
the Region of Origin: 'Improving Access to Durable Solutions'", COM
(2004: 410).
8   Interviews with author, 2005 and 2006.
9   The "Sarkozy" Law of 26 November 2003.
10   From 2001 onwards, those who have attempted to reach Australia by boat
have been detained in either Nauru or Papua New Guinea whilst their claims
are processed.
11   Evidence to the House of Lords Select Committee, 1 February 2006.
12   Council Directive 2003/9/EC laying down the minimum standards for the
reception of asylum seekers.
13   Interview with author, November 2005.
14   Interview with author, February 2007.
15   Interviews with author, 2005 and 2006, for more details see Chapter 7.

7   Women asylum seekers and refugees: experiences from france

1   The interviews for this study were carried out during 2005 and 2006 with
asylum seekers from Algeria, Chechnya, Cote d'Ivoire, DR Congo, Guineau,

Mali, Sierra Leone, Sri Lanka and Turkey. The women interviewed were contacted first through the means of NGOs and agencies which help asylum seekers, and then through "word of mouth" with introductions to various friends and acquaintances of those already interviewed. Interviews were also conducted with NGOs including Amnesty International (French Section), CIMADE, FASTI, Femmes de la Terre, France Terre d'Asile, GRAF, RAJFIRE. Some of these associations provide specific support for women asylum seekers, including special women only consultation sessions, others make no special provision for women asylum seekers. Finally, officials and other actors in the asylum determination process were interviewed including officers working at the Ofpra (Office de protection de réfugiés et apatrides), assessors and judges at the CRR (Commission de recours de réfugiés), lawyers involved in representing asylum seekers at hearings at the CRR and representatives of the UNHCR in France. All of the interviews were carried out in French or in English, and were all tape recorded, transcribed and analysed. All translations into English are my own. To respect the privacy of respondents, all of the interview material is used anonymously.

2   The judges who represent the UNHCR are not always permanent employees of the organisation but are often drawn from a circle of academics or researchers and are appointed on a temporary basis to represent the UNHCR at the CRR. One former judge believes that the UNHCR office in Paris is likely to appoint people who know very little about asylum and immigration, so that they will not have any preformed views on the issues involved in judging asylum claims, and will be more readily adaptable to the institutional norms of the CRR.

3   Source: UNHCR.

4   For a discussion of the problems of definition of what is "political", see chapter four.

5   Ellerman makes a similar point concerning the need to have a more nuanced account of "public opinion" on immigration and asylum based on her study of public opposition to deportation policies (Ellerman, 2006).

6   Fédération des Associations de Soutien aux Travailleurs Immigrés.

7   Including Femmes de la Terre, GAS (Groupe Accueil Solidarité) and GAMS (Groupe pour l'abolition des mutilations sexuelles).

8   Meeting of the CFDA, 21 September 2005.

9   Interview, January 2006.

10   Interview, February 2006.

11   Several sittings are held concurrently every day and are open to the public, except if the asylum seeker being heard asks for a private session.

Bibliography

Abdi, A. W. (2006), "Refugees, Gender-based Violence and Resistance: A Case Study of Somali Refugee Women in Kenya", in E. Tastsoglou and A. Dobrowolsky (eds), *Women, Migration and Citizenship*, Aldershot: Ashgate.

Abiri, E. (2000), "The Changing Praxis of 'Generosity': Swedish Refugee Policy during the 1990s", *Journal of Refugee Studies*, 13, 1, pp. 11–28.

Adamson, F. (2005), Global Liberalism versus Political Islam: Competing Ideological Frameworks in International Politics, *International Studies Review*, 7, pp. 547–569.

Adelman, H. (1999), "Modernity, Globalization, Refugees and Displacement", in A. Ager (ed.), *Refugees: Perspectives on the Experience of Forced Migration*, London: Continuum.

Adelman, H. (2001), "From Refugees to Forced Migration: The UNHCR and Human Security", *International Migration Review*, 35, 1, pp. 7–32.

Ager, A., Ager, L. and Long, L. (1995), "The Differential Experience of Mozambican Refugee Women and Men", *Journal of Refugee Studies*, 8, 3, pp. 265–287.

Agier, M. (2002), *Aux bords du monde, les réfugiés*, Paris: Flammarion.

Agier, M. (2003), "La main gauche de l'Empire: Ordre et désordres de l'humanitaire", *Multitudes*, 11, janvier 2003, http://multitudes.samizdat.net/La-main-gauche-de-l-Empire.html.

Agier, M. and Valluy, J. (2007), "Le HCR dans la logique des camps", in O. Le Cour Grandmaison, G. Lhuilier and J. Valluy (eds), *Le retour des camps? Sangatte, Lampedusa, Guantanamo*, Paris: Autrement.

Alison, M. (2007), "Wartime Sexual Violence: Questions of Masculinity", *Review of International Studies*, 33, 1, pp. 75–90.

Al'Rassace, S. and Falquet, J. (2006), "Les femmes parties de leur pays en raison de leur lesbianisme: un état des connaissances en France aujourd'hui", *Asylon(s)*, 1, http://terra.rezo.net/article483.html.

Amnesty International (2004a), *It's in Our Hands: Stop Violence Against Women*, London: Amnesty International.

Amnesty International (2004b), *Russian Federation: Nowhere to Turn to – Violence Against Women in the Family*, London: Amnesty International.

Amnesty International (2005a), *Temporary Stay, Permanent Rights: The Treatment of Foreign Nationals Detained in Temporary Stay and Assistance Centres*, London: Amnesty International.

Amnesty International (2005b), *Europe: Treatment of Refugees and Asylum Seekers*, London: Amnesty International.

Amesty International (2006), *Sexual ViolenceAgainst Women and Girls in Jamaica: "just a little sex"*, London: Amnesty International.

Andric-Ruzicic, D. (2003), "War Rape and the Political Manipulation of Survivors", in W. Giles et al. (eds), *Feminists Under Fire: Exchanges Across War Zones*, Toronto: Between the Lines.

Ankenbrand, B. (2002), "Refugee Women Under German Asylum Law", *International Journal of Refugee Law*, 14, 1, pp. 45–56.

Anthias, F. and Yuval-Davis, N. (1992), *Racialized Boundaries: Race, Nation, Gender, Colour and Class and the Anti-Racist Struggle*, London: Routledge.

Ascoly, N., Van Halsema, I. and Keysers, L. (2001), "Refugee Women, Pregnancy and Reproductive Health Care in the Netherlands", *Journal of Refugee Studies*, 14, 4, pp. 372–393.

Audit Commission (2000), *Another Country: Implementing Dispersal Under the Immigration and Asylum Act 1999*, London: Audit Commission.

Audit Commission (2002), *Another Country: Implementing Dispersal Under the Immigration and Asylum Act 1999*, London: Audit Commission.

Bach, R. and Carolle-Seguin, R. (1986), "Labour Force Participation, Household Composition and Sponsorship Among Southeast Asian Refugees", *International Migration Review*, 20, 2, pp. 381–404.

Baines, E. K. (2004), *Vulnerable Bodies: Gender, the UN and the Global Refugee Crisis*, Aldershot: Ashgate.

Barnett, M. (2001), "Humanitarianism with a Sovereign Face", *International Migration Review*, 35, 1, pp. 244–278.

Barsky, R. (1994), *Constructing a Productive Other: Discourse Theory and the Convention Refugee Hearing*, Amsterdam: John Benjamins Publishing Company.

Bauman, Z. (1998), *Globalization: The Human Consequences*, Cambridge: Polity Press.

Bellas Cabane, C. (2006), "Fondements sociaux de l'excision dans le Mali du XXIème siècle", *Asylon(s)*, 1, http://terra.rezo.net/article485.html.

Bexelius, M. (2001), *Women Refugees: An Analysis of Swedish Asylum Policy 1997–2000*, Stockholm: Swedish Refugee Advice Centre.

Bexelius, M. (2006), *Swedish Law and Practice and Gender Persecution: Summary Conclusions and Comments*, unpublished document provided by author.

Bhabha, J. (2004), "Demography and Rights: Women, Children and Access to Asylum", *International Journal of Refugee Law*, 16, 2, pp. 228–243.

Bigo, D. (2001), Migration and Security, in V. Guiraudon and C. Joppke (eds), *Controlling a New Migration World*, London: Routledge.

Binder, S. and Tosic, J. (2005), "Refugees as a Particular Form of Transnational Migrations and Social Transformations: Socioanthropological and Gender Aspects", *Current Sociology*, 53, 4, pp. 607–624.

Bloch, A. (1999), "Refugees in the Job Market: A Case of Unused Skills in the British Economy", in A. Bloch and C. Levy (eds), *Refugees, Citizenship and Social Policy in Europe*, Basingstoke: Palgrave.

Bloch, A. and Levy, C. (eds) (1999), *Refugees, Citizenship and Social Policy in Europe*, Basingstoke: Macmillan.

Bloch, A. and Schuster, L. (2005), "At the Extremes of Exclusion: Deportation, Detention and Dispersal", *Ethnic and Racial Studies*, 28, 3, pp. 491–512.

Bloch, A., Galvin, T. and Harrell-Bond, B. (2000), "Refugee Women in Europe: Some Aspects of the Legal and Policy Dimensions", *International Migration*, 38, 2, pp. 169–190.

Blue, S. (2005), "Including Women in Development: Guatemalan Refugees and Local NGOs", *Latin American Perspectives*, 32, 5, pp. 101–117.

Boltanski, L. (1993), *La souffrance à distance*, Paris: Métaillie.

Boswell, C. (2000), "European Values and the Asylum Crisis", *International Affairs*, 76, 3, pp. 537–557.

Boswell, C. (2001), *Spreading the Costs of Asylum-Seekers: A Critical Assessment of Dispersal Policies in Germany and the UK*, London: Anglo-German Foundation.

202   *Bibliography*

Boswell, C. (2003), "The 'external dimension' of EU immigration and asylum policy", *International Affairs*, 79, 3, pp. 619–638.

Bousquet, E. (2006), *Le droit d'asile en France: politique et réalité*, Working paper no. 138, New Issues in Refugee Research, Geneva: UNHCR.

Bouteillet-Paquet, D. (2002), "Quelle protection subsidiaire dans l'Union européenne?", *Hommes et Migrations*, 1238, pp. 75–88.

Boyd, M. (1993), *Gender Concealed, Gender Revealed: The Demography of Canada's Refugee Flows*, Working Paper, Center for the Study of Population, Florida State University.

Brachet, O. (2002) "La condition du réfugié dans la tourmente de la politique d'asile", *Hommes et Migrations*, 1238, pp. 45–58.

Bunch, C. (1995), "Transforming Human Rights from a Feminist Perspective", in J. Peter and A. Wolper (eds), *Women's Rights, Human Rights: International Feminist Perspectives*, New York: Routledge.

Butler, J. (1990), *Gender Trouble: Feminism and the Subversion of Identity*, New York: Routledge.

BWRAP and WAR (2006), *Misjudging Rape: Breaching Gender Guidelines and International Law in Asylum Appeals*, London: Crossroads Books.

Callamard, A. (1996), "Flour is Power", in W. Giles, H. Moussa and P. Van Esterik (eds), *Development and Diaspora*, Dundas: Artemis Enterprise.

Callamard, A. (2002), "Refugee Women: A Gendered and Political Analysis of the Refugee Experience", in D. Joly (ed.), *Global Changes in Asylum Regimes*, Basingstoke: Palgrave Macmillan.

Canadian Council for Refugees (2005), *Closing the Front Door on Refugees. Report on the First Year of the Safe Third Country Agreement*, Montreal: CCR.

Carey-Wood, J., Duke, K., Karn, V. and Marshall, T. (1995), *The Settlement of Refugees in Britain*, Home Office Research Study, London: Home Office.

Carpenter, R. C. (2004), "Some Other Conceptual Problems: A Reply to Winter, Thompson and Jeffrey's Critique of the UN's Approach to HTPs", *International Feminist Journal of Politics*, 6, 2, pp. 307–311.

Carpenter, R. C. (2005), " 'Women, Children and Other Vulnerable Groups': Gender, Strategic Frames and the Protection of Civilians as a Transnational Issue", *International Studies Quarterly*, 49: pp. 486–500.

Carpenter, R. C. (2006), *"Innocent Women and Children": Gender, Norms and the Protection of Civilians*, Aldershot: Ashgate.

Castells, M. (1996), *The Rise of the Network Society*, Oxford: Blackwells.

Castles, S. (2003), "The International Politics of Forced Migration", *Development*, 46, 3, pp. 11–20.

Castles, S. (2004), "Why Migration Policies Fail", *Ethnic and Racial Studies*, 27, 2, pp. 205–227.

Castles, S. and Loughna, S. (2005), "Trends in Asylum Migration to Industrialized Countries, 1990–2001", in G. Borjas and J. Crisp (eds), *Poverty, International Migration and Asylum*, Basingstoke: Palgrave Macmillan.

Castles, S. and Miller, M. (1998), *The Age of Migration: International Population Movements in the Modern World*, Basingstoke: Palgrave.

Castles, S., Korac, M., Vasta, E. and Vertovec, S. (2001), *Integration: Mapping the Field*, Oxford: Refugee Studies Centre.

Castles, S., Crawley, H. and Loughna, S. (2003), *States of Conflict: Causes and Patterns of Forced Migration to the EU and Policy Responses*, London: IPPR.

Ceneda, S. (2006), "RWRP's campaign to improve the use of gender guidelines in the UK", *Asylon(s)*, 1, http://terra.rezo.net/article499.html.

Center for Reproductive Rights (2003), *Body and Soul: Forced Sterilization and Other Assaults on Roma Reproductive Freedom*, New York: Center for Reproductive Rights.

Charlesworth, H. and Chinkin, C. (2000), *The Boundaries of International Law: A Feminist Analysis*, Manchester: Manchester University Press.

Charlesworth, H. et al. (1991), "Feminist Approaches to International Law", *American Journal of International Law*, 85, pp. 613–664.

Chimni, B. S. (1998), "The Geopolitics of Refugee Studies: A View from the South", *Journal of Refugee Studies*, 11, 4, pp. 350–374.

Cimade (2004), *Rétention administrative des étrangers. Un an après la loi Sarkozy*, Paris: Cimade.

Cimade (2006a), *Centres et locaux de rétention administrative – rapport 2005*, Paris: Cimade.

Cimade (2006b), *Votre voisin n'a pas de papiers: paroles d'étrangers*, Paris: La Fabrique.

Clarence, E. (2003), "Ignored and Isolated: Women and Asylum Policy in the United Kingdom", in J. Freedman (ed), *Gender and Insecurity: Migrant Women in Europe*, Aldershot: Ashgate.

Cockburn, C. (2004), "The Continuum of Violence: A Gender Perspective on War and Peace", in W. Giles and J. Hyndman (eds), *Sites of Violence: Gender and Conflict Zones*, Berkeley: University of California Press.

Community Care (2001), "Isolated by Gender", *Community Care*, November 22.

Community Care (2002), "Denial of Milk Tokens Exposes Babies to HIV Risk, Claim Campaigners", *Community Care*, February 14.

Copelon, R. (1994), "Intimate terror: Understanding domestic violence as torture", in R. Cook (ed.), *Human Rights of Women: National and International Perspectives*, Philadelphia: University of Pennsylvania Press.

Copelon, R. (1995), "Gendered War Crimes: Reconceptualizing Rape in Time of War", in J. Peters and A. Wolper (eds), *Women's Rights, Human Rights: International Feminist Perspectives*, New York: Routledge.

Crawley, H. (1999), "Women and refugee status: beyond the public/private dichotomy", in D. Indra (ed.), *Engendering Forced Migration: Theory and Practice*, Oxford: Berghahn.

Crawley, H. (2001), *Refugees and Gender: Law and Process*, Bristol: Jordan.

Crawley, H. and Lester, T. (2004), *Comparative Analysis of Gender-Related Persecution in National Asylum Legislation and Practice in Europe*, Geneva: UNHCR.

Créac'h, X. (2002), "Les évolutions dans l'interprétation du terme réfugié", *Hommes et Migrations*, 1238, pp. 65–74.

Crépeau, F. (1995), *Droit d'asile. De l'hospitalité aux contrôles migratoires*, Bruxelles: Bruylant.

Cusimano Love, M. (2007), *Beyond Sovereignty: Issues for a Global Agenda*, Belmont: Thomson.

Daniel, E. V. (1996), *Charred Lullabies: Chapters in an Anthropology of Violence*, Princeton: Princeton University Press.

Dorf, J. and Careaga Perez, G. (1995), "Discrimination and the Tolerance of Difference: International Lesbian Human Rights", in J. Peters and A. Wolper (eds), *Women's Rights, Human Rights: International Feminist Perspectives*, New York: Routledge.

Dorlin, E. (2006), *La matrice de la race – Généalogie sexuelle et coloniale de la nation française*, Paris: La Découverte.

Donato, K. M., Gabaccia, D., Holdaway, J., Manalansan, M. and Pessar, P. (2006), "A Glass Half-Full? Gender in Migration Studies", *International Migration Review*, 40, 1, pp. 3–26.

Drumm, S., Pittman, S. and Perry, S. (2001), "Women of War: Emotional Needs of Ethnic Albanians in Refugee Camps", *Affilia*, 16, 4, pp. 467–487.

Duffield, M. (2001), *Global Governance and the New Wars: The Merging of Development and Security*, London: Zed Books.

Dufour, E. (2006), "Comment s'est constitué historiquement et comment a évolué récemment le rôle de France Terre d'Asile (FTDA) dans le ≪ dispositif national d'accueil?", TERRA-Editions, Collection ≪ Synthèses ≫, http://terra.rezo.net/article544.html.

Düvell, F. and Jordan, B. (2002), "Immigration, Asylum and Welfare: The European Context;", *Critical Social Policy*, 22, 3, pp. 498–517.

Eagle, A. et al. (2002), *Asylum Seekers' Experiences of the Voucher Scheme in the United Kingdom – Fieldwork Report*, London: Home Office Research, Development and Statistics Directorate.

ECRE (2005), *The EC Directive on the Reception of Asylum Seekers: Are Asylum Seekers in Europe Receiving Material Support and Access to Employment in Accordance with European Legislation?* Brussels: European Council on Refugees and Exiles.

Ellerman, A. (2006), "Street-Level Democracy: How Immigration Bureaucrats Manage Public Opposition", *West European Politics*, 29, 2, pp. 293–309.

Enloe, C. (1989), *Bananas, Beaches and Bases: Making Feminist Sense of International Politics*, Berkeley: University of California Press.

Enloe, C. (1993), *The Morning After: Sexual Politics at the End of the Cold War*, Berkeley: University of California Press.

Enloe, C. (2000), *Maneuvers: The International Politics of Militarizing Women's Lives*, Berkeley: University of California Press.

Erdman, J. N. and Sanche, A. J. (2004), "Talking About Women: The Iterative and Dialogic Process of Creating Guidelines for Gender-Based Refugee Claims", *Journal of Law and Equality*, 3,1, pp. 70–83.

Fanning, B. et al. (2001), *Beyond the Pale: Asylum Seeking Children and Social Exclusion in Ireland*, Dublin: Irish Refugee Council.

Favell, A. and Geddes, A. (2000), "Immigration and European Integration: New Opportunities for Transnational Political Mobilisation?", in R. Koopmans and P. Statham (eds), *Challenging Immigration and Ethnic Relations Politics: Comparative European Perspectives*, Oxford: Oxford University Press.

Ferhati, B. (2006), "La lutte contre l'excision des fillettes et des femmes au Soudan: entre politiques volontaristes, mondialisation et résistances sociales", *Asylon(s)*, 1, *http://terra.rezo.net/article503.html*.

Fesshaye, S. (2003), "Rape, Hunger and Homelessness" *The Guardian*, 1 November 2003.

Finnemore, M. and Sikkink, K. (1998), "International Norm Dynamics and Political Change", *International Organization*, 52, 4, pp. 887–917.

Folkelius, K. and Noll, G. (1998), "Affirmative Exclusion: Sex, Gender, Persecution and the Reformed Swedish Aliens Act", *International Journal of Refugee Law*, 10, 4, pp. 607–636.

Forbes-Martin, S. (2004), *Refugee Women*, Maryland: Lexington Books.

Franguiadakis, S., Jaillardon, E. and Belkis, D. (2004), *En quête d'asile: Aide associative et accès au(x) droits*, Paris : LGDJ.

Franz, B. (2003), "Bosnian Refugee Women in (Re)settlement: Gender Relations and Social Mobility", *Feminist Review*, 73, pp. 86–103.

Freedman, J. (ed) (2003), *Gender and Insecurity: Migrant Women in Europe*, Aldershot: Ashgate.

Freedman, J. (2004), "Introduire le genre dans le débat sur l'asile politique: l'insecurité croissante pour les femmes réfugiées en Europe", in M. Hersent and C. Zaidman (eds), *Genre, Travail et Migrations en Europe*, Paris: Cedref.

Freedman, J. (2007a), "Women, Islam and Rights in Europe: Beyond a Universalist/Culturalist Dichotomy", *Review of International Studies*, 33, 1, pp. 49–70.

Freedman, J. (2007b), "Women Seeking Asylum: The Politics of Gender in the Asylum Determination Process in France", *International Feminist Journal of Politics* (forthcoming).

Geddes, A. (2000a), "Denying Access: Asylum Seekers and Welfare Benefits in the UK", in M. Bommes and A. Geddes (eds), *Immigration and Welfare: Challenging the Borders of the Welfare State*, London: Routledge.

Geddes, A. (2000b), *Immigration and European Integration: Towards Fortress Europe?*, Manchester: Manchester University Press.

Ghorashi, H. (2005), "Agents of Change or Passive Victims: The Impact of Welfare States (The Case of the Netherlands) on Refugees", *Journal of Refugee Studies*, 18, 2, pp. 181–198.

Gibney, M. (2001), "The State of Asylum: Democratization, Judicialization and Evolution of Refugee Policy in Europe", Working paper no. 50, Refugee Studies Centre, University of Oxford.

Gibney, M. (2004), *The Ethics and Politics of Asylum: Liberal Democracy and the Response to Refugees*, Cambridge: Cambridge University Press.

Gibney, M. and Hansen, R. (2005), "Asylum Policy in the West: Past Trends, Future Possibilities", in G. Borjas and J. Crisp (eds), *Poverty, International Migration and Asylum*, Basingstoke: Palgrave Macmillan.

Giles, W. (1999), "Gendered Violence in War: Reflections on Transnationalist and Comparative Frameworks in Militarized Conflict Zones", in D. Indra (ed), *Engendering Forced Migration: Theory and Practice*, Oxford: Berghahn.

Giles, W. and Hyndman, J. (eds) (2004), *Sites of Violence: Gender and Conflict Zones*, Berkley: University of California Press.

Giles, W., de Alwis, M., Klein, E. and Silva, N. (eds) (2003), *Feminists Under Fire: Exchanges Across War Zones*, Toronto: Between the Lines.

Goodwin-Gill, G. (1996), *The Refugee in International Law*, Oxford: Oxford University Press.

Gray, E. and Statham, P. (2005), "Becoming European? The Transformation of the British Pro-migrant NGO Sector in Response to Europeanization", *Journal of Common Market Studies*, 43, 4, pp. 877–898.

Hammerstad, A. (2000), "Whose Security? UNHCR, Refugee Protection and State Security after the Cold War", *Security Dialogue*, 31, 4, pp. 391–403.

Hansen, L. (2000), "The Little Mermaid's Silent Security Dilemma and the Absence of Gender in the Copenhagen School", *Millenium: Journal of International Studies*, 29, 2, pp. 285–306.

Hansen, R. and King, D. (2000), "Illiberalism and the new politics of asylum: Liberalism's dark side", *Political Quarterly*, 71, 4, pp. 396–403.

Harrell-Bond, B. (1986), *Imposing Aid: Emergency Assistance to Refugees*, Oxford: Oxford University Press.

Harrell-Bond, B. (1999), Interview with Doreen Indra, in D. Indra (ed.), *Engendering Forced Migration: Theory and Practice*, Oxford: Berghahn.

Harrell-Bond, B. (2002), "Can Humanitarian Work with Refugees be Humane?", *Human Rights Quarterly*, 24, pp. 51–85.

Harrell-Bond, B. (2004), "Weapons of the Weak", *Journal of Refugee Studies*, 17, 1, pp. 27–29.

Harris, N. (1995), *The New Untouchables: Immigration and the New World Worker*, London: Penguin.

Hathaway, J. (1991), *The Law of Refugee Status*, Toronto: Butterworths.

Held, D., McGrew, A., Goldblatt, D. and Perraton, J. (1999), *Global Transformations: Politics, Economics and Culture*, Cambridge: Polity Press.

Heyman, M. G. (2005), "Domestic Violence and Asylum: Toward a Working Model of Affirmative State Obligations", *International Journal of Refugee Law*, 17, 4, pp. 729–748.

Hotham Mission (2003), *Welfare Issues and Immigration Outcomes for Asylum Seekers on Bridging Visa E*, Melbourne: Hotham Mission.

Human Rights Watch (1992), *Double Jeopardy: Police Abuse of Women in Pakistan*, New York: Human Rights Watch.

Human Rights Watch (1999), *Crime or Custom: Violence Against Women in Pakistan*, New York: Human Rights Watch.

Human Rights Watch (2000), *Seeking Protection: Addressing Sexual and Domestic Violence in Tanzania's Refugee Camps*, New York: Human Rights Watch.

Human Rights Watch (2004a), *"Political Shari'a"? Human Rights and Islamic Law in Northern Nigeria*, New York: Human Rights Watch.

Human Rights Watch (2004b), *Honoring the Killers: Justice Denied For "Honor" Crimes In Jordan*, New York: Human Rights Watch.

Human Rights Watch (2006a), *Netherlands: Asylum Rights Granted to Lesbian and Gay Iranians*, New York: Human Rights Watch.

Human Rights Watch (2006b), *Stemming the Flow: Abuses against Migrants, Asylum Seekers and Refugees*, New York: Human Rights Watch.

Humphrey, M. (2003), "Refugees: An Endangered Species?", *Journal of Sociology*, 39, 1, pp. 31–43.

Huysmans, J. (2006), *The Politics of Insecurity: Fear, Migration and Asylum in the EU*, London: Routledge.

Hyndman, J. (1998), "Managing Difference: Gender and Culture in Humanitarian Emergencies", *Gender, Place and Culture*, 5, 3, pp. 241–260.

Hyndman, J. (2000), *Managing Displacement: Refugees and the Politics of Humanitarianism*, Minneapolis: University of Minnesota Press.

Hyndman, J. (2004), "Refugee Camps as Conflict Zones: The Politics of Gender", in W. Giles and J. Hyndman (eds), *Sites of Violence: Gender and Conflict Zones*, Berkeley: University of California Press.

IDMC (2006), *Internal Displacement: A Global Overview of Trends and Developments in 2005*, Geneva: Internal Displacement Monitoring Centre.

Indra, D. (1989), "Ethnic Human Rights and Feminist Theory: Gender Implications for Refugee Studies and Practice", *Journal of Refugee Studies*, 2, 2, pp. 221–242.

Indra, D. (ed.) (1999), *Engendering Forced Migration: Theory and Practice*, Oxford: Berghahn.

International Commission of Jurists (2003), *Violence Against Women in Bangladesh: A Legal Assessment of Acid Attacks and Domestic Violence*, Geneva: International Commission of Jurists.

IOM (2000), *World Migration Report*, Geneva: IOM.

Jaubany-Baucells, O. (2002), "The State of Welfare for Asylum Seekers and Refugees in Spain", *Critical Social Policy*, 22, 3, pp. 415–435.

Jacksic, M. (2007), "De la victime idéale de la traite des êtres humains à la victime coupable. La production sociale d'une absence", *Cahiers Internationaux de Sociologie* (forthcoming).

Joachim, J. (2003), "Framing Issues and Seizing Opportunities: The UN, NGOs and Women's Rights", *International Studies Quarterly*, 47, pp. 247–274.

Joly, D. (1996), *Haven or Hell? Asylum Policies and Refugees in Europe*, Basingstoke: Macmillan.

Joly, D. (ed) (2002), *Global Changes in Asylum Regimes*, Basingstoke: Palgrave.

Kälin, W. (1986), "Troubled Communication: Cross-Cultural Misunderstandings in the Asylum Hearing", *International Migration Review*, 2, 2, pp. 230–241.

Keck, M. and Sikkink, K. (1998), *Activists Beyond Borders: Advocacy Networks in International Politics*, Ithaca: Cornell University Press.

Keck, M. and Sikkink, K. (1999), "Transnational Advocacy Networks in International and Regional Politics", *International Social Science Journal*, 51, 159, pp. 89–101.

Kelley, N. (2002), "The Convention Refugee Definition and Gender-Based Persecution: A Decade's Progress", *International Journal of Refugee Law*, 13, 4, pp. 559–570.

Kelly, L. (2000), "Wars Against Women: Sexual Violence, Sexual Politics and the Militarised State", in S. Jacobs, R. Jacobson and J. Marchbank (eds), *States of Conflict: Gender, Violence and Resistance*, London: Zed Books.

Kennedy, P. and Murphy-Lawless, J. (2003), "The Maternity Care Needs of Refugee and Asylum Seeking Women in Ireland", *Feminist Review*, 73, pp. 39–52.

Kennedy-Pipe, C. (2000), "From Cold Wars to New Wars", in C. Jones and C. Kennedy-Pipe (eds), *International Security in a Global Age: Securing the Twenty-First Century*, London: Frank Cass.

Kibreab, G. (1985), *Reflections on the African Refugee Problem*, New Jersey: Africa World Press.

Kneebone, S. (2005), "Women Within the Refugee Construct: 'Exclusionary Inclusion' in Policy and Practice – The Australian Experience", *International Journal of Refugee Law*, 17, 1, pp. 7–42.

Kobelinsky, C. (2006), "Les figures du demandeur d'asile", unpublished paper transmitted to author.

Kofman, E. (2005), "Gendered Global Migrations: Diversity and Stratification", *International Feminist Journal of Politics*, 6, 4, pp. 643–655.

Kofman, E., Phizacklea, A., Raghuram, P., Sales, R. (2000), *Gender and International Migration in Europe*. London: Routledge.

Koopmans, R. and Statham, P. (1999), "Political Claims Analysis: Integrating Protest Event and Political Discourse Approaches", *Mobilization*, 4, 2, pp. 203–221.

Korac, M. (2003), "Integration and How We Facilitate It: A Comparative Study of the Settlement Experiences of Refugees in Italy and the Netherlands", *Sociology*, 37, 1, pp. 51–68.

Koser, K. (2001), "New Approaches to Asylum?", *International Migration*, 39, 6, pp. 85–100.

Kreitzer, L. (2002), "Liberian Refugee Women: A Qualitative Study of Their Participation in Planning Camp Programmes", *International Social Work*, 45, 1, pp. 45–58.

Lavenex, S. (2001), *The Europeanisation of Refugee Policies: Between Human Rights and International Security*, Aldershot: Ashgate.

Legal Action for Women (2006), *A "Bleak House" in Our Times: An investigation into Women's Rights Violations at Yarl's Wood Removal Centre*, London: Crossroads Books.

Legoux, L. (1995) *La Crise de l'asile Politique en France*, Paris: Ceped.

Legoux, L. (1996) "Crise de l'asile, crise de valeurs", *Hommes et Migrations*, 1198–1199, pp. 69–86.

Lentin, R. (2003), "Pregnant Silence: (En)gendering Ireland's Asylum Space", *Patterns of Prejudice*, 37, 3, pp. 301–322.

Lesselier, C. (2007), "Femmes, exil et politique: vécu et action de femmes exilées en France depuis 1970", Paper presented at Conference: Exhumer l'histoire des femmes exilées politiques, Brussels, May 2007.

Liedtke, M. (2002), "National Welfare and Asylum in Germany", *Critical Social Policy*, 22, 3, pp. 479–497.

Light, D. (1992), "Healing Their Wounds: Guatemalan Refugee Women as Political Activists", *Women and Therapy*, 13, pp. 297–308.

Locher, B. and Prügl, E. (2001), "Feminism and Constructivism: Worlds Apart or Sharing the Middle Ground", *International Studies Quarterly*, 45, pp. 111–129.

Loescher, G. (1993), *Beyond Charity: International Cooperation and the Global Refugee crisis*, Oxford: Oxford University Press.

Loescher, G. (2001), *The UNHCR and World Politics: A Perilous Path*, Oxford: Oxford University Press.

Luoparjarvi, K. (2003), *Gender-Related Persecution as Basis for Refugee Status: Comparative Perspectives*, Abo Akademi University: Institute for Human Rights.

Lyth, A. (2002), *Where are the Women? A Gender Approach to Refugee Law*, Lund: Lund University.

Macklin, A. (1995), "Refugee Women and the Imperative of Categories", *Human Rights Quarterly*, 17, 2, pp. 213–277.

Macklin, A. (1998), "Cross-Border Shopping for Ideas: A Critical Review of United States, Canadian and Australian Approaches to Gender-Related Asylum Claims", *Georgetown Immigration Law Journal*, 13, pp. 25–71.

Macklin, A. (1999), "A Comparative Analysis of the Canadian, US and Australian Directives on Gender Persecution and Refugee Status", in D. Indra (ed), *Engendering Forced Migration: Theory and Practice*, Oxford: Berghahn.

Malkki, L. H. (1995), *Purity and Exile: Violence, Memory and National Cosmology Among Hutu Refugees in Tanzania*, Chicago: University of Chicago Press.

Malkki, L. H. (1996), "Speechless Emissaries: Refugees, Humanitarianism and Dehistoricization", *Cultural Anthropology*, 11, 3, pp. 377–404.

Malloch, M. and Stanley, L. (2005), "The Detention of Asylum Seekers in the UK: Representing Risk, Managing the Dangerous", *Punishment and Society*, 7, 1, pp. 53–71.

Manderson, L. et al. (1998), "A Woman without a Man is a Woman at Risk: Women at Risk in Australian Humanitarian Programs", *Journal of Refugee Studies*, 11, 3, pp. 267–283.

Mann, C. (2006), *Traditions et Transformations dans la Vie des Femmes Afghanes des Camps de Réfugiés au Pakistan Depuis le 11 Septembre*, unpublished doctoral thesis, EHESS Paris.

Marfleet, P. (2006), *Refugees in a Global Era*, Basingstoke: Palgrave Macmillan.

Matas, D. (2001), "Refugee Determination Complexity", *Refuge*, 19, 4, pp. 48–54.

Maternity Alliance/Bail for Immigration Detainees (2002), *A Crying Shame: Pregnant Asylum Seekers and Their Babies in Detention*, London: Maternity Alliance.

Matsuoka, A. and Sorensen, J. (1999), "Eritrean Canadian Refugee Households as Sites of Gender Renegotiation", in D. Indra (ed.), *Engendering Forced Migration: Theory and Practice*, Oxford: Berghahn.

McLeish, J. (2002), *Mothers in Exile: Maternity Experiences of Asylum Seekers in England*, London: Maternity Alliance.

Medical Foundation for the Care of Victims of Torture (2000a), *Response of the Medical Foundation for the Care of Victims of Torture to the National Asylum Support Service Vouchers Review*, London: Medical Foundation for the Care of Victims of Torture.

Medical Foundation for the Care of Victims of Torture (2000b), *Asylum Detention is Not Fair (Policy Statement)*, London: Medical Foundation for the Care of Victims of Torture.

Meertens, D. (2004), "A Life Project Out of Turmoil: Gender and Displacement in Colombia", in P. Essed, G. Frerks and J. Schrijvers (eds), *Refugees and the Transformation of Societies: Agency, Policies, Ethics and Politics*, Oxford: Berghahn.

Mohanty, C. T. (1991), *Third World Women and the Politics of Feminism*, Bloomington: Indiana University Press.

Moller-Okin, S. (ed) (1999), *Is Multiculturalism Bad for Women?* New Jersey: Princeton University Press.

Molyneux, M. and Razavi, S. (eds) (2002), *Gender Justice, Development and Rights*, Oxford: Oxford University Press.

Montazami, Y. (2007), "Souffrance psychique des femmes demanderesses d'asile et des femmes sans papier", paper presented at a conference *Est-ce ainsi que des femmes vivent?* Paris: January 2007.

Montgomery, E. and Foldspang, A. (2005), " 'Predictors of the Authorities' Decision to Grant Asylum in Denmark", *Journal of Refugee Studies*, 18, 4, pp. 454–467.

Morokvasic, M. (1984), "Birds of Passage Are Also Women", *International Migration Review*, 18, 4, 886–907.

Morris, L. (2002), "Britain's Asylum and Immigration Regime: The Shifting Contours of Rights", *Journal of Ethnic and Migration Studies*, 28, 3, pp. 409–425.

Morrison, J. (2001), "The Dark Side of Globalisation: The Criminalisation of Refugees", *Race and Class*, 43, 1, pp. 71–82.

Niarchos, C. (1995), "Women, War and Rape: Challenges Facing the International Tribunal for the Former Yugoslavia", *Human Rights Quarterly*, 17, 4, pp. 649–690.

Noiriel, G. (1991), *Réfugiés et sans-papiers. La République face au droit d'asile*, Paris: Calmann-Lévy.

Ofpra (2006), *Rapport d'Activité 2005*, Paris: Ofpra.

Oosterveld, V. L. (1996), "The Canadian Guidelines on Gender-Related Persecution: An Evaluation", *International Journal of Refugee Law*, 8, 4, pp. 569–596.

Oswin, N. (2001), "An Exploration of Feminist Approaches to Refugee Law", *International Feminist Journal of Politics*, 3, 3, pp. 347–364.

Oxfam (2005), *Foreign Territory. The Internationalisation of EU Asylum Policy*, Oxford: Oxfam.

Oxfam and the Refugee Council (2002), *Poverty and Asylum in the UK*, London: Refugee Council.

Papademetriou, D. (1993), "Confronting the Challenge of Transnational Migration: Domestic and International Responses", in OECD (ed.) *The Changing Course of International Migration*, Paris: OECD.

Pearce, H. (2003), "An Examination of the International Understanding of Political Rape and the Significance of Labeling it Torture", *International Journal of Refugee Law*, 14, 4, pp. 534–560.

Pelosi, A. (1996), *Intercultural Communication in the Refugee Hearing*, Montreal: McGill University.

Peterson, V. S. and Runyan, A. S. (1993), *Global Gender Issues*, Colorado: Westview.

Pettman, J. J. (2002), *Worlding Women: A Feminist International Politics*, New York: Routledge.

Phizacklea, A. (ed.) (1983), *One Way Ticket: Migration and Female Labour*, London: Routledge.

Pirouet, L. (2001), *Whatever Happened to Asylum in Britain? A Tale of Two Walls*, Oxford: Berghahn.

Piper, N. (2006), "Gender the Politics of Migration", *International Migration Review*, 40, 1, pp. 133–164.

Pittaway, E. and Bartolomei, L. (2003), "An Examination of the role of Identity and Citizenship in the Experiences of Women in Kakuma Refugee Camp in Northern Kenya", *Development*, 46, 3, pp. 87–93.

Pittaway, E. and Bartolomei, L. (2006), *The Case for an UNHCR Conclusion on "Refugee Women at Risk"*, Sydney: Centre for Refugee Research.

Pittaway, E. and Pittaway, E. (2004), " 'Refugee Woman': A Dangerous Label", *Australian Journal of Human Rights*, 10, 1, pp. 119–135.

Preston, R. (1999), "Researching Repatriation and Reconstruction: Who is Researching What and Why?", in R. Black and K. Koser (eds), *The End of the Refugee Cycle? Refugee Repatriation and Reconstruction*, Oxford: Berghahn.

Rajaram, P. K. (2002), "Humanitarianism and Representations of the Refugee", *Journal of Refugee Studies*, 15, 3, pp. 247–264.

Rao, A. (1995), "The Politics of Gender and Culture in International Human Rights Discourse", in S. Peters and A. Wolper (eds), *Women's Rights, Human Rights: International Feminist Perspectives*, New York: Routledge

Raper, M. (2003), "The Changing Role of NGOs in Refugee Assistance", in L. Adler and U. Gielen (eds), *Migration, Immigration and Emigration in International Perspective*, Westport: Greenwood.

Ratner, H. (2005), *Refugee Women and Stories of Sexual Violence: Agents in their Victimisation?*, Unpublished manuscript, Copenhagen: Institute for Antropology.

Reed, A., (2003), "Gendering Asylum: The Importance of Diversity and Context", *Feminist Review*, 73, pp. 114–118.

Refugee Action (2002), *Is it Safe Here? Refugee Women's Experiences in the United Kingdom*, London: Refugee Action.

Refugee Council (1996), *Women Refugees*, London: Refugee Council.

Refugee Women's Resource Project (Asylum Aid) (2003), *Women Asylum Seekers in the UK: A Gender Perspective*, London: Refugee Women's Resource Project.

Refugee Women's Resource Project (Asylum Aid) (2005), *Gender Issues in Asylum Claims: Spreading Good Practice Across the European Union*, London: Refugee Women's Resource Project.

Refugee Women's Resources Project (Asylum Aid) (2006), *"Lip service" or implementation: The Home Office Gender Guidance and women's asylum claims in the UK*, London: Refugee Women's Resources Project.

Reynolds, A. (2007), "How Anti-Terror Laws Hurt Asylum Seekers", *New Amercian Media*, *http://news.newamericanmedia.org/news/view*.

Rousseau, C. (2000), "Les réfugiés à notre porte: violence organisée et souffrance sociale", *Criminologie*, 33, 1, pp. 185–201.

Rousseau, C., Crépeau, F., Foxen, P. and Houle, F. (2002), "The Complexity of Determining Refugeehood: A Multidisciplinary Analysis of the Decision-Making Process of the Canadian Immigration and Refugee Board", *Journal of Refugee Studies*, 15, 1, pp. 43–70.

Sales, R. (2002), "The Deserving and the Undeserving? Refugees, Asylum Seekers and Welfare in Britain", *Critical Social Policy*, 22, 3, pp. 456–478.

Sales, R. and Gregory, J. (1998), "Refugee Women in London: The Experience of Somali Women", *Refuge*, 17, 1, pp. 16–20.

Schuster, L. (2003), "Common Sense or Racism? The Treatment of Asylum-Seekers in Europe", *Patterns of Prejudice*, 37, 3, pp. 233–255.

Schuster, L. and Solomos, J. (2004), "Race, Immigration and Asylum: New Labour's Agenda and Its Consequences", *Ethnicities*, 4, 2, pp. 267–300.

Sen, G. and Correa, S. (1999), *Gender Justice and Economic Justice*, New York: UNIFEM.

Seu, B. I. (2003), "The Woman with the Baby: Exploring Narratives of Female Refugees", *Feminist Review*, 73, pp. 158–165.

Shahidian, H. (1996), "Iranian Exiles and Sexual Politics: Issues of Gender Relations and Identity", *Journal of Refugee Studies*, 9, 1, pp. 44–72.

Shaw, M. (2002), *The Nationality, Immigration and Asylum Bill: Immigration and Asylum*, Research Paper 02/26, London: House of Common Library.

Sitaropoulos, N. (2002), "Refugee Welfare in Greece: Towards a Remodeling of the Responsibility-Shifting Paradigm?", *Critical Social Policy*, 22, 3, pp. 436–455.

Spijkerboer, T. (2000) *Gender and Refugee Status*, Aldershot: Ashgate.

Spire, A. (2006), "Le pouvoir discrétionnaire des agents de prefecture", Paper presented at seminar *Les nouvelles frontières de la société française*, Paris, March 2006.

Statham, P. (2003), "Understanding Anti-Asylum Rhetoric: Restrictive Politics or Racist Publics?", *Political Quarterly*, pp. 163–177.

Steans, J. and Ahmadi, V. (2005), "Negotiating the Politics of Gender and Rights: Some Reflections on the Status of Women's Human Rights at 'Beijing Plus Ten'", *Global Society*, 19, 3, pp. 227–245.

Steiner, N. (2001), *Arguing About Asylum: The Complexity of Refugee Debates in Europe*, Basingstoke: Palgrave.

Stevens, M. (1993), "Recognizing Gender-Specific Persecution: A Proposal to Add Gender as a Sixth Refugee Category", *Cornell Journal of Law and Public Policy*, pp. 179–219.

Stivens, M. (2002), "Gender Politics and the Reimagining of Human Rights in the Asia-Pacific", in A. Hildson et al. (eds), *Human Rights and Gender Politics: Asia-Pacific Perspectives*, London: Routledge.

Suhrke, A. (1997), "Uncertain Globalization: Refugee Movements in the Second Half of the Twentieth Century", in W. Gungwu (ed.), *Global History and Migrations*, Boulder: Westview.

Swidler, A. (1986), "Culture in Action: Symbols and Strategies", *American Sociological Review*, 51, 2, pp. 273–286.

Szczepanikova, A. (2005), "Gender Relations in a Refugee Camp: A Case of Chechens Seeking Asylum in the Czech Republic", *Journal of Refugee Studies*, 18, 3, pp. 281–298.

Thobani, S. (2001), "Benevolent State, Law-Breaking Smugglers and Deportable and Expendable Women: An Analysis of the Canadian State's Strategy to Address Trafficking in Women", *Refuge*, 19, 4, pp. 24–33.

Tickner; J. A. (2005), "What Is Your Research Program? Some Feminist Answers to International Relations Methodologigal Questions", *International Studies Quarterly*, 49, pp. 1–21.

Toubia, N. (1995), "Female Genital Mutilation" in J. Peters and A. Wolpe (eds), *Women's Rights, Human Rights: International Feminist Perspectives*, New York: Routledge.

Tran, T. V. and Nguyen, T. D. (1994), "Gender and Satisfaction with the Host Society among Indochinese Refugees", *International Migration Review*, 28, 2, pp. 323–337.

Tuitt, P. (1996), *False Images: Law's Construction of the Refugee*, London: Pluto.

Turner, S. (2004), "New Opportunities: Angry Young Men in a Tanzanian Refugee Camp", in P. Essed, G. Frerks and J. Schrijvers (eds), *Refugees and the Transformation of Societies: Agency, Policies, Ethics and Politics*, Oxford: Berghahn.

UNHCR (1990), *Policy on Refugee Women*, Geneva: UNHCR.

UNHCR (1991), *Guidelines on the Protection of Refugee Women*, Geneva: UNHCR.

UNHCR (1995a), *An Overview of Protection Issues in Western Europe*, Geneva: UNHCR.

UNHCR (1995b), *Sexual Violence Against Refugees: Guidelines on Prevention and Response*, Geneva: UNHCR.

UNHCR (2001), *Respect Our Rights, Partnership for Equality: Report on the Dialogue with Refugee Women, Geneva, Switzerland, 20–22 June 2001*, Geneva: UNHCR.

UNHCR (2002), *Guidelines on International Protection: Gender-Related Persecution Within the Context of Article 1(A)2 of the 1951 Convention and/or its 1967 Protocol Relating to the Status of Refugees*, Geneva: UNHCR.

UNHCR (2003), *Sexual and Gender-Based Violence Against Refugees, Returnees and Internally Displaced People: Guidelines for Prevention and Response*, Geneva: UNHCR.

UNHCR (2005), *2004 Global Refugee Trends*, Geneva: UNHCR.

UNHCR (2006a), *The State of the World's Refugees*, Geneva: UNHCR.

UNHCR (2006b), *Measuring Protection by Numbers*, Geneva: UNHCR.

UNHCR (2006c), *Guidelines on International Protection: The Application of Article 1A(2) of the 1951 Convention and/or 1967 Protocol Relating to the Status of Refugees to Victims of Trafficking and Persons at Risk of Being Trafficked*, Geneva: UNHCR.

USCR (2004), *Refugee Reports*, Washington: US Committee for Refugees.

USRC (2005), *World Refugee Survey 2004*, New York: USRC.

Valentine, D. (1996), *Charred Lullabies*, Princeton: Princeton University Press.

Valji, N. (2001), "Women and the 1951 Refugee Convention: Fifty Years of Seeking Visibility", *Refuge*, 19, 5, pp. 25–35.

Valluy, J. (2004), "La fiction juridique de l'asile", *Plein Droit*, 63, Décembre 2004.
Valluy, J. (2005), "La nouvelle Europe politique des camps d'exilés: genèse d'une source élitaire de phobie et de repression des étrangers", *Cultures et Conflits*, 57, pp. 13–69.
Valluy, J. (2007), "De la dépendance étatique dans l'accueil des demandeurs d'asile à l'affaiblissement des réseaux de solidarités avec les exilés", unpublished article.
Van Wetten, J. et al. (2001), "Female Asylum-Seekers in the Netherlands: An Empirical Study", *International Migration*, 39, 3, pp. 85–98.
Vayrynen, R. (2001), "Funding Dilemmas in Refugee Assistance: Political Interests and Institutional Reforms in UNHCR", *International Migration Review*, 35, 1, pp. 143–167.
Wallace, R. and Holliday, A. (2005), "The Application of the Gender Guidelines with the UK Asylum Determination Process", AIT Legal and Research Unit Update, Issue 12, June 2005, London: AIT.
Waylen, G. (1996), "Analysing Women in the Politics of the Third World", in H. Afshar (ed.), *Women and Politics in the Third World*, London: Routledge.
WCRWC (1997), *Liberty Denied: Women Seeking Asylum Imprisoned in the United States*, New York: Women's Commission for Refugee Women and Children.
WCRWC (2002), *UNHCR Policy on Refugee Women and Guidelines on Their Protection: An Assessment of Ten Years of Implementation*, New York: Women's Commission for Refugee Women and Children.
Welch, M. and Schuster, L. (2005), "Detention of asylum seekers in the UK, France, Germany and Italy: A Critical View of the Globalizing Culture of Control", *Criminal Justice*, 5, 4, pp. 331–355.
Whitworth, S. (1997), *Feminism and International Relations: Towards a Political Economy of Gender in Interstate and Non-Governmental Institutions*, Basingstoke: Palgrave Macmillan.
WHO (2000), *Female Genital Mutilation*, Fact sheet no. 241, Geneva: WHO.
Wihtol de Wenden, C. (2002), "La crise de l'asile", *Hommes et Migrations*, 1238, pp. 6–12.
Winter, B., Thompson, S. and Jeffreys, S. (2002), "The UN Approach to Harmful Traditional Practices: Some Conceptual Problems", *International Feminist Journal of Politics*, 4, 1, pp. 72–94.
Youngs, G. (2004), "Feminist International Relations: A Contradiction in Terms? Or: Why Women and Gender are Essential to Understanding the World 'We' Live in", *International Affairs*, 80, 1, pp. 75–87.
Yuval-Davis, N. (1997), *Gender and Nation*, London: Sage.
Yuval-Davis, N. and Anthias, F. (eds) (1989), *Woman, Nation, State*, Basingstoke: Macmillan.
Yuval-Davis, N., Anthias, F. and Kofman, E. (2005), "Secure Borders and Safe Haven and the Gendered Politics of Belonging: Beyond Social Cohesion", *Ethnic and Racial Studies*, 28, 3, pp. 513–535.
Zetter, R. (1996), "Indigenous NGOs and Refugee Assistance: Some Lessons from Malawi and Zimbabwe", *Development in Practice*, 6, 1, pp. 37–49.
Zetter, R. and Pearl, M. (2000), "The Minority Within the Minority: Refugee Community-Based Organisations in the UK and the Impact of Restrictionism on Asylum-Seekers", *Journal of Ethnic and Migration Studies*, 26, 4, pp. 675–697.
Zlotnik, H. (2003), "The Global Dimensions of Female Migration", *Migration Information Source*, March 2003, Migration Policy Institute.

Zurek, Y. (2004), "The Experiences of Women in Australian Immigration Detention Centres", *Forced Migration Review*, 20, pp. 37–39.

Zwingel, S. (2005), "From Intergovernmental Negotiations to (Sub)National Change: A Transnational Perspective on the Impact of CEDAW", *International Feminist Journal of Politics*, 7, 3, pp. 400–424.

Index